QUALITY

Manchester gangster tales from the sixties

JOHN LUDDEN

Manchester: a city inhabited by rogues, villains,
Kind hearts and black souls.
Welcome to Quality.

PROLOGUE:

We begin in the present day.

Manchester: Just after 2.00pm on a rainy and miserable windswept, Sunday afternoon, a white transit van turns left off Deansgate in the city centre and heads over a bridge across the river Irwell, into neighbouring Salford. The van radio is playing Arabic music. It comes to a halt opposite a run-down pub with boarded windows and graffiti covered walls. Inside music can be heard.

The Smiths are playing on a juke box.

There is a light that never goes out

....The pub is the Brass Anchor.

Across the road a mass of wasteland. Burnt out cars and twisted metal. Concrete overran with grass weeds. Needles and beer cans strewn all around.

Empty wine and whisky bottles lie dumped as two small dogs are scampering around for scraps.

A smashed up bus shelter nearby with the letters *MUFC* lovingly scrawled across it.

One love.

A little further on over the River Irwell is Salford's big brother. Manchester.

A grey northern Mancunian skyline covets the horizon, whilst the distant rattle of a Metrolink tram trudging south over Castlefield railway bridge echoes in the wind....

The van driver is thirty-three-year old Azil Aturak. He plies an illegal trade for a newly arrived Syrian criminal gang desperate to make their mark on the Manchester drugs trade. The Syrians have a simple bloodcurdling policy. Eliminate the opposition and first on the hit list. Easier said than done. Salford.

Azil's task is to deliver the cargo, nothing more. Once the job is done the cargo is on its own. They are deemed expendable for the pool of hired guns arriving daily from an exploding Middle East is never-ending. He goes to open the van's back doors, letting out the two young boys carrying Uzi machine pistols, with hoodies covering their faces. Fifteen-year olds Hassan Sharim and Ali Khalil. Both are illegal immigrants and desperate for visas for themselves and their families.

The price they have to pay awaits inside the Brass Anchor. For a new life they have been ordered to kill all in there.

Azil faces them. 'My boss wants their blood. Now we have your families and if you want them brought to this country make sure he gets his wish. You leave nobody alive and then make your way to the meeting spot for me. From there we shall get you to safety and start preparations to bring over your loved ones from the homeland. Do you understand'?

Looking extremely apprehensive they nod and clutch tight on their weapons. Both are sweating profusely. Azil tries to offer a reassuring smile, but it appears more like a grimace.

'It's time, now may God be with you. Go'!

He points towards the pub and pushes them onwards. 'Think of your families when you press the trigger. Of your mothers and sisters.'

Then with an unholy haste Azil races back to the van, starts the engine and swiftly drives off.

There is no guilty conscience, just relief that the first part of the job is done and now he waits. Whether the boys succeed or fail matters little, the war has begun and Hassan and Ali are already dead. Or soon will be.

Inside the Brass Anchor it is relatively quiet. Only the usual small collection of Sunday afternoon drinkers are gathered in a tattered nondescript vault. In one corner of the room three elderly men sit playing dominoes. They are arguing amongst themselves. Seventy-five year old Tommy Keenan is loudest amongst them. The other two are of the same age. Eddie Hopkins and Eric Taylor. However Tommy's still, film star looks, silver grey hair and sparkling blue eyes give him the look of a man fifteen years younger.

A smiling Tommy loves teasing his friends. Both whom he has known for over fifty years. 'Right you pair of cheating bastards, this is where I take your pensions and your false teeth off you. No more fooling around. This is serious.'

'We shall see big mouth,' grins Eddie.

'More front than bloody Blackpool, Tommy Keenan. Always have had,' adds Eric.

At the bar are four much younger men, whilst another two around the same age across the room are playing darts. All are members of

Salford's most notorious crime gang. Amongst them is their boss, a dark-haired lean handsome figure. Thirty-three years old Paul Brady. He comes across as easy going with a quick smile, but in manners of family business, like his father and uncle before him, when required Brady is utterly ruthless.

A murderous individual who has inherited a natural air of leadership, Paul Michael Brady rules Salford with an iron fist in a velvet glove.

Suddenly the gentle demeanour of a Sunday afternoon drinking session is exploded as the Syrian shooters charge through the door blazing. One fires towards the lads drinking at the bar, but misses wildly and succeeds only in putting two bullets into a juke box to silence Morrissey. The other fails to pull the trigger properly and is swiftly seized upon and dragged to the floor.

As madness ensues Tommy, Eddie and Eric are grabbed hold of and quite literally thrown under the table by a gang member. He covers their bodies with his own.

The others rush to overpower the second Syrian and he too is disarmed and pushed to the ground. Once secured Brady motions with his hands for calm.

He looks down. 'Some fucking entrance. Right who are you working for'?

Hassan starts to plead for his life in Arabic.

Brady's best friend and second in command, thirty-one year old Shaun Barlow, screams at the confused and scared boy. 'What the fuck are you saying lad? Speak English. It just might save you.'

Still he continues on in his native tongue. Ali joins in and it's clear they are both pleading for their lives.

Brady stands over them.

He whispers quietly under his breath. 'I just can't have this. Not here, not this close to home. Not in Salford.'

Brady stares across to Barlow, who with one glance knows what his boss wants him to do.

He turns to two other members of the gang, twenty-six year old, Salford born, Stephen Marshall and twenty-year old Tony Rea. Ancoats born, a tough kid of Italian descent.

'Stephen, Tony, go and get the van. I don't want to see their fucking, ugly, faces again.

Do you understand'?

Initially both Marshall and Rea appear shocked. They look over to Brady who nods in their direction. Then it becomes crystal clear what is expected of them.

Marshall smiles at Rea. 'Okay Tom mate, looks like we have got work to do.'

They haul the Syrians to their feet and drag them out of the pub.

'Come on Laurel and Hardy,' says Rea. 'We are going for a little ride.'

Paul Brady goes across to the three old men whom are watching on in an air of quiet disbelief. 'No broken bones I hope gents'? asks a smiling Brady, as he bends down to pick all the Domino pieces off the floor, and place them back on the table.

He sits down. 'Sorry about ruining your game. To make up let me buy you all a drink.'

'Buy us a drink'? exclaims Tommy. 'I was winning that last bloody game.'

Brady leans across. 'Nobody saw anything right'?

Tommy looks him straight in the eyes. 'What from under the table? Don't be silly son. I'm just glad they took Morrissey out and shut him up'? Brady laughs whilst the other two shake their heads at Tommy's cool reply. He never changes.

'Nothing we haven't seen before Paul,' replies Eric, with a shrug of his shoulders.

'You can say that again,' laughs Eddie. Both are hardly strangers to what has just occurred. Like Tommy they are colourful veterans of Manchester's gangland. Another era maybe, but equally at times as grim, with never any medals handed out for valour.

'This used to be a normal Saturday night around here back in the sixties,' adds Tommy.

Paul Brady glances through the window to see Marshall and Rea leading the two tied-up shooters over towards a black transit van at gunpoint. They push and shove them through the rear doors and drive away.

Brady stands and walks back to the bar where a smiling Barlow passes him a beer.

'I think we are going to war Paul.'

'You don't fucking say,' he grins.

Inside the van, which is speeding down a Salford back road, the Syrians are still crying and begging for mercy. Marshall turns and stares at them from the passenger seat in utter disdain. They try desperate to make eye contact but receive short shrift and no sympathy.

'You should have thought of this before acting like a drunken Butch and Sundance. What do you expect us to do? We have a reputation to uphold and there's a price to pay for what you've just done.'

Rea looks across to Marshall. 'We'll take them to Brennan's warehouse and do it there okay'?

Marshall is cocking the barrel on his pistol. 'Perfect.'

And still they plead, but the Syrian's words are falling on deaf ears…..

Back in the Brass Anchor the damage has more or less been cleared up. Albeit the bullet riddled juke box, it has escaped relatively unscathed. A uneasy sense of normality has returned. Paul Brady goes back across to Tommy, who is now sat alone after Eric and Eddie have headed home after experiencing enough excitement for one day.

'Do you mind if I sit'?

'Be my guest.'

'Where are your mates'?

'Gone home to recharge their pacemakers and watch Countrywatch.'

Brady grins wide and takes a large swig from a beer bottle. He then checks his mobile phone for messages and places it on the table. Tommy watches him carefully. This is a young man with a lot on his mind, but he so reminds him of his Father. Michael Brady.

'Got problems lad'?

A smiling Brady is amused at the sarcastic tone. 'Nothing I can't handle.'

'I don't doubt it.'

He stares back at Tommy lighting a cigarette. 'Shouldn't you do that outside'?

Tommy inhales and then smiles. 'What are you going to do shoot me'?

A laughing Brady checks his mobile again. 'You knew my old man really well didn't you. Michael Brady'?

'We did a lot of business together in the sixties. Both Michael and your uncle Paul. Good lads, I miss them.'

'Me too,' replies Brady, his mask momentarily dropping. 'Every fucking day.'

'I remember my uncle saying you was a top man back then. A real gentleman. An old fashioned gangster. I've been told by so many people you are touched by greatness and there's a sprinkling of gold dust around you Tommy Keenan.

Truly a class act.'

'I was no gangster. I just made a living that's all. A bit like yourself.'

But Brady is adamant. 'Come on then Tommy, cards on the tables. What happened in 1963 when the Krays came to Manchester? What really went down? My old man nearly opened up one night just before he died. He was from the same school as you. Never said much and in the end he took most to the grave.

But you?

Your name popped up one too many times. Even from Dad's lips. You know the score, and you know who sent them home'?

'Tommy inhales again on his cigarette.

'Nothing to do with me son.'

Brady shakes his head in disbelief. 'You old timers. It's like *Omerta* on that subject.

This isn't Sicily, it's not even fucking Ancoats! My God, all these years and still you don't speak about it'?

He checks his phone once more, but still nothing,

so Brady continues. 'And there's so much other stuff. The Beatle's rumour. Did you really meet them and how close did we come to owning their contract?

Brady smiles. 'Was it really old man Quinn, dressed as a copper, who done Bobby Di Marco on the ferry cross the Mersey, to grab the fifty grand bounty on his head?

The mad and bad Paddy Costigan getting blown to kingdom come by Blind Billy and Boom? And then they got shot to pieces down by the canal. Gypsy revenge.

The Great Train Robbers? Jesus, that was incredible! Did we really hide Bruce Reynolds from the old Bill?

All the lads from the firms up on Saddleworth Moors helping the coppers find those poor kids murdered by Brady and Hindley?

And how close did Georgie Best really come to getting his legs broke for sleeping with Lenny Foyles' daughter'?
And that fucking sombrero!

It doesn't end there. Frank Sinatra and the missing diamonds? What the hell was that all about? And it goes on….Tommy, there's a book in all this. So come on mate.

Time to come clean.'

The van arrives at Brennans. An old abandoned warehouse sat on an Industrial wasteland. Around them is nothing but deserted/boarded up buildings and burnt out cars. Rea and Marshall drag the Syrians out of the van and take them kicking and screaming into the building. Inside it resembles a vast deserted airplane hangar.

Still Hassan and Ali are begging for their lives but it's wasted breath. They are pushed to the floor as Rea and Marshall take out their weapons and nonchalantly let fly a hail of bullets into the stricken Syrians. The guns go quiet and Marshall starts to film the bodies with his mobile phone.

'Stephen, what the fuck are you doing'? exclaims Rea.
'For my book,' Marshall declares smiling. 'My life in the Manchester gangland'!

Rea laughs. 'You are one sick bastard. Text Paul, tell him our unexpected visitors have decided to get their heads down. It's over.'

Brady's phone buzzes. He looks at the message from Marshall and smiles.
'So it begins. The sun is fucking shining again, so let me buy you a drink Tommy'?
'No thanks.'

'Why not'? asks Brady. 'You're not going anywhere. You practically live in here anyway.'

'Because I haven't got the money to buy you one back lad,' an embarrassed Tommy replies.

But Brady is adamant. 'Come on, let's me and you cut a deal. I buy the drinks and you tell me the truth about the sixties and what really went down. We have a little time, so let's have the stories.

What do you say'?

'I have them, but whether you chose to believe? It's been a long time. Even I find it difficult now to distinguish between the reality and the myth.'

Brady slaps Tommy on the arm. 'Hey, I'm a believer! He playfully points a finger at him, as if it's a pistol.

'Don't move or I'll shoot you.' He laughs whilst Tommy just smiles and shakes his head. 'Kids,' he mutters quietly under his breath.

Why the hell not tell Paul Brady what went on back then? He has got nothing else better to do and chances are the boy could be dead tomorrow. Besides he deserves to know. It is his heritage after all.

Brady returns with the beers and sits back down. He looks across to Tommy.

'Come on then legend, from the beginning.'

Tommy inhales then puts his cigarette in the ashtray. He takes a drink, his mind racing back to events what feel like a lifetime ago. Tommy smiles. 'They were quality days.

Once upon a time........

ACT ONE

ONCE UPON A TIME IN MANCHESTER

LONDON CALLING: 1963

In the empty snooker club, the Regal, in London's East end, in Bethnal green. Gangland bosses thirty-three year old twins Reggie and Ronnie are playing whilst discussing business. Top of the agenda is expanding their criminal empire across the country. The Kray's burning desire to rule nationwide is matched only by their ruthlessness to make it so, and together they make their plans.

'So what do you think Reg'?

'About going up to Manchester? I say yes. I was reading the other day if the Germans had won the war then Hitler was going to make the Midland hotel in Manchester his main headquarters for the North. If it was good enough for Adolf then it is for me. Besides I'm a Colonel, he was just a miserable Corporal.'

Reg smiles and takes his shot.

'So what are you getting at Ron. Are you really comparing us to the Germans?

Don't let Mum hear you say that.'

Ron laughs. 'I'm just saying that's all. There must be more to that city than cloth caps, chimneys and fucking pigeons.'

'Who do we know up there'? asks Reg.

'Paddy Mullen mainly. Our paths have crossed once or twice. He's a class act. Paddy owns the Cromford club, the best in Manchester. He's smart and goes under the radar, Not like the other bosses in that city. Easily somebody we can work with. Then there's his main boy, Tommy Keenan. We worked with Tommy last year. Another good lad, for a northerner that is. Tommy helped us shift those American cigarettes from the docks to make a tidy sum.'

Reg puts down his cue. 'Like you say, Paddy is somebody we can do business with. As for Tommy? He's small fry. A spoke in a wheel. But who's up there we can actually hit'?

Ron also stops playing. 'From what I'm told there are four main gangs. Salford, north and south Manchester and some run down dump called Moss side. The city is divided between them, but it's not London Reg. A few northern grease monkeys with lump hammers and chains. No class. We could put it all to bed in a night.' Reg grins. 'Just me and you. What do you think'?

Ron senses blood. 'let's do it Reg. Let's take the train up and surprise them. Educate the savages. We can book into the Midland, have a good drink then go and pay their top boys a visit. Shake the tramps up a bit and break a few heads.

Lay down some ground rules.'

Reg nods, he loves the idea. 'Show them there are two new sheriffs in town. The Kray twins. Men against boys. We'll show them how we do things in the big city.'

Ron is already planning ahead. 'Manchester, Liverpool, Leeds, Newcastle, even Glasgow. Invade Scotland and put the Jocks in their place.

We'll make the Mafia look small time.'

Reg is laughing. 'First we deal with Manchester Ron. One at a time.'

Suddenly Ron's eyes glaze over. 'Manchester. They call it the *'Rainy city'* don't they? Well it'll be raining fucking blood by the time we have finished with it.'

Ten Downing Street: Sir Peter Dowling, a senior member of the government and close personal friend of the prime minister, is sat in his office reading a highly classified document on the infamous Kray twins. The sixty-one year old Tory peer takes off his glasses and rubs his eyes. Dowling is mortified on what is in front of him. The Krays have become a monster that is out of control. Their influence poisonous and spreading and becoming a danger to the establishment.

The order, the way of things for the privileged few.

It has been made known to Dowling from the highest authority that they must be dealt with by 'whatever means necessary.' And it has fallen for him to make it so. The gloves have come off in the battle against this pair of East end villains, whose power now reaches into the inner sanctums of Parliament. A number of his fellow politicians, friends, over keen to enjoy the services of rent boys and other minors provided by the Krays at parties, and whom are now being blackmailed for their actions.

Caught on camera and in some situation filmed. Two in particular, one a member of cabinet and another of royal blood in scenes so horrific that if ever made public, could not just bring down the government, they could topple the monarchy and have them all, politicians and royals hanging from lamp posts.

Even more worrying for Dowling, he is amongst the worried band of brothers of whom the twins have pictures that would end his career in an eye blink. With a jail sentence a certainty to follow if they came to light, a man of his standing in years would simply not be able to endure. So this is more than personal for Dowling it is a crusade. Life and death.

His. They have to go.

Dowling hears a knock on his door. Entering is head of C11, fifty-eight year old Charles Worthing. A close ally of Dowling, they are former Eton boys and long standing friends. C11 are an elite highly secretive branch of Scotland Yard, whom operate beyond where the normal arm of British justice is not allowed to reach. A law unto themselves and the select band from whom they take orders.

A smiling Worthing walks across to Dowling who stands to shake his hand.

'Good to see you again Peter. No guesses for why you have sent for me'?

Dowling goes to his drinks cabinet and makes them both a large gin and tonic. He hands Worthing a glass. 'It appears our mutual friend has given us the red light. I assume you have the necessary people available to carry this out Charles'?

Worthing nods. 'The very best. And I believe something has just come up which could help us reach our goal A little unexpected and we'll have to work fast but it is possible.'

'Go on,' answers Dowling.

Worthing continues. 'Well we received word from our operative within the Kray's organisation that they are planning on making a surprise trip up north to Manchester this coming Monday. It appears our worse fears of them planning to expand their empire have come to fruition. But there is some good news for it has opened up a door of opportunity, one which just may be the answer to our problems.'

'You have my undivided attention Charles,' smiles Dowling. Worthing grins wide. 'It's quite simple really. We end this farce in the north. I have already briefed our northern brethren to warn them the Krays are heading up. I spoke to their best man up there. A Detective inspector George Collins. He'll be our liaison. With your permission I'd like to expand on what just may occur when those two vermin step foot off the train in Manchester.'

Dowling raises his glass. 'So long as they don't get back on it, you have a free hand to do whatever is required to rid us of this pestilence.'

Worthing joins Dowling in the toast.

He smiles. 'Then we have an understanding. The Krays don't leave Manchester alive'?

Dowling nods and the two men chink their glasses.

'End this fucking nightmare Charles.

        End it.'

THE GATHERING OF THE CLANS

It is night time in the north and from across a darkened Manchester, cars carrying the city's leading gangsters head towards the Portland hotel in Piccadilly. All have been summoned to a mystery meeting on the understanding it's in their very best interest to attend.

From across the river in Salford comes thirty-eight year old Michael Brady. Tall with jet black hair and sparkling blue eyes. A studious, deep thinking man but also a ruthless individual. Sat alongside him, his young sibling, thirty-four year old Paul. Medium build with choir boy looks that hide, like his older brother, a ferocious and frightening temper when roused.

From the north comes the *'Irishman,'* fifty-seven year old, Mayo born, John Flannery. Short of stocky build. A large forehead with fading curly hair. Green Irish smiling eyes. Outwardly mild mannered, but dangerous if underestimated.

For he too possesses a murderous nature when needed.

From Moss side comes the Jamaican, thirty-two year old, Jimmy *'the weed'* Da Silva.

A huge man with cold eyes but the possessor of a quick smile. So full of life, an extrovert, Da Silva is wearing a ridiculously expensive sheepskin coat, with diamond rings on most fingers and is feared and respected across the city

From the south comes forty-six year old Harry Taylor. Medium height, a rounded but handsome face with lively eyes, slicked back hair and a permanent cigarette in his mouth. A smooth operator whose calm persona and likeable personality also hides the capacity when required to wreak blood and carnage on his enemies.

Outside the Portland hotel two smartly dressed concierges stand idly chatting at the main entrance. They are twenty-three year old local lads from Ancoats, Peter Coates and Brian Ashley. Their attention is suddenly taken by a Rolls Royce pulling up. 'Here we go again,' says Coates, and they both immediately leap into action. Ashley strides up to greet the guest. He opens the car door.

'Good evening Sir.'

'How are you two doing tonight'? he replies.

The man takes out his wallet and hands Ashley a five pound note. He then walks over to Coates, who nods in acknowledgement, and he too is given the same amount. The man smiles. 'Keep up the good work boys.' Coates and Ashley stand and stare at each other in shock, clutching their tips as he disappears through the lobby.

'Was that who I think'? asks Coates.

Ashley grins wide. 'It certainly was. Bloody hell what's going on in there? We've got every fucking villain in the city inside.'

The man in question and last to arrive is Manchester's most famous gangster, Harry Taylor.

He swaggers into the hotel with all eyes upon him. Staff stop in their tracks and paying guests stare at this man who never seems to be out of the newspapers. Taylor makes his way over to the reception desk.

An attractive long blond-haired, twenty-one year old receptionist, Sara O'Farrell watches him approach. Sara has been aware he was due and has been looking forward to meeting the charismatic Taylor. She gives him her best smile. 'Good evening Mr Taylor, we have been expecting you. Please follow me.'

She leads Taylor into the lift and presses the button. The door shuts. Taylor smiles and offers her a cigarette. Sara shakes her head. 'No thank you, I'm on duty sadly sir. But I get off at two'?

He moves towards her. 'Hopefully I'll see you later then'?

Sara grins wide. 'Maybe'?

Taylor continues. 'You never know your luck in a big city girl……..'

He leans in to kiss her when suddenly the doors open.

Sara motions with an arm towards the corridor. A close call she thinks.

'Follow me sir.'

But in all reality Sara could not help herself. There is something about this man she finds so attractive.

Both step out of the lift with Sara in front and Taylor watching her walk off down the corridor. They stop halfway. She points to the door and inside voices can be heard.

Sara turns to Taylor and smiles. 'Well have a nice evening.'

Taylor winks at her. 'Keep it warm lady, I'm not going away.'

Inside and glaring at him, soon as he opens the door, are the rest of Manchester's underworld leaders. Taylor grins wide. 'Hello lads, no show without punch as they say. Does anyone know what the bloody hell this is all about'?

'Hey Harry,' replies Flannery. 'Welcome to our little party.'

'It's Errol fucking Flynn,' laughs Da Silva. 'Harry man, good to see you.'

The Brady brothers eye Taylor with a little suspicion due to a recent clash over the ownership of a popular pub on the city limits of their Salford and his Stretford territory. Settled finally but leaving a little bad blood and many bruised bodies.

Taylor stares across to the Brady brothers. 'Michael, Paul, good to see you lads. No hard feelings I hope'?

Michael smiles. 'None at all. Water under the Irwell Harry.'

'It's finished Harry,' adds Paul. 'In the past.' The Brady's walk over towards Taylor and they shake hands. He offers out cigarettes and glances around the lavish suite and especially at a long serving table with huge plates of sandwiches and bottles of wine and beer laid out.

'Someone has gone to a lot of trouble to arrange this little get together,' he says. 'We might as well get stuck in lads, until we figure out what's going on. If it's a hit we might as well go out on a full stomach.'

Suddenly the suite door opens and the host arrives.

The bosses face's drop in shock.

There stands veteran, fifty-four year old Police Detective-Inspector George Collins. A small but stocky figure with a world weary face. He is smiling wide. Collins takes off his trilby.

'The gathering of the Mancunian clans. Gentlemen how nice to see you getting along so well. It moves even my black heart. He pulls out his pockets.

'Look no handcuffs, so nobody panic.'

Flannery does not appear impressed on seeing Collins. 'George I'm a fucking busy man. What are you playing at'?

Taylor, cool as ever, laughs whilst putting both hands in the air. 'It's a fair kop George, I'll come quietly.'

'I've a hot date tonight George,' grins Da Silva. 'And I don't want my lady going cold if you know what I mean.'

The Brady brothers look the most tense of all present at Collins' sudden appearance into their midst. He notices this. 'Don't worry lads, a truce. I come in peace.'

Collins points across to a table. 'Shall we be seated? You are all going to want to hear this.'

They sit down with him at the head of the table.

'Please don't tell me you are retiring George,? Laughs Flannery. You'll break my cold stone Mayo heart.'

'Unfortunately for you I'm going nowhere John. How can I possibly consider retirement when you undesirables are still on the streets? I couldn't sleep at night. Besides,' he says smiling. 'I would miss you all too much.

But now down to business.

In just three days' time on Monday morning, those cockney loudmouth's, Ronald and Reginald Kray, will be departing on the 8-20 from Euston station and heading our way.

This is no social call. Their aim is to stake a claim up here in the north. Preferably....Manchester.'

For a second there is stunned silence before Michael Brady speaks up.

'You can't be serious George? I have it on good authority those two psychopaths never move out from the East end.'

'Too far away from their mum,' Paul adds. 'Fucking mummies boys. And one is a fag by all accounts. They wouldn't dare come up here causing trouble.'

Collins shakes his head. 'I don't know who's giving you boys your information but you are both wide off the mark. This is gospel. The Krays are coming. They are power mad and see themselves as kings of the realm. A criminal empire stretching from Land's End to John O'Groats that takes in all points north, far as Newcastle. And maybe even Glasgow. Yes the fucking Jocks. But you gentlemen, we,

are set to be their first port of call.'

'Why are you telling us this'? asks Taylor. 'The last time I looked we were on different sides.'

'Because we can't stop them coming Harry, for despite my better judgement on the matter, England remains a free country. So my hands are tied but yours aren't. You lot here tonight can do something about it. I need you to put your considerable immoral brains together and come up with a viable solution to keep these lunatics out. I'm open to all suggestions. Mad, bad and utterly fucking outrageous.'

'Do your job for you George,' remarks Flannery. 'Is that what you mean'?

Collins sighs heavily. 'Look Manchester isn't the big smoke. The politics and practicalities of fighting crime is different up here. Shall we say it suits all parties if everyone just keeps their heads down and gets along. Now you all know me, I'm a hard faced bastard, but I'm Manchester's hard faced bastard. I'm your hard faced bastard.

Nothing would give me greater pleasure in life than nicking you lot and throwing away the key in Strangeways. Because I love this fucking city. Hitler tried to bomb us back into the dark ages, but we survived, and I'll be damned if two cockney wide boys with their sharp suits and razors are going to turn the streets of Manchester red with blood in a gang war.

No chance. Not on my fucking watch.

Now, I and the gentlemen I'm here to represent are willing to do whatever necessary to ensure such a scenario does not occur. Let's just say there exists from this moment on an unofficial truce whilst this matter is resolved. And I have been told to inform you if this goes well, we'll be looking, shall we say a little more favourably on all your business interests. But if this doesn't work out as required, we'll come down on everyone here like a fucking ton of bricks.'

'What happens if they don't want to listen to reason George'? asks Da Silva.

He is now deadly serious. They all are as a business-like air fills the room.

All eyes intently on Collins.

'Like I said,' he replies. 'From the highest authority.'

'Are the Krays coming alone'? asks Taylor.

'Of course Harry,' smiles Collins. 'Those two think they are fucking bullet proof and believe it's divine providence that allows them to throw their weight around. But let me assure you, they are flesh and blood and bleed like everybody else. '

'I heard a story the twins have half the coppers in the Met on their payroll'? asks Paul Brady.

'Only half'? quips Collins. Everybody smiles.

He continues. 'Meet them at the station. Find someone you trust and agree on to explain in no uncertain terms that the Mancunian air is bad for their health. Too much smog and smoke gets on their soft southern chests. Tell them you can't buy fucking jellied eels in this city.'

'And you promise,' says Flannery. 'That if it gets bloody, no comebacks'?

'Collins nods. 'You have my word and everybody here knows I'm good for it.'

Flannery looks around at the faces of the other bosses. One by one they nod towards him. 'That's enough for us George.'

Collins claps his hands together. 'Right gentlemen give me some names'?

'There's only one,' replies Taylor.

'Tommy Keenan,' says Da Silva. Taylor nods in agreement.

'Agreed,' adds Flannery. 'Tommy can handle this pair of freaks.'

Michael Brady nods. 'Me too, I go along with old Irish here. Tommy is the man'

'No contest,' remarks his brother Paul. 'The only problem I see is if the Krays cut up rough. Maybe this particular job requires a more persuasive character? Paddy Costigan maybe'?

All present stare at Paul Brady like he is mad.

'Come off it Paul,' says Collins. 'Paddy's idea of gentle persuasion would be to blow up the fucking train as it arrives in Manchester.'

They all laugh but Collins is serious.

'Paul has a point George,' adds Da Silva. 'If events take a turn for the worst and these London boys don't play ball, it'll be people like

Paddy who settle this. Let's be realistic, the Krays will not go quietly.'

'Preferably with a sawn off in his hand,' says Michael Brady. Collins addresses Brady. 'For the next few days I see no evil, I hear no evil Michael, so I never fucking heard that. Right then I'm going to leave you thieves, rascal and vagabonds alone. Eat and drink and be merry courtesy of the Manchester Police. Last word before I depart this den of Mancunian inequity. Sort this out gentlemen.

This is our city. Don't let Manchester become just an extension of the Kray's empire. The twins are rotten bad fellows. They are vile, they are poison and they corrupt. And most important for you lot are bad for business. And on that note I'll bid you all goodnight.' Collins tips his hat towards the bosses before leaving the room.

Taylor watches as Collins shuts the door behind him. He turns to the others.

'Collins is right about one thing, if the Krays get their foot in the door we'll never get rid of them. This has to be nipped in the bud.'

'I agree,' says Flannery. 'They obviously think we are a soft touch. If not the case why don't they move on Liverpool, Leeds or Newcastle. Glasgow even? No they fancy it here.'

Michael Brady nods in agreement. 'I say we hit them so hard that they wake up on the Old Kent road looking for their fucking fingernails. Make a statement of intent so that no one from London ever dares contemplates trying it on again. We've got to stand our ground. Stay tight. Give them two choices, get back on the train or a first class ticket to the fucking graveyard.'

'By the way,' smiles Flannery. 'Talking of Paddy Costigan, I have him waiting in the hotel bar.' Everybody stares in annoyance at Flannery. He simply shrugs his shoulders. 'Well you never know, I thought maybe one of you was planning some kind of a hit. Let's be honest we have all had our moments here.'

'Oh come on John,' says Da Silva.

Taylor is not impressed. 'That man is an animal, a wild dog John. You've heard the story. I don't know how you tolerate having him around.'

'Don't play the saint with me Harry Taylor,' snaps Flannery. 'What are you a priest? What does Billy Tarr do for you, the fucking cleaning'? Men like Costigan are worth their weight in gold. In our line of business even wild dogs as you say, have their worth.'

Taylor shakes his head. 'I draw the line with scum like Costigan.'

Da Silva breaks up the argument. 'Will you two leave it? If Costigan is here let's use him to go pick up Tommy. It's Friday night, he shouldn't be too hard to find.'

'He'll be on the tables at Paddy Mullen's place, the Cromford club,' smiles Paul Brady.

'Tommy practically lives in there.'

'Don't you think it makes more sense if one of us goes to pick him up'? asks Taylor.

'No need to attract attention and if Costigan causes grief with the doormen or Mullen's clientele it could spell unwanted trouble. Paddy isn't someone we want to upset. Especially at the minute with the balloon set to go up.'

'No let's send Costigan,' says Michael Brady.'

'I just had a thought,' adds Da Silva. 'Why isn't Mullen here'?

'Paddy keeps his own council,' answers Taylor. 'He moves in much different circles to the rest of us and has also done business in the past with the Krays. He wouldn't put up with this. Maybe Collins thought he couldn't trust him'?

Flannery shakes his head. 'No Harry, more likely Collins doesn't want to lose his table at the Cromford club. If we are all agreed I'll go and tell Costigan to pick up Keenan'?

'Go tell him fetch,' says Taylor, in a sarcastic tone. Flannery eyes Taylor angrily before leaving the suite.

'Don't needle him Harry,' smiles Paul Brady. 'The Paddies are naturally paranoid. It's their fucked up history. They blame us for everything. Besides we have a couple of tooled up lads in the next room'!

'Me too,' grins Da Silva.

Taylor shakes his head in disbelief. 'I don't fucking believe it. Whatever happened to good old fashion traits like honesty and trust'? Anyone would think we were common criminals.' After a second they all laugh.

Even Taylor. 'Right then,' he says. 'If you boys will excuse me for a moment there's a young lady in reception who I need to have a quick word with for later on.'

Da Silva smiles. 'Errol Flynn is at it again man.'

Sat nursing a large glass of whisky at the hotel bar is thirty-one year old Paddy Costigan. A brute of a man, huge in size with a bulldog pug-nosed, badly scarred face. A dark nasty aura surrounds him. Costigan gives off a stench of violence. A young couple sat quietly in the corner of the room cannot help but stare at him. Costigan catches their eyes and they both swiftly look away in mortal fear.

John Flannery approaches him.

'I have a job for you Paddy. One that involves a little delicacy.' Costigan is listening intently. 'Whatever you say Mr Flannery.'

'I need you to find Tommy Keenan at the Cromford club and bring him back here. Tell him it's a matter of urgency. But, and I cannot stress this enough Paddy, There must be no trouble. Do you understand? I can't afford to be made to look bad in this matter.'

Flannery is still rather unsure whether his message is getting through.

'Tommy is a good friend of mine, as is Mr Mullen the owner. Be firm but be polite.'

Costigan nods. 'Yes Mr Flannery, no trouble. Just bring Keenan back here.'

'No broken bones Paddy or blood on the pavement'?

'No Mr Flannery, no broken bones or blood on the pavement.'

'Good lad,' Flannery smiles. 'Now away with you son.'

Costigan stands to go. He heads out of the hotel and pushes the two concierges out of his path as he leaves. Both end up in a huddle on the floor.

'Get out of the fucking way,' growls Costigan, as he ventures off into the Manchester night.

'What's his problem'? asks Ashley. As he gets back up, brushing himself down.

'I don't know,' replies Coates.

'But I fucking hope and pray it's never me.'

THE CROMFORD CLUB

Paddy Costigan makes his way towards the Cromford club. Here gangsters, priests, movie stars, famous singers, footballers and politicians mix happily. Entrance is by invitation only and the sight of Costigan coming towards them has the Cromford's three burly doormen twitching.

'What the hell does this lunatic want'? whispers one, well out of Costigan's earshot.

'Who's going to tell him he can't come in'? replies another.

'Calm down lads,' exclaims the third and senior doorman, Thirty-five year old ex-boxer Jimmy Toolan. 'He's probably just here on business.' Costigan approaches the doormen. 'Evening boys, how are you doing'?

Remembering his boss Flannery's warning, Costigan attempts a friendly smile, but it only makes him appear even more menacing.

'Evening Paddy. Look no offence, we don't want any trouble, but you know Mr Mullen's strict door policy? Guests only on a Friday, no exceptions.'

'I have an urgent message for Tommy Keenan,' says Costigan. Toolan relaxes and steps forward towards Costigan. 'Come with me Paddy.'

He escorts Costigan into the club foyer where the powerful voice of a woman singing can be heard coming from the next room. Those guests present in the foyer stare rather worryingly at Costigan. 'Paddy please stay here for a minute whilst I go and find Mr Mullen.'

Costigan hands Toolan a murderous stare. 'Hurry up I haven't got all fucking night.'

Toolan is no shrinking violet and can seriously take care of himself, but Costigan is known for being a maniac. He goes over to him. 'Just stay calm yeah? I'll be back in a minute.'

That said Toolan steps through an entrance into the luxurious inner sanctum of the Cromford club.

Costigan catches a slight glimpse through a half open door. What he sees is a lavish room bedecked out in the finest surroundings. Dimly lit, shrouded in cigarette smoke, a mysterious other world. Tables are evenly scattered around where diners and drinkers sit gossiping and laughing. Others deep in business talk. On the stage an aspiring young Welsh lady singer called Shirley Bassey is bringing the house down.

This is the Cromford club. Manchester's classiest joint.

Sat on one of the side tables is the owner, fifty-four year old, Paddy Mullen. A tall and impressive man. Elegantly suited and clearly a much respected figure. Mullen is in conversation with two of his best friends. Owner of a Mancunian gambling empire, forty-four year old, Lenny Foyle and the Manchester United manager, Fifty-three year old, Matt Busby. Both are equally sartorially dressed as Mullen and also kings of their domains.

The doorman approaches Mullen's table. 'Excuse me Mr Mullen.'

'Yes Jimmy'?

He leans down and whispers into his boss's ear. Mullen leans back on being told of Costigan's presence and request. Just the thought of having him on the premises makes his skin crawl. 'Get that damn Costigan out of the foyer and away from the punters Jimmy. Take him to my office. I'll be with you shortly.'

'Yes sir.'

Busby notices his friend's sudden change of mood. 'Is everything okay Paddy'?

'I'm not sure yet Matt. 'Will you lads excuse me for a couple of minutes'?

Mullen stands to go. 'Of course,' replies Busby.

'No worries Pat,' smiles Foyle. A man who operates in the same world as Mullen and knows automatically something is not right.

'Paddy has a problem Matt,' he says. 'I've seen that look before. Something isn't right.'

They watch on as Mullen makes his way through the dining room.

Paddy Mullen enters his office and stood waiting for him is Paddy Costigan. The two shake hands. Mullen smiles but he feels uneasy. 'Patrick it's so good to see you. How are the family'?

Costigan shrugs his shoulders. 'Last I heard they were fine Mr Mullen.'

That's good, now what's this about Tommy Keenan? What do you want with him? I'm sure you and Mr Flannery are well aware he's a good friend of mine'?

'There's no problem Mr Mullen. None at all. Mr Flannery and the other bosses just need to have a little chat with him regarding a business matter.'

Mullen lights up a cigarette. 'You know of my reputation Patrick'?

'Yes sir.'

'Regarding this so called business matter, I wouldn't be happy if anything unfortunate was to happen to Tommy. Not a scratch, a broken nose or an unlucky bang on his head. Do we understand each other'?

'We do Mr Mullen. I'd never lie to you.'
Mullen smiles. 'Good lad.' He picks up his phone.
'Have Tommy Keenan come up to my office.'

Twenty-seven year old Tommy Keenan, man about town, fixer, gangster. Black hair with striking blue eyes and movie star looks is enjoying himself on the Blackjack tables. Swamped by a crowd of admirers, Tommy is on a winning run and the chips are piled high in front of him. Suddenly a croupier taps Tommy on the shoulder and whispers into his ear.
'Tommy, Paddy needs you upstairs in his office straight away.'
He stares at his mountain of chips. 'Cash me in please Charlie.' He hands him a handful of chips then turns to walk back through the hub of backslappers. Tommy heads towards his girlfriend. A young blond lady, twenty-four year old Alison Jones. Waif like beauty. An English rose.
Tommy kisses Alison. 'I have to go and see Paddy. I shouldn't be too long.'
'What does he want'? asks Alison.
'Oh he probably just wants to know if I have any good tips for the horses.'
Alison kisses Tommy on the cheek. 'Of course he does. I love you Tommy Keenan.'
He smiles. 'Then I'm the luckiest man in the world.'

Tommy knocks on Mullen's office door, enters and his smiling face turns to
stone when he sees Paddy Costigan standing staring at him. Tommy warily addresses Costigan. 'How's your luck Paddy'?
Costigan totally ignores him.
Paddy Mullen is sat behind his desk. 'It appears young Keenan, your presence is required elsewhere and quickly.' Tommy points towards Costigan.
'With him'? Mullen nods.
'John Flannery and the other bosses would like a chat about a subject I know nothing of, but Paddy here has given me his word he'll look after you.'
Mullen stares daggers at Costigan. A look that unnerves even him.

'He has indeed been kind enough to guarantee his own good health upon the fact. Now Paddy could you wait downstairs please? Tommy will be with you shortly.'

'But Mr Mullen....' Mullen's tone is firm but measured with a hint of a threat.

'Paddy Costigan, this is my club, my rules now get out.'

Costigan reluctantly turns to leave the room and glares angrily at Tommy on the way.

Tommy is relieved to see him go. 'Oh great you have gone and upset him now.'

An exasperated Mullen stands from his chair. 'Tommy what's going on'?

He shrugs his shoulders. 'I was hoping you'd know'?

Mullen looks worried. 'Nothing happens in this city without my knowledge, but I have to admit I'm out of the loop on this one and that makes me very nervous. Something isn't right.

Have you been behaving'?

Tommy smiles and sits down on Mullen's desk.

'You know me, fooled around a bit but nothing dangerous.'

'Are you working on anything that might have put somebody's nose out of joint'?

He shakes his head. 'Nothing to rattle Flannery or the others.'

'Right, listen up. Go to the meeting. They all know you are under my protection. Then come straight back here later and fill me in. I can smell trouble son. There is something rotten in the air.'

Tommy stands to leave. 'Paddy one other thing, I've left Alison downstairs.'

Mullen smiles. 'Don't worry I'll invite her onto mine, Len's and Matt's table until you return. We have some of the United lads calling by later, so we'll ensure they make a big fuss of her. She'll be treated like a princess.'

Tommy sighs. 'Oh great, whilst I'm about to disappear into the night with the craziest Mick ever to come out of Ireland, my girlfriend is being serenaded by a bunch of randy footballers.'

Mullen laughs. 'I'll keep a good eye, now get going before Costigan starts tearing my bloody doormen apart limb by limb.'

A foul mood Paddy Costigan with Tommy Keenan behind him leaves the Cromford club. Tommy looks around. 'Where's the car'?

'It's ten minutes by foot you lazy bastard,' scowls Costigan.
'So come on Paddy, what's going on'? Costigan ignores him and keeps walking.
'Oh come on Pat,' pleads Tommy.
'I haven't got a clue. I was told to just come and pick you up and that's it.'
'Am I in trouble?'
Costigan smiles. 'You're always in fucking trouble. Too much to say for yourself. Always have had. A big fucking mouth Keenan.'
Tommy laughs. 'You don't like me do you Paddy?'
An irritated Costigan grunts. 'I don't like anybody, now just shut up and walk.'
But Tommy can't resist winding him up. 'I like you Paddy,' he says with a huge grin. Costigan snaps and in a fit of rage has him by the lapels on his suit.
'You mouthy bastard. You just don't know when to shut up do you? You are going to talk yourself into an early grave Keenan. Luckily for you I'm under orders, now for the last time just fucking walk and don't even breathe loud. Otherwise,
  so help me God'?
Costigan let's go of Tommy and strides off. He shrugs himself down, straightens his tie and decides to stay quiet. Tommy does not want to risk being murdered this very night.
  The concierge's are still on duty outside the hotel when the bulky figure of Paddy Costigan comes into view hurtling towards them. He pushes them aside.
  'Evening lads I feel your pain,' smiles Tommy, following close behind.
  Costigan leads him towards the suite. They both stand outside the door. He knocks and opens it slight enough for Tommy to walk through.
  'In you go smart mouth, I'll see you later.'
' Not if I see you first,' says Tommy. Before hastily walking inside before a mad eyed Costigan has a chance to reply.

FOR THE ANGELS
  A nervous looking Tommy Keenan enters and all eyes are upon him. A smiling John Flannery approaches. 'Tommy Keenan, thank you so much for coming.' Flannery puts an arm around Tommy's

shoulders and leads him over to a table where they are all sat. Obviously still pensive, Tommy takes in all the faces staring back at him. It's an A list of Manchester's underworld.

'Okay gent's, cards on the table. What do you want from me?'

Harry Taylor speaks first. 'Tommy, last year you did some work for the Krays in London. What did you make of them'?

He shrugs his shoulders. 'Good lads, I had no problems. Everything went smooth as clockwork, the job got done, it got done well. We shock hands and they paid up.'

Michael Brady is next. 'What Harry means is should we fear them'?

'Who's we'? asks Tommy.

'Manchester, Tommy boy,' smiles Da Silva.

Tommy is confused. 'What's going on here'?

Michael Brady passes Tommy a glass of wine. 'On Monday morning they are coming up from London with the intention of taking over. Got it in their retarded heads we are soft and ripe for plucking and will give in at the sight of their fucking Saville Row suits.'

'Walk all over us,' says Flannery.

'We can't have it Tommy,' jumps in Da Silva. 'We just can't have it.'

Tommy goes to have a cigarette, but his lighter isn't working. Taylor strikes a match and offers to light it for him. He does so.

'We need you to have a little chat with them. Explain discreetly but firmly that they should just get back on the train and go home. The weather is rough. We wouldn't want them to catch a cold. Call it northern hospitality.'

'And how exactly do I go about this'? asks Tommy.

Taylor smiles. 'Come on Tommy, you have a silver tongue and can charm the birds out of the trees.'

'It will be better coming from you,' adds Flannery. 'A friendly face, someone they know and have done business with. And most importantly, whom they trust.'

'And what if they refuse to listen'? says Tommy.

'Then it becomes our problem,' replies Michael Brady.

A shocked Tommy cannot believe what he is hearing. 'You seriously can't be contemplating hitting the Krays?'

Taylor shakes his head. 'Tommy, Tommy you really surprise me. Don't be so naïve son. You have been around long enough to know anybody can be got rid of, if the will and the firepower is there to achieve it. Kings and Queens, Prime Ministers. Hell somebody managed to hammer a couple of bullets through John F Kennedy's skull last month. The President of the fucking United States was put down. So who on this earth is going to give a moment's grief about those two lunatics? Nobody will care, I promise you. Apart from their Mother of course. Who I'm told is a lovely lady'?

But Tommy has major doubts and is convinced they are all mad to even consider this.

'Lads, I've worked down there. I know, I've seen it. They control the entire East End and huge swathes of club land over across the city. This is such a huge call that I'd urge you all to think again. The twins have great influence in London that even extends into Parliament. Politicians, bent coppers high in the met who dance to their tune. They collect dirt on the establishment like a schoolboy collects stamps.

They love it and they bloody well use it.'

Taylor listens intently but he is not impressed. 'True, but if the Krays go down they'll all run for cover. The twins pollute everything and everyone they come into contact with. Trust me, no one will care Tommy. Indeed we'll be doing the country a favour.'

Tommy remains unsure. 'People call them crazy Harry, but I'm telling you they have a sixth sense. The twins can smell trouble and if it does turn nasty you are going to have to cut their heads off to stop them coming for you.'

'Like we said before Tommy,' replies Da Silva, in rather ominous tone.

'Our problem.'

'They are staying at the Midland,' says Flannery. 'You turn up and switch on the charm and none of this has to come to pass.'

'What about Paddy'? asks Tommy.

Flannery looks nervously at the others. 'This isn't Mullen's problem Tommy. He has no need to know, for it'll only complicate matters. Best for him and us,

and you in particular that he's kept in the dark until we sort this problem out.'

Tommy stares long and hard at Taylor. 'Okay, so the worse scenario I fail. What then'?

Flannery looks around and they all nod back to him.

'Then this is how it will be. We'll have four shooters within spitting distance of the room. Depending on how it goes the twins either walk out of the hotel and back to the train station breathing and in one piece.'

Or they leave in body bags,' adds Paul Brady. 'With blood staining their fucking Saville Row suits.'

Taylor notices Tommy's deep concerns and attempts to douse cold water on this bloodcurdling scenario. 'But hopefully Tommy, with you whispering sweet nothings in their cockney ears we'll never have to make that call'?

'It's all down to you Tommy boy,' smiles Da Silva. 'The Angels have decided this beautiful city of ours is in your hands.'

Flannery laughs. 'The Man who saved us from the Krays. You'll go down in

folklore son. A legend.'

Tommy cannot help but smile. 'So I'm doing this for the angels? I'm filling up. One thing more, do I actually have a choice in this'?

'All life is a choice Tommy lad,' replies Flannery. 'Either you chose to live or you chose to die.'

Taylor pats Tommy on the back and refills his wine glass. 'Get working on your speech son.' Tommy looks around the table and lights another cigarette. He inhales deeply, puts his head back and sighs.

The night has suddenly taken a turn for the unexpected and the worse.

THE BOY WITH NO SHOES

Tommy Keenan enters back into the packed Cromford dining room and walks over towards Paddy Mullen's table. Sat with Mullen are also now Manchester United footballers Denis Law and Paddy Crerand. A smiling Keenan nods to acknowledge their presence and sits down next to Mullen. 'Well how'd it go'? he asks.

'It was nothing at all,' replies Tommy. 'Flannery has got hold of some bootleg whisky from home. He wants me to spread the word.'

Mullen eyes Tommy and does not look convinced. 'And that's it, all this fuss'?

'That's it,' replies Tommy. 'Not worth worrying about. It's one step up from potcheen at best.'

Mullen smiles. 'You can take the man out of Mayo'?

Tommy laughs. He lights up a cigarette. 'Still a farmer's boy at heart is our John. In his head he's never left Belcarra.' Mullen stares long and hard at Tommy. It unnerves him.

.....'What'? he says, appearing ruffled.

'And the others'?

'Nothing, there's nothing else.'

'Just that'? asks Mullen.

'Nothing I swear,' answers Tommy. Inside his heart is racing. He has never before lied to Mullen and had no intention of ever doing so.

Until now.

Mullen's granite features suddenly break into a smile and he points towards the dance floor. There Matt Busby is dancing with Tommy's girlfriend Alison.

'Matt has kept her busy,' smiles Mullen. 'He thinks he's Fred bloody Astaire! Another ten minutes and they'll run off together.'

Busby leads a beaming Alison by the hand back over to the table. Everybody stands up to greet them. 'You are a lucky man Thomas Keenan,' he says.

'You take good care of this lass.'

Tommy smiles. 'I intend to and thank you Mr Busby.'

Busby kisses Alison's hand before passing it over to Tommy. 'Now go and dance this beautiful lady's feet off lad.'

Tommy and Alison return to the dance floor and Mullen and Foyle watch them go.

'Is everything sorted now Paddy'? he asks.

Mullen's eyes are locked on Tommy.

'I hope so Len,' he says. 'I truly hope so.'

Tommy holds a smiling Alison close. 'So what was so important that you had to leave me in the charming arms of the most famous man in Manchester'?

He laughs. 'The usual stuff. Curing lepers and blind kids. All sorted now though. I'm all yours.'

'Tommy, why don't you ever tell me what you do for a living'?

He grins wide. 'I just told you I cure....' Alison puts her hand gently over Keenan's mouth to stop him talking. 'Just dance Saint Thomas, Just dance.'

Tommy kisses Alison and whispers into her ear.

'I love you.'

The next morning Tommy Keenan jumps off the back of a double decker bus on Deansgate, Manchester, and goes into a busy cafe. It is busy and *All my Loving* by the Beatles is playing on the radio. The smell of sizzling bacon fills the air. Tommy spots Paddy Mullen already sat down with his breakfast and goes over to join him.

'Morning Paddy.'

'Are you thirsty'? replies Mullen.

'Excuse me'? answers a surprised Tommy.

'Here have my coffee.' He slides his cup of coffee over to Tommy.

'Are you hungry'? continues Mullen. He then picks up his full breakfast plate and throws it across the table. 'How about my wallet, do you want my money'? Mullen takes out a large bundle of notes and slams then down on the table.

Suddenly Tommy realises what is going on. 'Paddy please'?

But an angry Mullen is seething. 'How about the clothes off my back'?

Here's my tie.' He rips it off and throws it in Tommy's face.

'Go on put it on,' he says.'

Tommy goes to pick it up only for Mullen to snatch it back off him. 'You lied to me boy.'

Tommy's head is down. 'I'm sorry.'

'Look at me,' insists Mullen. Keenan stares towards his boss. He has never seen him this angry. 'I'm going to tell you a story lad and you'd do well to listen.

There was this kid from Collyhurst.

He was twelve-years old. Eight stone wet through. His Father would knock him around like a spinning top. His mother was a drunk. Only ever cared where the next drink was coming from. So this poor kid, one day I'm out and about in town and I see him sat on a bench in Piccadilly. He's crying so I go up to him and ask what's wrong? He points to his shoes and both of them have big holes in the soles.

He tells me with tears falling down his face that if he went home with his shoes in this state his father would take the belt to him. So I take him into Manchester's finest shoe shop and picked him out the best pair of shoes they had. And then this kid smiled. We said our goodbyes and he went home.

The next day I'm in town again and I see this same kid, sat on the same bench. Wearing the same old shoes. And again he's crying. He tells me that he'd gone home and his father had accused him of stealing the new shoes. To teach the kid a lesson he then kicked him around
the house and slashed him with a buckle belt. Then he threw the new shoes into the fire. This kid was badly bruised. A black eye, busted lip.

Well I got mad.

First I bought him another pair of shoes and then made him take me to his house. The kid was terrified when we knocked on the door. His father appeared, a big brute of a man, but a bully. You know the type, only picked on women and kids. I told the boy to go inside whilst I spoke to his old man. I asked him if he knew who I was and he nodded.

I told him that if he ever even shouted at the kid again I'd personally break every bone in his body. And do you know what happened'?

'He never touched the kid again,' says Tommy.

His eyes firmly fixed on Mullen and close to tears.

'Correct,' continues Mullen. 'That same kid, when he was sixteen came knocking at my door looking for a job. He began by running errands and sweeping up around the club. I always told him to watch what goes on. Listen and learn. Always show respect. To keep his nose clean and I'd look after him. The kid graduated and I grew to love him like a son.

He spread his wings, flew the nest. He became a man, respected. I had a father's pride in how he treated people and did business. I only ever had one rule. An eleventh commandment. Never lie to me. And last night Thomas Keenan,

you broke it.'

Tommy interrupts. 'Paddy, I had no choice. It was for your own good. I didn't want you involved in this madness.'

'So you did lie to me'? replies Mullen.

Tommy appears shell-shocked. 'You tricked me'?

Mullen says quietly, but with clear intent. 'I'll ask you this one last time Tommy. Tell me what's going on'?

Left with little choice he opens up. 'They are going to hit the Krays.'

'Say that again'? utters a stunned Mullen.

Tommy continues. 'On Monday morning the Krays are arriving from London. They have it in their thick heads to take over. Flannery, the Brady brothers, Da Silva and Taylor have been given the all clear by the Old Bill to deal with it. I've have been given this one chance to reason with the twins, and if that doesn't work,

they are dead men.'

'Shooters'? asks Mullen.

'The best we have.'

'If I can't get them back on the train, five minutes after I leave their hotel room the balloon goes up and they go down.'

'Why you'?

Tommy shrugs his shoulders. 'I've no idea. Look Paddy, nobody wants you involved because this isn't your problem. Please, this one time, for me. Just keep your distance. I don't want you mixed up in this.'

'So my Mancunian brothers in arms don't trust me'? replies Mullen.

Tommy shakes his head. 'No it's not that, they are just businessmen playing the odds. To them you are an outsider. You operate on a different level.'

But Mullen is not convinced. 'I'll tell you why the others didn't want me involved, It's because I'd have told them this is sheer bloody stupidity,

and I'd have ended it.'

'Paddy this came from the police, it's political. If I fail the gangs have been given the red light to do their dirty work for them. It's a rubber stamped hit. An assassination. Stay out of it. Please, I can do this thing. I can end it peacefully with no bloodshed.'

'The kid with the holes in his shoes,' laughs Mullen. 'Who was scared of his own shadow is going to make everything right'?

'I'm not a kid anymore. I've listened and learnt from the best. I can do it.'

Mullen stares hard at Keenan. In his eyes he still sees the same scared young kid beaten to a pulp by his father. Finally he smiles. 'Pass me my wallet.'

Tommy hands it over.

'And my breakfast.' Tommy laughs and passes the plate back.

Mullen leans over the table. 'I want to know everything you know and if it satisfies me you just might leave here in one piece.'

'Yes sir,' Says a smiling Tommy, as he lights up a cigarette.

'And another thing,' says Mullen. Suddenly he slaps him on the head and snatches the cigarette out of his mouth and throws it onto the floor.

'He glares at a shamefaced Tommy. 'You ever lie to me again I'll put you back on that bench in Piccadilly where I found you. Now what are you having for breakfast'?

Tommy feels it safe to smile and catches the merest glimpse of forgiveness in Mullen's eyes. But one thing is certain.

He'll never lie to him again.

Paddy Mullen and Tommy Keenan are walking along the banks of the River Irwell. Nearby is the docks with huge freight ships from all over the world loading and unloading their cargos. The two stop for a moment and stare over the water.

'From across the planet they come here Tommy,' says Mullen. 'The United States, China, Africa, Japan, Russia and never one bit of hassle. And yet two mouthy cockneys with delusions of grandeur and a mother fixation from the East End can cause us such grief'?
So what are you going to say to them'?

Tommy appears transfixed by the ships. He turns to look at Mullen.

'Well it isn't Shakespeare I can tell you that. I've a speech in mind Paddy, but I feel I only have it in me to deliver once. Do you know what I mean'?
Mullen smiles. 'I hear it from the theatre types the entire time son. It'll be alright on the night? I pray for your sakes you don't get tongue tied, because those two crazy bastards will cut it out. '

Mullen clenches his fist. 'The Krays respect only one thing Tommy. Power. Real power. Oh they'll have done their homework with the result being they consider Manchester ripe for the taking. Your words have to resonate loud with them that they are set to make the biggest mistake of their lives.

Leave a lasting impression, not just to get them on the train, but to ensure they never come back. No half measures. Anything else, if you come across in any way weak or unsure they'll see through you and the game is over.

And the shooting will begin.'

Tommy has not taken his eyes off Mullen. 'Paddy you have to promise whatever happens you won't step in'?

Mullen shakes his head. He is disgusted with himself for not hot being able to help this boy, who is his son in all but blood 'This thing is already in motion. Even if I wanted to I couldn't. No it's down to you Tommy. You have to kill them with words.'

Mullen stops and puts his hand on Tommy's shoulder. 'Send them home.'

The two men look across at the docks. It feels like the gentle calm before a raging storm. No more words are necessary.

THE HITMEN

Welcome to Salford: Saturday Afternoon: The Brady brothers, Michael and Paul drive through the gates of Monroe's scrapyard on the borders of Salford and Manchester. Around them huge mounds of old cars reach high. A crane is busy flattening scrap metal. The workers whom they drive past all nod in acknowledgement, but the Brady's ignore them. Michael suddenly spots the owner, fifty-six year old fat, balding and permanently in a bad mood, Eric Monroe. Michael motions for Paul to pull over.

Wearing a hard hat Monroe is deep in conversation with his foreman.

He is raging. 'Sack the idiot, this is his second day off sick in a year. I'm not a fucking charity.' Monroe notices the Brady's walking towards him.

He mutters under his breath. 'Oh no, what the fucking hell do these two clowns want'?

Monroe smiles wide as the brothers draw closer. 'Michael, Paul it's good to see you. What brings you down here on a Saturday afternoon'?

'We are looking for Damien Quinn'? replies Paul.

'Is he around'?

Monroe points up towards the crane. 'He's up there.'

'Well fucking go and get him down here then,' snaps Michael.

A shaken Monroe motions to his foreman to go and fetch Quinn.

'Your payments are late Monroe'? says Paul.

'Things are a bit tight at the moment Paul. No bugger is paying up. You know what they are like around here.'

Michael smiles and shakes his head. 'Come on Eric, you are working on a Saturday afternoon for Christ's sake. You must be rolling in it, so don't mess us around. I want two grand by Friday, otherwise you'll find yourself at the bottom of one of these fucking piles. Understand'?

Monroe nods his head.

The foreman returns with twenty-three year old Damien Quinn. A Salford lad. Slim build with cropped black hair and large blue eyes. Cool, scared of nothing and a devil may care attitude. However where Quinn differs is in his ability to handle a shotgun and kill for money.

Paul Brady stares at Monroe and his foreman. 'Fuck off.'
The two men shuffle off quickly leaving Quinn alone with the Brady brothers.

'How are you keeping Damien'? asks Michael.
'Fine thanks Mr Brady. It's good to see you both.'

'We have a job for you,' says Paul. 'It'll pay well, but it may mean you having to leave Manchester for a while.'

Quinn laughs and looks around at the scrapyard. 'You mean having to leave all this behind? No problem I'm in.'
Michael smiles. 'Good lad, we'll pick you up tomorrow at three and explain more. Be ready.'

Paul Brady winks at Quinn and smiles. 'Nice to be working together again Damian.'

'Likewise,' he replies.

The brothers get back in the car and drive off. Quinn is watching them go, when suddenly Monroe walks back over, until only inches from his face.

'Eh Quinn, I don't pay you to stand around. Now get back to fucking work soft lad.'

Quinn eyes Monroe, as if sizing him up for a future target, before simply smiling and declaring. 'Anything you say Mr Monroe.'

One day soon Quinn has just decided he is going to kill Monroe.

Welcome to Moss Side: Saturday night: With bodyguards on either side of him Jimmy
'the weed' Da Silva, steps out of his car opposite the Nile Club. He stares with disdain at the run down building. Situated on the first

floor, the main entrance is blocked by two burly, black doormen. They swiftly move aside as he goes upstairs.

On entering Da Silva can hardly see through the thick swirling Marijuana and tobacco smoke. A saxophone player is performing live and the dance floor is packed. He clicks his fingers and a pretty young girl from behind the bar in a mini skirt and beehive haircut comes over. Da Silva talks into her ear and the girl points a finger to pick out a table through the haze.

Sat holding court is twenty-eight years old Leon *'Pearly'* Spence. Dressed immaculate in a tailor-made suit and handmade shoes, Spence's devilish good looks and charm is currently being used on three female admirers, hanging onto his every word. Spence is Jimmy
'the weed's' most deadly hired hand and a born killer.

Da Silva only uses him sparingly because of his disturbing nature, and the fact Spence actually appears to enjoy killing. A smiling Da Silva approaches his table.

'Leon my man'!

He leans down and shakes a beaming Spence's hand.

'What are you doing in here Jimmy'? replies Spence. 'This isn't your scene.'

'We need to talk,' says Da Silva. 'Can we go outside'?
'Sure,' he replies. Both men head out of the club. They are followed down the stairs by Da Silva's bodyguards.

Da Silva offers Spence a cigarette. 'We have to go to work on Monday Leon. I need you at your best, for this is huge. We cannot have any mistakes.'

'Who is it'? inquires Spence.
'They are two brothers. Twins. You'll be working with three other men.'

'Twins? It's not the Krays is it'? laughs an excited Spence.

Da Silva stares and says nothing.

'Fucking Hell Jimmy, is it'?
'It's not a certainty Leon. They have one chance to get back on the train, if not, well you and the others blast them into the next life to meet their ancestors.'

'Guns? I was hoping I'd get the chance to carve them up.'

Da Silva suddenly remembers why Spence turns his stomach. 'Stay by your phone tomorrow. I'll be in touch. Now go back to your ladies.'

'Hey man I can smell blood and it excites me. They could get lucky tonight.'

As Spence heads back upstairs Da Silva watches him go. 'He turns to his bodyguards. 'That bastard makes my skin crawl.

Come on I need a drink.'

Welcome to Collyhurst: In Billy Greens Pub, Paddy Costigan is sat at the bar drinking whisky when in through the door walks his boss, John Flannery. The pub is crammed and in a state of mayhem. An Irish fiddle and accordion band is playing the *Fields of Athenray.* Every table is packed. A fist fight breaks out and pint pots and bottles fly before it is swiftly broken up and taken outside.

Rousing sing songs are in full flow. Drowning out the brave efforts of the band to be heard. At Costigan's feet a dog is licking clean a bowl of beer gifted to it by the locals. It's Saturday night in Billy Greens and you can't get a seat to save your life.

A smiling Flannery sidles up to an unsuspecting Costigan. 'How are you Patrick, you up for a large one'? Flannery motions the barmaid over towards them. 'Two large whiskies,' please my dear.'

Costigan nods in gratitude. 'Thank you Mr Flannery.'

The barmaid hands both men their drinks. Flannery clutches his glass and smiles at Costigan. 'Who'd you like to drink to Patrick'?

'I'm not sure,' he replies.

'How about to our friendship'? answers Flannery.

Costigan smiles wide, he raises his glass. 'To our friendship.' The two men clink glasses and down the whisky in one.

Flannery leans close to Costigan. 'Patrick, I need you. I need a friend and someone I can completely trust to perform a difficult task.'

'Anything Mr Flannery.'

'It may mean you'll have to leave England for a while. Go back to Ireland until I give you the all clear.'

'That'd be grand, I have some things I need to fix back there. I left in a hurry, a little family problem. All got a little messy.'

Suddenly Flannery is intrigued. He knows all but nothing of Costigan's background.

'Tell me what happened Patrick'?

'Well I lost my temper and crippled my cousin.'

A shocked Flannery stares open mouthed. 'How the fuck did that happen'?

'He owed me money and was refusing to pay, so I put a kitchen knife through his hand. He was a writer, a good one as well they say, but he had to give it up after that.'

'Could he not use the other hand'? asks Flannery.

'Not really,' replies Costigan. 'He lost it in the war.'

Flannery is stuck for words. He tugs the passing barmaid's arm. 'Two more large ones please.'

Flannery hands Paddy his drink and offers up a toast. 'To families, fuck em'!

Costigan raises his glass.

'Fuck em.'

Welcome to Ancoats: Rea's funeral Parlour: Paddy Mullen enters into the office of fifty-five year old Salvatore Rea. A large bulky figure with fierce Sicilian features. Piercing eyes, large moustache and greased back oily hair. Rea and Mullen are close friends, they share a close bond. Brothers in all but blood. They embrace and both are smiling.

'How's the funeral business doing Salvatore'?

'Thriving Patrick. People keep dying, for luckily God in his divine wisdom forbids us to live forever. I soothe my soul by commiserating with the crying widows and daughters. I serve them good wine and pay due respect. And I grow a little richer with every loss. A sad but true fact of life. But that's me, how goes the way of things in your world'?

Paddy sighs. 'Very complicated.'

'Something is wrong, what is it'? asks Salvatore.

'There's a storm coming my friend. One that may well blow us all away.'

Salvatore puts his arm on Paddy's shoulder. 'How long have we known each other, thirty years? If you have a problem, it becomes my problem. Our families have shared births, marriages and loss. Great days and bad. We survived a war. You looked after my wife and children when your government felt it wise to intern me. This whilst I had two sons fighting in their army. The windows on our houses was smashed on the day that idiot Mussolini declared an alliance with the Germans.

And you, what did you do?

You went and boarded up the broken windows and stood outside my home all night armed with an iron bar. And nobody dared come near. I don't forget this. We are brothers Patrick. Now tell me what's wrong'?

'Let's just say that if events over the next few days spill out like I think, then your profits are set to soar.'

Salvatore stiffens his stance. He stands tall and straightens his braces.

'There is going to be a war? If you are in trouble I shall stand by your side. You know my true nature Patrick Mullen. I bring much more to the table than simply hugging old widows. We have large numbers. We have guns and much ammunition. Not only in Ancoats, but across the city and elsewhere. I can have a small army at your disposal. You just say the word and we'll smash this enemy.'

If it comes to a war Salvatore,' says Paddy. 'There's no one more I'd have stood by me than you, a brave son of Sicily. But in this particular matter I think a little of that famous Sicilian cunning is called for.'

Rea nods and smiles wide. 'I will bring us a bottle of my island's finest red and we shall talk long into the night.'

Welcome to Stretford: Harry Taylor is on the touchline watching his twelve-year old son play for a local football team. Alongside him are fellow Dads, either shouting advice or abusing the referee. Stood next to Taylor, watching his son also is forty-six year old William *'Billy'* Tarr. Balding with glasses, an unremarkable appearance, but a Victoria Cross holder earned during D-day. Tarr taking out an entire German bunker on his own and killing all inside.

He is also one of the most feared henchmen in Manchester.

An old wartime pal, he is recognised as Taylor's second in command, and whilst he is the respected public face of their business, Tarr is the General in the field. And when required the assassin. He also shows unswerving loyalty to Taylor. This stemming from a time when Taylor saved his life in the retreat to Dunkirk. They are discussing who from their firm to use as the hitman in the Kray job.

'So who do you think'? asks Taylor. 'Who do we give the golden ticket to'?

'Harry, we've gone through all the lads and the one person perfect for it you haven't even mentioned'?

A quizzical Taylor stares at his old friend. 'Who'?

'Me.'

'You must be fucking joking,'?

'What do you mean'? replies Tarr.

Taylor is adamant. 'There's no way you get this gig Billy. You are my oldest mate and I love you. So forget it and watch the boys play football.'

'But Harry there's nobody else.'

Taylor remains quiet and keeps his eyes focused on the pitch. He knows Tarr is right but does not want to admit it.

Tarr continues. 'What happened at Dunkirk is irrelevant, because you'd have done the same for me. No, it's strictly business. And on this matter, you are simply not thinking straight.'

This comment irks Taylor, he does not want his friend involved, for he fears events are set to spiral out of control.

'You do realise if Tommy cannot talk those lunatics round, then your lad out there on the pitch, and mine also will probably be forced to grow up without a Dad? Once we hit the Krays a firestorm is going to blow up the likes we haven't seen since the fucking Luftwaffe filled their boots with Manchester.

Now I trust Collins, he's a goodun, but who's behind him? No doubt they'll be London Met, you can guarantee that. And probably even higher up to make a call like this. MI5 or some other secret group we don't know about. Who's to say these people will not decide to get rid of those doing their dirty work. Me and you and everyone involved in this fucking madness?

No, something stinks. This is a damned hornet's nest Billy, and if you shake it hard enough, God knows what'll fall out. This is not the country I fought for. We'd come home to a nation fit for heroes, the establishment promised us? What a joke that was. England is now nothing more than a fucking banana republic.'

Tarr shakes his head. He hears Taylor but remains steadfast in his opinion.

'All you say I agree with, but still it makes no odds. Face it, I'm your man Harry. We have nobody else good enough for a number like this. And deep down you know it. Let's just do this thing then get back to normal.'

Taylor offers a resigned smile. 'I should have left you in that fucking ditch in France, you hard headed bastard.'

Always been your trouble Harry,' laughs Tarr. 'A heart bigger than your brain.'

The two continue to watch the football in silence. Taylor eyes Tarr out of the corner of his eye and is clearly not happy, for he fears for his friend.

CONFESSION

Sunday evening: Tommy Keenan enters the huge doors of Saint Patrick's church in Collyhurst. He was expecting it to be empty but instead notices the Irish parish priest, seventy-one year old Father John Kelly lighting the candles. A small man, slim with a mischievous, friendly, wizened face.

A smiling Tommy makes his way towards him. 'I hope you are lighting one for me Father'?

Father Kelly turns around. 'I'll need more than one to save your soul Thomas Keenan.'

He approaches Tommy, then breaks into a huge smile and shakes his hand warmly.

'How long has it been my son? Are you still performing the devil's work for Paddy Mullen'?

'Come on Father,' Tommy grins. 'You know my heart is pure and intentions mostly honourable. At least that's what the judge said.'

'What brings you here today Thomas? You are a little too old and wise in unworldly ways to resume your role as an altar boy. I'm not sure I can sell that to the Bishop.'

Tommy laughs and looks around at the church. He appears deep in thought.

'I just wanted to see the old place.'

'Are you going away'? says Father Kelly. His dry sense of humour never failing to amuse a smiling Tommy.

'Father can I ask you a favour'?

'You can ask Thomas but I have sufficient Communion wine and enough cigarettes for myself. As for women, sadly it's a vice I'm not allowed.'

An exasperated Tommy knows he has met his match. 'Father please'!

'I'm teasing Thomas, ask away.'

'Will you hear my confession'?

A surprised Father Kelly is taken aback. 'Of course, but....'

Tommy points to the confessional box. 'We can talk better in there.' Both men make their way. Tommy climbs in with Father Kelly behind the veil.

'Father forgive me, it's at least ten...'

'Fifteen,' replies the priest.

A smiling Tommy continues. 'It's at least fifteen years since my last confession. I've pulled quite a few strokes. Not all legal. In fact most of them not. I've broken the odd nose, but only if they had it coming to them. I've stolen, swindled and fooled around. I've drunk and swore. But I never told lies Father. Well apart from this one time and that was for good intentions.'

An open mouthed Father Kelly listens on. 'Small mercies Thomas. I'm glad to hear it.'

'I've a dangerous profession and sadly my vocation and calling in life takes me down roads I'm sure you don't approve of. But I've never hurt anyone and I've only ever stole off those whom could afford it.'

'Ah the angel of Collyhurst has granted me with his presence,' smiles the priest.

Tommy goes quiet for moment.

He takes a deep breath. 'Father have you heard of the Kray twins'?

'I'm a darned priest Thomas not a monk. What about them'?

'Okay then here goes. Cards on the table. Tomorrow morning they are coming to Manchester with the intention of taking over, but Flannery and the other gangs are not backing down. There's going to be hell to pay. Unless'?

'Unless what'? asks Father Kelly. 'Please don't tell me you are involved'?

'In this one Father, believe it or not I'm the cowboy in the white hat,' smiles Tommy.

'There is, shall we say a window of opportunity. I've been given one chance to talk them around and put the twins back on the train alive. Otherwise,

they never go home'?

Father Kelly listens on in both astonishment and horror. 'You could go to the police'?

'No chance Father, they are the ones loading the bullets.'

'Christ have mercy'! exclaims the priest. 'This is bloody Manchester not Chicago. Is Paddy involved'?

Tommy shakes his head. 'He knows nothing about it.'

'Don't lie to me Thomas. I've known you since you were five-years old. Something tells me he knows, but is against it, and hates the idea of you having anything to do with this madness.'

'Paddy's hands are tied. Things have moved too fast, he can't stop it without making matters worse. I was hoping in the unlikely event of an unhappy ending, you may have a word? I owe everything to him.

This little talk we are having here is,

I suppose my last will and testament. I need you to prevent him from going crazy. He'll listen to you. Please'?

'Hold on a minute, you think that because I'm a man of God, I may have some hold over a man like Patrick Mullen? All the saints and angels in heaven will not be able to stop him should you be killed. I can promise you now that such would be his retribution, the devil would fear to allow him entry into hell.'

'Knowing such what I have told you today Father, can you still give me full absolution of my sins? Not that I deserve it mind, but perhaps maybe for old time's sake'?

Father Kelly heaves a deep sigh of disbelief. 'Ten Our Father's and ten Hail Mary's. In their entirety I might add and he'll be listening, so no cheating.'

Tommy is shocked. 'Is that it'?

'Consider yourself lucky Thomas, God is in a good mood today.'

'Thank you Father, you take care of yourself.'

Tommy stands and steps out of the confessional box. He makes the sign of the cross then turns to go.

'And Thomas. I'll light a candle for you in the morning,' says Father Kelly. Unaware he has already left.

'Thomas, are you still there'?

Suddenly the Priest hears Tommy's departing footsteps.

'Go with God Thomas Keenan…...'

GREETINGS FROM THE BIG SMOKE

178 Vallance Road-Bethnal Green: London. The Kray twins are in the bedroom preparing their suitcases for the trip to Manchester. Reg pulls out two hand guns hidden in the back of a wardrobe and shows them to Ron.

He smiles. 'Which one do you want'?

'No guns,' replies Ron.

'Are you serious'?

'You said it yourself Reg, northern monkeys.'

'Pack some bananas instead yeah'? laughs Reg. 'Grease monkeys with bows and arrows.'

The Krays crack up with laughter whilst carrying on packing.

At Bootle Street Police Station, it is late Sunday evening, and Inspector George Collins is sat in his office reading an intelligence report on the Kray's imminent arrival in Manchester. There is a knock on the door and in walks C11 officer, forty-one year old, Charles Lewis. A tall imposing figure. A snobbish individual, proud of his Eton background and feeling like he is in another world in Manchester.

Alongside him is his partner, forty-three year old Robert Flynn. A streetwise, short, burly figure with an unhealthy view of everything outside the capital.

'Working late George'? asks Lewis.

Flynn smiles as George looks up. 'We have appreciated all your help in this matter. I know it couldn't have been easy. These types of jobs never are. But remember you are on the side of the good guys. No matter what happens tomorrow, Manchester wins.'

In the short time he has known them Collins already cannot stand either of the two men.

'What you really mean is London wins? We are simply doing your dirty work. Let the boys from the provinces soil their hands with this filth. Well it doesn't sit right with me. Never has done.'

'A little late to develop a conscience,' says Lewis.

'These are big boy's games now,' adds Flynn. 'Not your normal mickey mouse policing, dealing with small town hoods and nicking ferret shaggers. If you can't handle it, go home and put on your fucking carpet slippers.'

Collins finally snaps. 'You patronising fucking, cockney wide-boys. Let me tell you something. You think you can come up here with your flash Harry suits and arrogant manner and strut around and tell me how to run my city? All this has nothing to do with policing, this is politics, pure and dirty politics. The Krays have got too powerful for you. You can't handle them. They have pictures and film of powerful men in power sleeping with rentboys and abusing kids. Some so high up, that if it ever got out this government would fall.

And God knows what other dirt they have? The Met, C11? Fuck me if you lot were any more bent down there you'd be ringing bells and shagging Esmeralda!

Now I bit my tongue before. If the Krays have to go then so be it. They are scum so blow those two bastards to kingdom come. They hurt people and I can swallow it. But tomorrow is not the end of it for us, because if Keenan cannot talk them back on the train, and it gets bloody. we'll be cleaning up this mess for years. Long after you two have gone back to whatever London gutter you crawled out of.

So a little advice gentlemen, if you want to keep your teeth don't ever look down on me or my home town again, because I won't have it. This is still my watch, my city and my fucking Manchester.'

Flynn claps his hands in mocking style. 'A nice speech George. It has brought a tear to my ear. You should run for sheriff in this fucking town. We all know your man has not got a prayer in hell of succeeding and that the Krays are going to slit him ear to ear before he has a chance to open his mouth. Personally I hope the twins do slot Keenan and the shooters go in.

For me then it's case closed, we can go home to civilisation, and it's your fucking problem.'

Collins shakes his head. His heart is filled with disgust for this man.

'You boys from the big smoke. We fought a war against bastards like you.'

'You just don't understand George,' says Lewis. 'Dealing with the Krays is a new type of war. There are no rules and you are right it is political. Am I comfortable with that? No not really but they are evil and they are out of control. A new type of villain. They'll have to be dealt with, if not tomorrow, then on another day.'

'Go home George,' adds Flynn. 'Go home, you are so out of your league it's embarrassing.' Collins smiles. 'Go home? I am fucking home. And to say I'm out of my league? Jesus H Christ, you look so far down your noses at us that you can't see what's in front of you up here.'

He laughs. 'You really do have no idea who you are dealing with do you? There are forces out there, not a stone throw from where we are speaking now whom could eat you fuckers for breakfast. But anyway, like you say, I'm out of my league. And so I bid you goodnight and us all good luck tomorrow gentlemen. For I fear we are going to need it.'

'It'll have nothing to do with luck,' says Lewis.

Collins looks puzzled. 'What are you trying to say? Has something changed I don't know about'?

Lewis sports a huge grin. 'Goodnight George, sleep the dream of the good copper. We'll speak tomorrow.'

And then the penny drops with Collins.

He says nothing more, just stands from the desk, puts on his overcoat and hat and steps out the office. Lewis and Flynn watch him go.

'Can he be trusted'? asks Lewis.

'Ignore him,' answers Flynn. 'He's upset. Nothing but cowboys this far north.

Northern fucking cowboys.'

'And our insurance is arranged'?

Flynn smiles. 'No one gets out of there alive Charlie boy. No matter what.'

OLD MAN KABEL

George Collins is ringing Paddy Mullen from a public phone box on a quiet deserted Deansgate.

'Hello Paddy, George Collins. We need to talk'?

Mullen is in his office at the Cromford club. 'You've got some nerve George. The normal spot in an hour,' he replies and hangs up.

George Collins pulls up in a black taxi cab on the Old Trafford forecourt of Manchester United Football club. It is late and there is not a soul around. He pays and steps out the cab, before walking through a side entrance left unlocked for him to go inside. Collins heads up the tunnel. The floodlights are on. He glances around the empty grandstands then onto the pitch.

Paddy Mullen stands waiting for him in the centre circle.

'Sorry to drag you away from the club at this late hour Paddy.'

'Stuff on your mind George? Stuff like the Kray twins'?
Collins offers a wry smile. 'When did it all get so complicated Pat? When we were younger it was good and bad guys. Black and white and no shades of grey. Today, everything, all of it is fucking grey. I cannot tell the difference anymore.'

'Your choice,' says Mullen. 'Nobody forced you to go along with this crazy charade.'

'I could never have the Krays in this city Paddy. The consequences of those two psychopaths let loose on the people of Manchester. I heard a story. A true story from one of the boys at the Met. How they crucified a punter in one of their clubs because they claimed he didn't show enough due respect.

He nudged one of them at the bar for Christ sake and didn't apologise so they put nails through his fucking hands. Our lot are angels, fallen maybe, compared to that. But there's a line, a difference between simple villainy and sheer evil. Those two operate as if even God's laws don't exist and I couldn't have that here. Whatever the cost to my career or my conscience. I just couldn't stomach it.'

Mullen is not impressed. 'I think you need to speak to a priest George. I can't help you with this.'

'I want your word Paddy that if it all goes wrong and Tommy goes down then you won't retaliate'?

Mullen lights a cigarette and inhales slowly before answering.

'You've already set fire to the rain George. Now you expect me to let my own blood be sacrificed. For what, so some faceless bastards in London can sleep a little easier at night'? You know me better than that. Tommy is my son in all but name. He comes out of this alive or, you lot think the Krays would have been your biggest nightmare? If this kid gets hurt I won't rest until.....'

Collins cuts him short.

He is smiling. 'I thought not.

Do you remember the old Jew who owned the pawn shop on Nelson street? Ronnie Kabel? The time when the Salford boys came across the river looking for easy pickings'?

'What about it'? replies Mullen. 'That was a long time ago.'

Collins continues. 'How old was you, sixteen or seventeen? You waited for them as they came across the swing bridge. You was on your own. No knife, no gun I saw you. I watched everything. I followed you, but never let you see me because I didn't have your guts to stand up to them. But I watched it all unfold.

The entire gang walked up to you and whatever you said made them turn around and head back to Salford. And they never ever came back across that bridge again to bother old man Kabel. Whatever you said that day put the fear of God into them. One kid from Collyhurst against ten. What was it Paddy, what did you say'?

Mullen smiles at the memory. 'Old man Kabel was always good to my family. My Mother went in the shop once and tried to pawn her wedding ring because we simply had no food on the table. Do you know what the old man did, bless him? He refused to take it and gave my mother ten pounds from his own pocket. He told her she was a good woman and not to worry about paying it back.

Well she came home with two bagful's of groceries and wept tears of joy at the kitchen table.

I never forgot that and so I picked out the biggest one and told him I was the old man's son, and they'd have to kill me to get at him. But before that happened I'd kill one of them. They looked at each other like I was crazy but I was deadly serious.

I was ready to kill. They obviously never fancied finding out so they turned around and went home.'

'They were right to do so,' says Collins. 'You were crazy back then.'

'I don't like bullies George, never have or will. I've always looked after my own.'

Collins gazes around the stadium. In the distance there is the rattle of freight trains roaring past Trafford Park.

'I'm a blue myself,' he says. 'I love Matt, but I never could abide this place.'

'I know,' smiles Mullen. 'That's why I always arrange to meet you here.

It was his idea.'

'What would Matt make of this mess'?

Mullen shakes his head. 'A parallel universe. I'd not dare mention it and he has too much class to ask me.'

'So tomorrow is in the hands of our fallen angels,' says Collins. 'I pray Tommy can pull this off.

'The path to hell is paved with bad intentions George. I pray so too because I'd hate us to fall out.'

Suddenly Collins becomes animated. He cannot lie much longer.

'Okay, fuck the knighthood I have a confession Paddy, but one not to be heard by a priest or anyone else in fucking uniform. Listen up, I'm going to tell you a story......'

COMING NORTH

It is early Monday morning before the city has come to life, and at the Midland Hotel's staff entrance a black transit van pulls up. The driver steps out and goes to open the back doors. Four men jump out each carrying bags under their arms. They are the hitmen, Damien Quinn, Leon *'Pearly'* Spence, Paddy Costigan and William *'Billy'* Tarr. The four are swiftly ushered inside by a man wearing a waiter's uniform.

In his Altrincham home, Tommy Keenan gets out of bed, and as he does so stares back at the still sleeping Alison. He leans back and gently kisses her on the forehead before heading into the bathroom. He starts to shave, but stops momentarily, and looks long and hard at his reflection in the mirror. A pensive Tommy breaks into a resigned smile.

'You have one chance Tommy boy,' he says to himself.

'Don't mess it up.'

At Euston Railway Station, the Kray twins dressed in matching suits are strutting down the platform carrying small suitcases. A path opens up from the star struck fellow passengers, one that they stride purposely through. Fully aware every eye is upon them. A smiling Reg ruffles the head of a young boy no older than ten who hands him a pen and piece of paper for an autograph which he signs.

In the railway carriage the twins both have their backs to the door as they load the suitcases onto compartments above the seats. Two other men enter. Both talking and laughing loud. Young and cocky teddy boys. Ron turns around to confront them.

'Not in here lads. Find yourselves another carriage yeah'?

One of them, wholly unaware of who he is speaking to blurts out. 'We paid for these fucking seats mate and will sit where we want. Besides who are you to tell us what to do'?

Reg now also turns around and seeing the two Krays side by side, the teddy boys suddenly realise they have just made the biggest mistake of their lives.

Reg appears ready to explode. 'Fuck off now.'

The frightened teddy boys pick up their suitcases and head back towards the door. Scared stiff, shocked and full of remorse. One turns around to Reg. 'I'm so sorry Mr Kray. We had no idea who you were.'

Reg says nothing and they swiftly scramble out of the carriage and into the relative safety of the train hallway.

'You bloody idiot! You could have got us fucking killed.'

'Shut up and just keep walking,' says the other, as they head far away as possible from the Krays.

The twins smile and sit down facing. 'I've never been this far north,' remarks Reg.

Ron laughs. 'We should have had jabs.'

'Do you remember when we were kids'? We used to think the West End was a foreign country.'

'It is Reg,'

'Do they definitely not know we are coming up'?

Ron shakes his head. 'Not got a fucking clue. We'll be a wonderful surprise for our northern brethren. We hit their top people hard, make our mark and show these amateurs just what real power means.'

A smiling Reg likes the sound of this. 'The Krays will reign in the rainy city.'

Ron gazes long and hard out of the train window. He appears lost in his thoughts. Very quietly he whispers almost to himself. 'We will drown them in their own blood.'

A fully dressed Tommy Keenan is in his kitchen just finishing off a cup of coffee and preparing to leave, when in walks Alison. 'Where are you going'? she asks him. 'Why did you not bother to wake me'? Tommy smiles. 'You looked so peaceful I didn't want to disturb you.'

Alison is worried. 'Tommy what's going on'? He motions for her to sit down.

She takes one seat, him the other. Tommy holds her hand.

'There's absolutely nothing for you to worry about,' he says.

Alison looks into his eyes and knows he is lying. 'Thomas Keenan you are the worse liar in the world.'

Tommy sighs. 'So I've been finding out lately.'

'Whatever you are up to, just be careful Tommy, and promise me you'll be home later.' Tommy cannot look Alison in the eye.

'Promise me Tommy.'

'I can't,' he replies.

'Fine then,' she says, now angry. 'If you'd rather stay out drinking with your friends then you can make your own tea'! Alison jumps up and storms out of the kitchen and back up the stairs. From the top of the stairway she lets rip a last riposte.

'And don't forget your key'! The bedroom door bangs shut. This sound makes Tommy jump. He smiles and lights up a cigarette.

If only life was always this simple.

DOUBLE CROSS

In the Midland Hotel cellar, the hitmen are sat around smoking and drinking coffee.

It is a dark and grimy room, lit by candle light. Entering comes their handler. Forty-two year old Frankie *'the horse'* Johnson. A gangly figure with a long face and mistrustful eyes. He is watched intently by the four men as they wait eagerly for news. Johnson claps his hands for attention.

'All right lads listen up. The Krays are due to arrive in Manchester in around an hour's time. From the station they'll come to the hotel, where Keenan will go to see them in their hotel room. When he comes out he gives me the nod to go or cancel. If it's go, I come down and fetch you lot, and you blow those two cockney bastards to kingdom come. Straight in and out, we have other people in place to move the bodies.

When done you come back down here where there'll be a van waiting. One thing, be certain. Head shots, under no circumstances can either be allowed to live.'

Tarr is concerned. It sounds to him as if it has already been decided that the Krays are dead men walking. 'And if it turns out a no go'? he asks.

'If Tommy talks them back onto the train what then'?

Johnson smiles. 'let's fucking hope so eh Billy. Same applies. I come down and tell you and we all go home. And everybody still gets paid the full rate.'

Spence starts to laugh. 'Come on Billy, you being a war hero and all that. Don't you miss the killing man? The smell of blood. A chance like this to make history. Maybe they'll give you another medal'?

An angry Tarr reacts. 'I was fighting for my country Spence. For my family and friends. I was defending our freedom against tyranny. The notion of patriotism is something you could never understand. Probably couldn't even fucking spell it.'

'So why do you this shit now? The war is over Billy man. You beat the Germans. The Nazis are gone, Hitler is dead.' An irritated Spence does not take kindly to be spoken down to by this old man. 'I think you missed the taste of blood. We are the same, you just hide it better.'

'That's enough Spence,' shouts Johnson.

'I don't mind Frank,' says Tarr. 'The man is an idiot. It's water off a duck's back for me.'

He turns to Spence. 'Anyone I've ever clipped had it coming to them. I'm a professional, I work for one man. Someone tries to hurt us, I hurt them. It's always been purely business. Whereas you? The stories I've heard. You get off on it, you are sick. That's the difference. You my boy are not right in the fucking head.'

An outraged Spence springs up and attempts to lunge at Tarr, only for Damien Quinn and Paddy Costigan to grab him. Johnson stands in front of Tarr, who is staring at Spence in utter contempt. Spence screams towards Tarr.

'You wait Tarr, when this is over we'll see who's the better man.'

Tarr simply smiles. He taunts Spence. 'Anytime boy. I'm not going anywhere.'

An irate Johnson comes between them and with the help of Quinn and Costigan order is finally restored and both men sit back down. Whilst continuing to give each other the evil eye.

'Enough'! shouts out a sweating Johnson. Wiping his brow. 'Calm down. We need clear heads. Now you don't have to like each other, but you have to work together, so this ends now. Peace in our fucking time okay? You are supposed to be professional so damn well act like it.'

Johnson glares at both Spence and Tarr who both nod in acknowledgement.

'Good.' He breathes a huge sigh of relief. 'Right I'm off. Next time you hear from me will be to say whether we have the red light or not.

So do me a favour please gents. Until then please try and refrain from killing each other.'

Johnson exits the cellar door and shuts it behind him.

Quinn smiles. 'Why do they call him the *'horse'*?

'Because he's got a fucking long face,' replies Costigan.

Spence starts to laugh and they all join in.

On Peter Street, opposite the Midland Hotel front entrance, and sat in an unmarked police car are Charles Lewis and Robert Flynn. They are waiting for the Kray's to arrive. From the hotel foyer a suited man appears. A C11 officer. He nods over to the car.

'All our chaps are in place,' says Lewis. 'Two doors down from the Kray's room. On word they go in.'

'They are clear on their orders'? asks Flynn.

'Absolutely, extreme prejudice. These are the best we have. They take out the twins and Keenan.'

'And the shooters in the cellar'?

Lewis looks at his watch. 'Johnson goes in five minutes. We tell them something has gone wrong and they have to leave the city for a short while.'

Flynn laughs. 'It never fails to amaze me how men like Johnson become so easy to turn. Put a few quid in their bank balance and they would sell their fucking kids. No morals up here. He goes too yes'?

Lewis nods. 'All of them. No exceptions, we clean it all up in one go.'

'Excellent,' smiles Flynn. 'Then we can go home and leave this miserable God forsaken city for good.'

Tarr, Spence, Quinn and Costigan are sitting quietly when the cellar door bursts open and a frantic looking Frank Johnson appears,

'Something has gone wrong we have to move now and quick. Get your stuff, there's a van waiting outside. It'll take you to a safe house in North Wales. Just for a day or so until things calm down.'

The four stand and head out of the door. Paddy Costigan is last and turns to face Johnson.

'I still want fucking paying.'

Johnson smiles. 'No worries Paddy, you are going to get everything that is due to you. I promise.' A satisfied Costigan grunts and leaves the cellar.

A worried Johnson watches him go. The clock is ticking as the hitmen jump into the back of the van. The C11 man is waiting and slams the door shut, before walking back to the driver's seat. He smiles at his fellow officer. 'The animals are in the cage.'
The van roars out onto Peter Street and past Lewis and Flynn. Neither take much notice of the one following shortly behind it.

'Hi ho, off to the slaughterhouse they go,' says Flynn ominously. Lewis checks his watch. 'The Krays should be arriving any time now.'

As they both look towards the Midland, Tommy Keenan is entering inside.
'Lewis smiles. 'This is coming together like child's play. It's just too fucking easy.'

Tommy walks into the foyer and is met by Frank Johnson. They shake and a smiling Johnson hands Tommy a note, with the room number in which the C11 hitmen are hiding.

He heads into the hotel restaurant area, whilst Johnson walks up to the reception and hands another piece of paper to a good looking young man stood behind it in a smart black suit. Dark hair, striking eyes, perfectly groomed and clearly of Italian decent.

He is Antonio Rea. Assistant manager of the Midland and nephew of Salvatore Rea.
The two exchange glances, then Johnson leaves whilst Rea glances at the paper and smiles.

He puts it in his pocket and picks up the phone.

'We have the room number. Get the boys ready.'

An announcement comes over the Piccadilly railway station tannoy. *The 8.20 From Euston station has just arrives on Platform nine.* The platform is packed as the doors to the train open and passengers start to step off the carriages. The Kray twins amongst them. As ever around the twins there is a flurry of excitement. All eyes upon them. A pretty young blond girl no more than twenty-years old smiles at Reggie and he winks back at her. The Krays walk business like down the platform with small suitcases in hand.

Nearby a policeman stands seemingly unaware of their presence. However in reality across the entire station, a small army of undercover detectives are monitoring their every step. A man in a bowler hat sitting on a bench reading a newspaper. Two porters unloading baggage and the young girl who previously smiled at Reggie. All police officers. On a mid-December morning they step out of Piccadilly station into daylight and it begins to rain.

Reg puts his hand out to catch the raindrops.

He looks up at the dark miserable Mancunian skies. Black clouds are gathered. He smiles and looks at Ronnie. The telepathy between the twins easy to read as Ron begins to laugh.

Easy pickings. It is a new day in the north.

......The Kray twins have come to Manchester.

The three assassins are sat quietly smoking in their hotel room, when suddenly there is a knock on the door, and one stands to answer it. Their guns are on the bed hidden under pillows and newspapers. On opening a waiter is stood with a food trolley.

He smiles. 'Good morning sir, Just a little welcome to Manchester.' As the waiter finishes talking, four men dressed all in black, wearing balaclavas and armed with baseball bats rush past him and overpower the three assassins.

Swiftly they are disarmed, gagged and tied up on the bed.

The alleged waiter grins wide. 'Be quiet lads. We wouldn't want to disturb the twins and Tommy whilst they are talking now would we'?

In the hotel restaurant Tommy is sat at a window table drinking a cup of coffee and looking out onto the busy road. He turns to see Antonio Rea approaching him. Rea reaches over and whispers into his ear. 'We have the shooters. Good luck mate.'

Meanwhile, a black cab is pulling up and out of it steps the Kray Twins.

Ron leans back into the driver's window and passes him the fare and a generous tip.

'Much obliged,' says the driver. He has a puzzled look on his face.

'Don't I know you gentlemen from somewhere'? The twins appear genuinely amused at this comment.

'Are you in the movies'?

They smile at each other and stride purposefully into the hotel foyer.

Tommy watches them enter from behind a newspaper at his table. The twins book in at the main desk where a pretty young receptionist smiles wide at them and hands the Krays their room key. A concierge goes to pick up the suitcases, but Ronnie puts his hand up to stop him.

He smiles. 'No need son, we'll carry our own.' Reg hands the concierge £10 anyhow.

'Thank you sir,' replies the concierge. Still appearing in shock at whom has just entered his normal, humdrum, daily existence.

Once in the room the twins are unpacking, when there is a knock at the door. They stiffen on hearing it. Reg goes to answer and stood there is Tommy Keenan.

Reg laughs. 'Well I'll be. Look what the fucking cat dragged in.'

Ron watches on. He looks surprised. Tommy steps inside and shakes Reg's hand. A suspicious Ron does similar. 'Nice to see you Tommy. But how did you know we were coming'?

Tommy smiles whilst lighting up a cigarette. 'Come on Ron. The Kray twins coming to Manchester? You cannot keep something like that quiet. It's like a visit from the Royal family. Or Elvis even.'

'Are you our welcoming committee'? asks Ron.

'In a manner of speaking. He points towards the suitcases. 'I've been sent to inform you not to bother unpacking.'

Tommy looks at his watch. 'There's another train back to London in an hour. I recommend you best both be on it.'

'Careful Tommy,' says Ron. 'This isn't your game. Choose your next words very carefully boy.'

The Krays appear frozen in mid rage, both ready to tear Tommy's head off.

He takes a deep breath and continues. 'Let me explain. Things have gone a little crazy lately with news of your visit. People talk both here and in London. News has got out about what you have in mind and many powerful noses have been put out of joint. I don't think you two realise how many enemies on both sides of the fence want you dead.

But luckily,' he grins wide. 'You have a guardian angel.'

'I don't believe in angels Tommy,' says Reg.

'Me neither,' adds Ron.

'Well you both better believe in this one. He's called Paddy Mullen and two doors down from here we have three London police shooters tied and gagged. They were set to do the three of us, but Paddy got word off the last good cop in the city, who luckily had developed a guilty conscience. Whoever you two had have upset, they were ready to pull the trigger on you. And me, which I have to tell you, I'm not too happy about.'

Ron is smiling but does not seem too convinced. 'Tommy you know me. If you are lying about all this, even though I like you, I'll have no qualms about cutting your fucking throat.

Are you following all this Reg'?

He nods. 'I am. Keep talking Tommy. It's what you are good at.'

An unsure Tommy thinks this could still go either way. He remembers Paddy's words about making his words resonate loud.

So that they stay with them.

'It's a lot more dangerous here than you two think. Believe me they protect what's theirs, and even if the Met had not decided to end you, it would only have been a matter of time before one of our lot had a pop, and you ended up food for the fishes in the canal.

Go home, you don't need this. Stay in your own manor. In London you are kings, up here you are just a pain in the arse. No offence but it's true. It's a different country in the north and reputations mean nothing. Especially those with an East End post code.

Believe me Reg, Ronnie. You are on a hiding to nothing.'

Tommy motions towards the door. 'Come with me I want to show you something.'

The three men step out and led by Tommy they walk down the corridor towards the assassin's room. Two burly looking guards stand outside. One acknowledges Tommy.

'You alright Tom, keeping well'?

He smiles. 'I'm Fine Eric, let us in mate.' Eric opens the bedroom door and stands aside.

Tommy and the Krays enter and see the three assassins bound and gagged on the floor.

Sat nearby are their Mancunian assailants. Now appearing remarkably relaxed, minus the balaclavas, sat chatting and playing cards.

And all clearly happy to see Tommy.

'It's good to see you mate,' one shouts over. A good friend of his by the name of Eddie Hopkins.

'Hello Eddie,' Tommy replies. 'Let me introduce you to a pair of legends. This is Reg and Ronnie Kray.'

A smiling Eddie stands and goes to shakes the twin's hands. 'A real pleasure gentlemen. Any friend of Tommy's is a mate of mine. Welcome to Manchester.'

'Much obliged,' replies Ron.

Thanks for all your help,' adds Reg.

'No problem Mr Kray,' answers Eddie. 'Glad to have been of service. We all are, now have a safe journey back to London eh'?

Ron turns to look at Reg who can't help but smile. They both glare at Tommy.

'I think we've seen enough,' says Ron.

Reg looks around the room at the faces of the other assailants and the assassin's guns on the bed. 'Thanks again for everything lads. If you are ever in London look us up.'

The assailants wave back in acknowledgement and return to their game of cards.

Tommy winks at his Mancunian brothers in arms and returns to the twin's bedroom.

He stands nervously near the door, whilst the Krays discuss in whispered tones at the window. He watches them closely. They finish their chatter and both stare across at him with features set in stone. For a second nothing is said, then, whilst Reg looks out of the window, Ron walks over.

'Looks like we have a train to catch.'

Tommy smile is one of relief.

Reg comes across also. 'Just one thing I need to know,' he asks.

'Go ahead.'

'No lies now Tommy, because I'll fucking know.'

He sighs hard. 'After this weekend, I'll never lie again.'

'Those lads of yours down the hall. Something tells me there's more to all this than meets the eye'?

'What was it Tommy'? inquires Ron.

He sits down on the bed, lights up another cigarette and stares up at the twins.

'I suppose you deserve to know. They, or should I say we, were ready to do you both in here. Originally, if I couldn't talk you back onto the train, then you were never going home.'

Ron's face has turned purple. 'Let me get this straight. If you couldn't sweet talk us back to London, then we were going to be hit right here. In this fucking room'?

Tommy nods. 'I wasn't happy about it, but business is business. It would have stuck in my throat. You know I like you two.'

Much appreciated,' says Ron. Utterly dumbstruck.

The twins stare at each other in disbelief. Secretly they admire the sheer nerve of what has gone down. 'It's like the fucking wild west,' says Reg.

'And what happens now if we change our minds and decide to stay'? adds Ron

'After all we've done for you'? smiles Tommy.

'We should kill you,' whispers Reg. With what appears real intent. His eyes suddenly void of colour.

'But we owe you instead' he adds. Much to Tommy's relief.

'You are one cool bastard Keenan, I have to grant you that.'

Tommy stands from the bed and stubs his cigarette out in a nearby ashtray.

'I had a good teacher. The best there is. Now go home eh. It's bad for your health up here. Far too much cold in the air, it gets in the bones.'

The twins look at each other and smile. 'Tell Paddy we are in his debt,' says Ron. 'He ever needs anything, just let us know.'

'Reg ruffles Tommy hair. 'That goes for you too. You ever get bored of living in the sticks playing cowboys and Indians, come down to civilisation and work for a proper firm.'

'I'll keep that in mind. Be lucky boys. Have a safe journey and give my regards to your mum.'

ENDGAME

The van carrying the four Manchester shooters is heading towards North Wales when suddenly a large haulage truck cuts across its path,

and it is forced to swerve off the road.

From out of the truck a large group of black clad men in balaclavas appear.

They drag the C11 operatives out of their seats and tie them up on the road side. Inside the back of the van the shooters have been flung onto the floor when the back doors are wrenched open. Stood there with their balaclavas removed and smiling wide are Harry Taylor, Paul Brady and Jimmy *'the weed'* Da Silva.

'Sorry about this lads,' smiles Taylor. 'Change of plan. I'll explain on the way home.'

The four hitmen look on in shock as they are helped out of the van. Paddy Costigan shakes himself down and approaches Taylor, Brady and Da Silva. They all stand wary. 'Hey Paddy man,' says Da Silva. 'We saved your skin. You were being took away to be killed.'
Costigan points over to the C11 operatives. 'What happens to those two'?

'They go back to London Paddy,' replies Paul Brady. 'They go back in one fucking piece. No missing ears or fingernails I'm afraid. Out of bounds. Paddy Mullen's say so.'
Costigan grunts in disgust and walks away.
Taylor goes across to talk to Tarr, who is sat nursing a cut head and wrenched arm.
'You alright Billy'?
'I'm getting too bloody old for this,' grins Tarr.
Taylor helps his friend to his feet. 'Come on mate, I'll buy you a drink and tell you all about it.'
An animated Paul Brady starts clapping to get everyone's attention.
'Right come on, job done. Let's get the fuck out of here.'

Outside the Midland hotel a waiter dressed in white shirt and black trousers appears with a tray holding two glasses of champagne. He crosses towards the car containing Lewis and Flynn. The two men watch in astonishment as the waiter approaches them.
'What the fuck is this'? asks Flynn. The waiter knocks on the window.
Lewis winds it down and the waiter leans in.
'Courtesy of Manchester sir.'
Lewis takes the tray and passes the drinks to Flynn. He notices a small note on the tray.
After reading it Lewis goes ashen faced.
'What's up'? says Flynn. 'What does it say'?

Lewis hands it over. *There is something that belongs to you in room 213*

Flynn and Lewis come crashing through the door to find the three assassins still gagged and bound. Their guns on the bed in full view with a note pinned reading *GO HOME*

Flynn has the look of a man who knows he is beaten. 'The game's up,' he says. 'I don't know how but the bastards have done us over.
This fucking city.'

At that moment the Kray twins step out the Midland hotel and enter into a waiting black cab. Watching them go from the other side of Peter Street is Tommy Keenan. As the cab disappears in the direction of Piccadilly, Tommy lights a cigarette and smiles.

He says quietly under his breath. 'Goodbye lads, don't rush back.'
And then Tommy walks away. Job done.
Paddy Mullen is sat at his desk in the Cromford club when the phone rings. He picks it up.
'Paddy Mullen.'
'Hello Paddy, George Collins. It's gone like clockwork. Tommy was superb. He's safe and the Krays are on their way home. As for Johnson, he played his double bluff to perfection and is on a plane to Spain as we speak, with an extra £500 in his pocket and a huge grin on his face. Speak soon.'
'Thanks George.'
Collins put down the phone and the line goes dead.
Mullen smiles and replaces the handle.

The Kray twins are boarding their train back to London. As they step on Ron turns around and takes a last gasp of Mancunian air. Reg watches his twin take a final look at the
'Rainy city.' 'Well so long you smog ridden hellhole.' He turns to Reg and smiles.
'Fucking miserable place anyway. I don't think we'll bother coming back.
Let's go home Reg.'

At the Cromford Club, the victorious bosses, leaders Harry Taylor, Tom Flannery, Michael and Paul Brady and Jimmy *'the weed'* Da Silva are sat with Paddy Mullen. All are celebrating the day's events and the atmosphere is one of euphoria.

'A toast lads, Manchester 1 London 0'! declares Harry Taylor for the entire club to hear.

Into the room comes Tommy Keenan linking his girlfriend Alison. They are immediately spotted by Paddy Mullen, who goes across to greet them.

'Alison, how are you my dear'? Mullen leans down and kisses her hand.

'I'm fine thanks Mr Mullen,' she replies, smiling wide.

Alison turns to Tommy. 'I'll see you at the bar.' Tommy kisses Alison and she walks off. He and Mullen watch her go. 'Marry that girl lad.'

Tommy laughs. 'Is that an order'?

'I had a phone call from Ronnie Kray thanking me but had no idea what for. He was singing your praises though. The twins want you in London, but my advice is stay here. After what has gone on they are on borrowed time.'

Mullen puts his arm around Tommy's shoulders and points across to the table where all the gang leaders are sat. 'Come and have a quick word. Get it over with.'

They head over to the table. First to spot Tommy is a cigar chomping Harry Taylor.

'Here he is, Tommy Keenan. The man who saved Manchester'!

The other men all applaud and cheer as Tommy and Mullen come close.

John Flannery speaks up. 'In years to come they'll talk about when the Krays came to Manchester and about how you, Tommy Keenan.'

Flannery points his finger at Tommy. 'How you put them back on the Train and sent them home.'

'You are a hero Tommy boy,' adds Da Silva. 'A true fucking light in the north.'

'One thing though Tommy,' adds Michael Brady.

'I don't want to rain on your parade, but no one will ever get to know what really happened. It'll be changed. The truth will get lost in the myth. It'll become urban legend. Once upon a time in Manchester. A Mancunian fairytale. But you'll know'!

'Hey Tommy,' says Paul Brady. 'Never mind how you done it, my question is why?

You could have cut and run from that room and just let the boys get on with it.

But you stayed. Why'?

All eyes are upon him as they wait for his answer.

'Why,' he replies. Tommy lights a cigarette and gazes across the table. He

stares at Mullen, who has the look of a proud Father. Tommy catches his eye.

He smiles. 'I did it for the angels.'

ACT TWO
IT'S A NORTHERN THING

WELCOME TO LIVERPOOL

January 1964: Liverpool docks: 6.30am: It is early morning as the mist rises off the River Mersey and from the Italian cargo ship *Vesuvio*, three serious faced young men all wearing cloth caps and carrying small suitcases exit down the gangplank. They hail from Naples and are greeted by a man in a smart black suit stood by a white Rolls Royce.

He steps forward and smiles wide. 'Benevento a Liverpool.' 'Ciao Bobby,' they each reply.

After much kissing of both cheeks and embracing he ushers them into the back of the car. and it drives away. As they reach the dock gates hundreds of men coming through to start their shift stare intently through the Rolls window.

One is thirty-nine year old freight loader Giuseppe Marchesi, who believes he recognises a face sat in the rear. For a moment eye contact is made before the man looks away and the car speeds off. Marchesi is certain the man inside is from his old neighbourhood back in Naples.

He watches the Rolls disappear down the back streets and out of view.

Originally from Naples, Marchesi came to Liverpool after the war where he has lived since. Many times Marchesi has returned to visit remaining family in the city of his blood.

He hails from the notorious backstreets of the *Forcella* district, and knows well of the infamous Neapolitan Mafia, the *Camorra*. Marchesi is certain the three men in the back of the white Rolls Royce are members of the notorious Di Marco clan.

Feared throughout all Naples, but what are they doing so far away from home.

In Liverpool?

LET IT BE

Two hours later the huge ominous figure of Paddy Costigan steps off the train at Lime Street Liverpool from Manchester. He has been sent by his Mancunian crime boss John Flannery to have a quiet word in the ear of nightclub owner Francis O'Connor to repay an unpaid debt of a thousand pounds. Now increased with interest to five.

Costigan has orders to return with either the money or the keys to his club. He checks again the piece of paper in his pocket with a name and address.

Francis O'Connor:10 Mathew Street: The Cavern club

It is a miserable and wretched January Monday morning and Costigan is in a bad mood. The rain is lashing down and Liverpool is reluctantly awakening to another working week. Outside the railway station a line of black cabs stand vacant waiting for business. A soaking Costigan pulls up the collar to his raincoat and walks swiftly to the front of the rank.

A bored driver sits reading his paper, when suddenly his attention is taken by Costigan's scarred and brutal features only inches from his face.

'Take me to the Cavern club on Mathew Street and don't try ripping me off, or I'll break your fucking Scouse nose.'

The shocked driver put downs his paper and starts the engine. 'Alright mate, just get in the back, no need for that talk.' Costigan growls at him then steps inside and slams the door shut.

The cab sets off through the busy traffic. The driver is nervous, he repeatedly checks out Costigan in his rear view mirror. A stranger and one obviously not here for sightseeing. The radio is playing the Beatles: *A Hard Day's Night.* 'Turn this rubbish off it's hurting my ears,' shouts out Costigan. Not wishing to upset this mad man the driver does as he is told.

No fare is worth this hassle.

Finally after only a five minute journey they arrive outside the Cavern. Costigan checks out the fare on the meter. He hands over the money. 'You robbing bastard,' he declares menacingly to a clearly perturbed driver, who in his worst nightmares could never have imagined this start to the week. He swiftly drives away leaving Costigan in the rain-sodden street facing the club. He eyes it with disdain.

'What a fucking dump.' Before tip-toeing through the huge puddles of water to enter through the main doors.

Facing Costigan as he walks in is a deserted medium sized dance floor with a small stage. 'What the hell,' he exclaims. 'This is not a club, it's a cave'? Costigan gazes around looking for signs of life, but the only sound is rain splashing hard onto the roof.

'Anyone home'? He spots the bar and decides to treat himself to an early livener. Costigan reaches over for a bottle of Jack Daniels and a glass and sits himself down on a stool before pouring.

Suddenly a voice calls out. 'Hey stranger are you going to fucking pay for that'?

The owner, fifty-four year old Irishman, Francis O'Connor approaches. An ex professional boxer with a broken pug nose and features not dissimilar to his visitor.

'Are you Francis O'Connor'? asks Costigan.

'What the fuck is it to you who I am, and what are you doing in my club'?

Suddenly Costigan notices O'Connor has in his hand a hurley. An Irish hurling stick, only this one has nails bolted into it. He is secretly impressed, a man after his own heart and judging by the accent,

like himself from County Mayo.

O'Connor continues. 'Well have you got a tongue in your head, answer me'?

Costigan smiles and reaches for another glass. 'Calm down friend, would you care to share with me'? An intrigued O'Connor relaxes a little; he lowers the hurley and walks towards Costigan who hands him a drink.

'A toast,' he proclaims. 'To the plain of the Yew Trees.'

O'Connor is curious. 'A Mayo man, I thought as much. '

He smiles as the two finish the whisky in one before slamming the glasses back down on the bar.

'From where do you hail'? asks Costigan, as he wipes his mouth on a sleeve.

'The beautiful town of Balla,' replies O'Connor proudly.

'And You'?

'Knock,' says Costigan, with what appears utter disdain.

O'Connor smiles. 'Ah the apparition. The town of miracles where the Holy Virgin Mary and the seven angels appeared and blessed all the local folk.'

'She never blessed me or mine,' answers Costigan bitterly, as he pours himself another drink.

'My parents used to say to me when I was a child. 'May the Devil say a prayer for you.'

They were both evil bastards so what chance did I ever fucking have?

Knock was cursed. I hated the place and couldn't get away from it fast enough.'

To help extinguish the memory Costigan downs the whisky in one. 'O'Connor eyes him with a renewed mistrust. 'Careful there, that's my whisky you are knocking back friend. It doesn't come cheap.'

Costigan turns to stare at O'Connor. 'Unless you give me five grand in cash now, this becomes my whisky. Or more to the point John Flannery's.'

O'Connor grins, he has been expecting such a visit.

'And John has sent you to collect I presume'?

Costigan nods. 'It's what I do.'

'And what happens if I told you I wasn't going to repay that no good son of Belcarra?'

'Well I'd be forced to take the keys from the club off you.'

O'Connor does not flinch. 'What's your name son'?

'Patrick Costigan.'

O'Connor's blood goes cold, this man before him is already the stuff of legend in the northern underworld. He knows the infamous story well, a tale so horrific many refuse to believe. And so he tightens his grip on the hurley stick.

Costigan notices. 'I'd not do that Mr O'Connor if I was you. It could be bad for your health.'

'And how do you figure that Patrick'? replies O'Connor, trying desperately to recover his earlier demeanour, but now knowing he is failing badly.

'Well I'd be forced to use it against you, and smash you over the fucking head with it.'   Said so matter of fact it totally unnerves O'Connor.

He is no coward but knows to try and fight Costigan would be useless.

'Does Flannery realise that if he comes here there are those in Liverpool whom will not take kindly to his presence? Mancunians are tolerated but not allowed to take liberties in this city.'

Costigan smiles. 'We are Irish Mr O'Connor, not Mancunians. The gypsy is in our soul, you know that. We go where we want and where the wind take us.

Besides let them fucking try.'

O'Connor is becoming desperate.

'Paddy, please let me explain something here. I just need a little more time. This is the home of the Beatles, this here, the Cavern is their birth right. I'm sitting on a goldmine now they have hit the big time. They are special Paddy, the girls love them, the boys love them. They are going to be absolute superstars. Bigger than Elvis even.

Next month after they fly to the States the Beatles name will be a licence to print money. There'll be no fucking limit to how much they can achieve.

Now listen up, this is the thing. I'm good friends with their manager Brian Epstein. I'm sure if I ask he'll get the boys to play a last gig here for old time's sake. What say I cut you in? I make you a partner in the club and we tell that peasant from Belcarra to fuck off?

Let it be Paddy. We come from Mayo boy, we are blood brothers and can sort this mess out between us'?

But Costigan is not for turning and shakes his head. He is loyal to John Flannery who is one of the few men alive along with Paddy Mullen he respects.

'Five grand or the keys to the club your choice'?

'Oh Paddy come on man I'm a fucking degenerate gambler. I'd bet on two flies racing up a wall. The truth is I don't have Flannery's money. All I have is these four walls.'

Costigan holds out his hand. 'Keys.'

For a second O'Connor contemplates the hurley, only to be stopped in his tracks by Costigan. 'I promise you all you have heard about me is true and more. If you raise that stick again this place will be painted in your blood. Now give me the keys.'

O'Connor hands them over to Costigan whose attempt to smiles makes him appear only even more sinister.

'The door is over there.' He says quietly to Francis O'Connor.

'Now get the fuck out of Mr Flannery's club.'

HERE COMES THE SUN

In Saint Patrick's church, Collyhurst, Father John Kelly says the immortal words and Tommy Keenan and Alison Jones become husband and wife. A packed congregation watch on and applaud as the happy couple make their way back down the aisle. On both sides the pews are packed with the great and the good and a certain unruly few of the Manchester club and gangland.

For this coming together between Tommy and Alison is as close to a royal wedding the Mancunian underworld could muster. Even attracting their fellow peers from Liverpool. Merseyside's three major powerbrokers Frankie Maguire, John Paul Harris and the up and coming Bobby Di Marco. All present and paying their respects to Paddy Mullen's first Lieutenant, and his new wife.

Amongst the guests are more recognisable faces such as Manchester United manager Matt Busby and players Denis Law and Paddy Crerand. Plus the new teenage sensation nineteen-year old George Best. Alison's four beautiful bridesmaids having spent the entire service desperately trying to catch George's eye.

They do not have to try too hard.

Representing her Majesty's police force is Detective Inspector George Collins. Secretly wishing he had brought his handcuffs, such is the rich array of villainy on show. But today a ceasefire is in place and Collins would never dare to antagonise Tommy's Keenan's best man, Paddy Mullen, after his help in ridding the city of the Kray Twins. Today belongs to Tommy and Alison and Collins is more than happy to keep his powder dry for now.

'Congratulations Mrs Keenan,' smiles Tommy to Alison as they leave the church.

'And to you,' she grins. They kiss to loud applause and cheers.

Alison throws her bouquet and amid the shrieks of the other girls it's caught by her youngest bridesmaid, seventeen- year old sister Emma. As she looks towards Tommy and Alison, Emma finally catches the eye of a grinning George, who waves in her direction. Only to receive a slap across the head for doing so off Paddy Crerand.

'Behave yourself George, she's out of bounds,' he declares, much to George's disappointment. 'Don't even think about it.'

John Flannery sidles up next to Paddy Mullen. They shake hands.

'A wonderful service Paddy,' says Flannery, as they watch the bride and bridegroom surrounded by well-wishers.

'Tommy is a good lad, you've raised him well.'

Mullen has the look of a proud Father. 'Maybe he's not my son in blood but in everything else he's my boy. But don't you go telling him that he'll think I'm going soft.

The lad is difficult enough to keep an eye on.'

Flannery laughs. 'I need to speak to you. Something has come up that I think you'll be interested in'? A partnership you may say. 'Come on John, is this really the time to talk business'?

Flannery sports a huge grin and continues on. 'This cannot wait. By good fortune I've just acquired the Cavern club in Liverpool and have no idea what to do with it. Now no one knows the club scene better than you. I thought maybe we could join forces? Put our respective talents together and make some serious cash.'

Mullen suddenly becomes all ears. Because of the Beatles, the Cavern is one of the most sought after clubs in England. This is one offer he simply has to take seriously.

'Let's speak later at the reception. Tell me, how on earth have you managed to get hold of that place'?

'The famous luck of the Irish,' grins Flannery. 'The fact the past owner Francis O'Connor, not knowing a jack from a fucking queen, and also having a terrible aversion to bet on donkeys helped me considerably. Add into the equation Costigan threatening to rip his head off and there you go. But there's something else Paddy.'

'Go on,' replies Mullen.

'Well My solicitor has been going through a host of paperwork left lying around the place and found something of interest regarding the Beatles.'

'Interesting in what way'?

'It appears all is not what it appears to be with this Brian Epstein who manages them. Ownership of the band could be up for grabs, for not all the dots were joined up in the contract.' Flannery smiles wide. 'There could be a way in old friend and we are talking millions.'

Suddenly Alison appears and gently grabs Mullen's hand.

She is laughing. 'Come on Paddy, we need you for best man duties. The dreaded group photograph.'

He kisses her on the cheek. 'Coming my girl.'

Mullen leans across to Flannery and whispers into his ear. 'We'll speak later in the Cromford club.' Flannery nods and watches him walk off with Alison. This man is crucial to his plans. He knows with Mullen on board the chances of managing the Beatles is no longer a pipe dream but a distinct possibility. There can be no greater ally alongside him in the entire north. A trusted powerful ally and an enemy to fear.

Mullen stands next to a grinning Tommy. 'What was Flannery rattling on about'?

'Oh just a bit of business. Somehow he's got hold of the Cavern Club.'

'You're kidding me,' answers a shocked Tommy. 'The Cavern is gold dust. How's the dumb ox wrangled that. Did he win it in a card game'?

Mullen smiles and shrugs his shoulders. 'Kind of. He claims luck of the Irish but reading between the lines, more likely he just set that pitbull Costigan on the owner.'

Their conversation is curtailed when a voice calls out from the rather camp photographer.

'Come on now, everybody smile and look towards the camera.'

'Anyway nothing to do with you my lad,' says Mullen.

He points across to Alison. 'Because you are going on honeymoon to Venice in two days' time with that beautiful young lady over there. Who, if you haven't already forgotten is now your wife.'

'Seriously Paddy, you know where we are staying. If you need me for anything ring the hotel. Okay'?

'Don't worry it'll hold,' replies Mullen. 'We'll speak more when you get home. Now for once in your life please just do as I tell you and say cheese'!

The camera flashes.

Father Kelly pulls Tommy and Alison to one side. 'I just wanted to wish you both future happiness and all the best of luck. Especially you Alison, now you are legally in the eyes of God, married to this vagabond.'

Tommy shakes his head as Alison bursts out laughing. 'I'll do my utmost best to keep him on the straight and narrow Father.'

With that she is whisked away to be congratulated elsewhere. The priest turns his attention to Tommy. 'As for you Thomas Keenan the dark days are over. Here comes the sun. I expect to see a lot more of you on Sundays now and I can only hope you find yourself, shall we say a more honest way to shift a shilling to support that young lady over there'?

'Thank you,' grins Tommy. 'I'll cancel the bank job and the hit on the bishop immediately and become a postman.'

Father Kelly pats Tommy gently on the arm. 'Good lad,' he smiles. 'In all seriousness time to wise up Thomas. You chanced your hand with the devil or should I say two of them not so long ago and walked away unhurt. Next time and knowing you like I do, there'll be another, you may not be so lucky.'

Tommy is listening intently. 'I can promise you no more dancing with the devil. Believe me I appreciate how close I came to meeting your boss. Never again Father. From now on I'm a simple wheeling and dealing business man.'

He winks at the priest

Father Kelly rolls his eyes. 'Quite, well the good lord loves a challenge Thomas Keenan and you are surely that.'

Later that evening in the plush and lavish surroundings of the Cromford club, where the wedding reception is taking place, it is time for the best man's speech. There is a call for quiet and Paddy Mullen stands. Every eye in the room is upon him. Tommy cannot help but think that this man who many years ago took him in when everybody else closed their doors. Who has raised and treated him like a son is now set to have some fun at his expense.

Mullen smiles and takes a piece of paper from his trouser pocket containing the speech.

'Tommy Kennan, a smile and a wink. A creature of the midnight hour. A Mancunian alley cat. He'll never settle down, they told me. Tommy loves the risk of an unturned corner and the never ending quest to get himself in trouble.

They all laugh as Mullen turns towards a smiling Alison. 'Well those days are over now,
because our Tommy has been struck by a thunderbolt in the manner of the beautiful Alison Jones. Or should I say Alison Keenan.'
Everybody applauds and Alison blushes.

Mullen continues. 'And now the alley cat is a pussycat with carpet slippers and whose only idea of excitement will be a hot cup of Bovril before he goes to bed. And if not I'll want to know about it.'

Again the guests laugh and for Tommy's the torment is far from over.

'Now I'm sure everybody in this room has at one time or another had dealings with Mr Thomas Keenan sat on my right. And that many of you have only turned up tonight to give him a good hiding before he jets off to Venice for the honeymoon. Now Tommy as you all know is never short of a word or two or three. Some might say he has the gift of the gab, that he could talk himself out of a locked cage with a gorilla. That doing business with Tommy is akin to tap dancing blindfold on a high wire.'

This is much worse than even Tommy imagined.

'But then there is his other side. The real reason you are all here tonight and why we love him. This boy who landed on my doorstep at sixteen-years old wanting a job, and has been by my side ever since. Tommy is somebody I trust with my life and those of my family. Who would give you his last pound and travel to the ends of the world to help out a friend. Whose loyalty and friendship is appreciated and loved by those of lucky enough to experience it.

Who I have watched with great pride grow from a boy into a man.

Who I'm glad to call my friend and would be proud to call my son.

Ladies and gentlemen, please stand and raise your glasses to the happy couple.

Tommy and Alison.'

Everybody stands and repeats Mullen's toast before breaking into huge applause.

Tommy embraces Mullen followed by a tearful Alison kissing him on the cheek.

'Thanks for that,' smiles Tommy

'You got away lucky lad,' replies Mullen laughing.

'At the last minute I decided not to use the juicy stuff'!

Later in the evening the tables have been moved, and the floor is cleared as the newly married couple step up for the first dance. As the opening bars of Gerry and the Pacemakers,

Don't let the sun catch you crying' begins, Tommy and Alison smooch cheek to cheek to polite applause from all present.

'Do you realise just how lucky you are to marry me'? whispers Tommy into Alison's ear.

She smiles. 'Thomas Keenan, if you were made from chocolate you'd eat yourself. Now dance and shut up.'

A grinning Tommy does as ordered.

Watching from a nearby table is Paddy Mullen, who is sat with the Manchester United contingent. Across from Mullen is George Best, who has the eye of every young female upon him. 'Dear me, how do you cope with it all George'? asks Mullen. Who has noticed Best's fan club staring across.

'Doesn't it ever drive you crazy, this weight of attention'?
Best grins wide. 'Not really Mr Mullen, to be honest I quite enjoy it.'
I bet you do you dirty bugger,' interrupts a smirking Paddy Crerand.
'Oh our George is a good boy aren't you son'? smiles Matt Busby.
'Nothing gets in the way of his football. There's a time and a place for the ladies isn't that right George? And it's not before the game.'
'Absolutely boss,' replies Best, with a straight face only to wink over at Crerand when Busby is not looking.

'Football comes first.' Crerand shakes his head and laughs.

Next to Mullen's table sits Salvatore Rea, Jimmy *'The Weed'* Da Silva, John Flannery, Harry Taylor and the Brady brothers, Michael and Paul. All are watching Tommy and Alison. 'When you think of the nerve of that guy to talk these two head case back on the train,' remarks Taylor. 'The lad could almost have West Indian blood,' smiles Da Silva.

'Cool as fucking ice man.'
'Tommy has the balls of a Sicilian,' Salvatore Rea announces grandly, much to the merriment of the giggling bridesmaids sat nearby.

Paul Brady speaks up. 'I heard a story that the Krays are going around telling everyone to give Manchester a wide berth. That we are a breed apart. Like the fucking wild west.'
'Coming from those two lunatics that is some statement,' answer Da Silva.

'It just shows what happens when we stand together eh lads'? adds Taylor.
'All for one,' he raises his glass in the air and the others do similar.
'To Manchester,' he toasts.
'And Salford,' answers Michael Brady.
'What, did you think you could have pulled it all off on your own without our Salfordian expertise'?
'Too fucking right,' says his brother Paul.
'Us boys from across the river held your fucking hands in all this.'

'And, last but not least, exclaims Harry Taylor. 'Let's not forget our friend from Ancoats and Sicily's finest.' He points in a smiling Salvatore Rea's direction. Taylor raises his glass towards him.

'Nothing to do with me I'm afraid boys,' replies Rea. Whereas the reality being without him and his family, the plan to rid Manchester of the Krays could never have worked.

Rea continues on with a half mocking smile upon his face.

'For I'm a simple funeral director. Indeed may God and you forgive me?

for I had already measured you up for your coffins.'

They all laugh.

With the wedding party in full swing Paddy Mullen retreats to his office with John Flannery. 'So you were saying about the Brain Epstein's contract with the Beatles'? asks Mullen, as he pours himself and Flannery a whisky.

'First to Tommy and Alison,' toasts Flannery. The two raise their drinks.

Mullen invites Flannery to sit facing him at his desk.

'So,' he begins. 'What's this all about'?

'Flannery smiles. 'God has shined his light upon us Patrick. We have had a huge slick of luck. My solicitor came across a copy of the contract and get this. It turns out the whole thing is littered with legal inaccuracies and would be proved worthless in a court of law. It seems all we have to do is make a direct approach to the band itself and sit back and let the lawyers do the rest. It'll be like taking candy off a baby.

Epstein has totally fucked this up.'

Mullen listens on intently. It all sound too good and easy to be true.

'Who have you got in mind to speak to them'?

Flannery pulls out a packet of cigarettes, he light one then inhales before answering.

'I was thinking maybe Tommy'?

'Impossible John, we'd have to move fast on this and he's going on honeymoon.

Who else'?

'Come on Paddy,' replies Flannery. 'There is nobody else. Tommy Kennan has the magic touch. The silver patter. He's already shown that with putting the Krays back on the train. It has to be him, there's nobody else comes near.'

Mullen knows Flannery is correct but is loathed to ask Tommy to postpone his honeymoon. 'They are due to fly out on Tuesday. Maybe I could have a word, Where are the Beatles performing at the moment'?

'They are in London for the next month then fly to America. These four boys are on the verge of conquering the world Paddy. The future of music belongs to them and we could be the ones pulling the strings and calling the shots.'

'What about our friends in Liverpool? The Cavern is their territory, what have they had to say on the matter'?

'Nothing as of yet, but in case of any misunderstandings, I have Costigan living in the place and the previous owner is looking after the day to day running.'

Flannery smiles. 'That old sheep herder Francis O'Connor is working for me now. Or should that be us. Well then, do we have a partnership'?

'Fifty percent'? says Mullen.

'Sixty, forty, come on Paddy,' smiles Flannery. 'Let's be fair now. I came to you with the idea.'

Mullen grins, offers Flannery his hand and the two men shake on the deal.

'Okay I'm in, but don't underestimate the amount of bad feeling this will generate on their territory. Scousers and Mancunians may not appreciate the fact but they are similar in so many ways. Remember how we felt when the Krays decided to gatecrash our little kingdom? It was so nearly carnage. Believe me there'll be a backlash John and I can assure and guarantee you'll definitely be hearing from a certain Bobby Di Marco, who has grand ambitions for that City. Bobby believes he's England's answer to Al Capone. He's obsessed with him and that's worrying.

We need to keep an eye on that young man.

Also don't let's forget those lunatics, the Clancy brothers? They are psychopaths and that makes them almost impossible to do business with.'

Flannery smiles. 'Ah don't worry about Bobby or Maguire and Harris. They are gentleman and more importantly businessmen. I'll sit down with them and cut a deal.

As for that bunch of gypsies, the Clancys? If they show their tinker faces, I'll have Costigan burn their fucking caravans down.

Relax none are a threat. This is a great opportunity Paddy. Surely you can see that'?

A reluctant Mullen cannot argue this point. 'I'll have a quiet word with Tommy tomorrow. But first we need to get Benny Green to speak to Epstein and give him a chance to cut a deal. Maybe even if he's willing we can have him working for us'?

'And if not'? asks Flannery.

'Then we cast him adrift and get Tommy to deal directly with the band.'

Flannery smiles. 'And how is the delightful Benjamin? I haven't seen him round for a while'?

'Benny is Benny,' smiles Mullen. He's in London trying to tie up that young Welsh lass Shirley Bassey on a long term contract. But no doubt most of his time will be spent in casinos and gin joints chasing some posh skirt he hasn't got a chance in hell with. And spending my money whilst doing so.'

Why do you allow him to get away with such things'? If he worked for me I'd watch him like a hawk.'

'Because he's a brilliant lawyer and I know that when it really matters I can rely on him

Benny has been by my side since the war. Along with Tommy I trust him more than anyone else in this city. No offence to present company of course.'

'None taken Paddy,' smiles Flannery.

'At least this time around Tommy doesn't have to worry about having his throat cut by a pair of psychotic twins.'

Mullen sighs and lights a cigarette. 'I'll pass this on to him John. I'm sure it'll help when he tries to square this with Alison on their honeymoon being postponed.'

It is four in the morning and Tommy is sat by his bedroom window in the Midland hotel. His view overlooks a deserted Manchester. He turns around and his new bride Alison is fast asleep with the moonlight shining on her face. This girl dreams in colour, Tommy is convinced.

He cannot help but pinch himself for Alison is to Tommy, beyond the stars, and the fact she was mad enough to marry him makes him the luckiest guy in the world.

That Tommy loves this lady beyond words is without doubt but secretly he has nagging doubts about their future together.

For Tommy's world is complicated, his is no nine to five existence.

Working hours begin and end when the lights have gone out in city and the sun is coming up in the morning. Tommy can never be truly honest with Alison about how he earns his living.

Sometimes he thinks it was a miracle pulling off the Kray job without being killed.

His talents are specialised, Tommy cannot move mountains or split the atom or turn water into wine but he can make people smile.

He can fix and he can get things done. Tommy Keenan can talk a stamp onto a letter and as he looks again at Alison sleeping, so precious and so lovely his thoughts turn to that this magical time cannot last forever. In his line of work nothing is straight forward.

Life in this city is a series of dramas.

Manchester: inhabited by rogues, villains and vagabonds. Some with kind souls others with cruel intent. Then there are men like Paddy Costigan with black souls ready to end your world with the same ease one makes the sign of the cross.

Tommy smiles. He will live for the day,

because who knows what tomorrow brings?

'Oh you have to be kidding me'? exclaims Tommy at the breakfast table the following morning, with Paddy Mullen sat facing. 'Alison is going to go spare. This could well be the fastest divorce in history.'

'It's only for a couple of days Tommy. She loves you and will understand,' replies Mullen. Clearly feeling and looking terribly guilty at having to ask this of the new bridegroom. But Flannery is correct, there is nobody else capable of the task.

'You leave tomorrow morning on the first train out of Piccadilly. Benny is already in London. I've arranged for you and him to meet Brian Epstein at the Dorchester on Tuesday at three o'clock. I've also sent word to Epstein we are coming and are giving him every opportunity to play ball. But if he turns us down Tommy, then I need you both to speak to the band direct. We'll offer them more money. God knows there'll be enough to go around.'

As a sweetener I'll send Alison and her parents to Blackpool for the week in my Rolls. All expenses paid at the Norbreck hotel. Hopefully that should soften the blow and save you earache and a black eye.'

'I wouldn't count on that Paddy, and what blow is this then'?

Unknown to both men Alison has been listening intently and with a scowl on her face. 'Is there anything you wish to tell me Tommy Keenan'?

Mullen stands to leave. 'If you'll excuse me, I'll let you two talk.' Alison hands him a scathing look before turning back to her husband.

'Well then'?

'Something important has come up. I need to go to London for a couple of days. In the meantime Paddy has arranged for you and your mum and dad to go to Blackpool. All expenses paid.' He smiles, badly misjudging his young wife's anger.

'Have a ride on a donkey and fish and chips on Paddy Mullen. Hell why not go mad and buy yourself a *'kiss me quick'* hat'? Don't worry about Venice, it's just a short delay. We'll be sailing down the Grand Canal in a gondolier before you know it. '

'And do I get a say in this'? she asks.

Tommy shakes his head. 'Like I say it's business. It's what I do. You knew this could happen when you married me.'

Suddenly a smile breaks out on Alison's face making Tommy relax. He starts to light up a cigarette.

'One thing you should know about me Thomas Keenan is don't ever take me for granted. Hopefully this will be a lesson for you.'

With that said, she picks up a jug of milk off the table and pours it over his head.

Tommy simply sits there whilst others around the restaurant stare across in disbelief.

Happy with her handiwork and point made,

Alison goes to walk off, only to suddenly turn around. 'Right then, I'm going to pack for Blackpool and don't expect a postcard. One more thing, if we are not in Venice by the weekend, I guarantee next time that will be hot coffee over your head.

Oh, and lastly.'

Alison smiles wide. 'I love you Tommy Keenan.'

With that said she strolls off.

Dripping in milk Tommy looks across to his audience. He grins wide.

'Normally I take it black.'

COME TOGETHER

On The following day it has just gone mid-afternoon in Liverpool and Francis O'Connor is stood behind the bar in an empty Cavern Club. He is cleaning out glasses with a white cloth and cuts a miserable figure. Now forced onto John Flannery's payroll, everything O'Connor owned and cherished has gone and now belongs to him.

Elsewhere in the building, the Cavern's temporarily new manager Paddy Costigan is sat with his feet up on the office desk reading a newspaper. On the radio The Beatles *Love me do* blares out and is annoying Costigan no end. To the extent he leans over and switches it off.

'That's fucking noise not music,' grumbles the Irishman. Wishing to be anywhere else but this depressing dank hole.

Hell bent on revenge for taking the club off him, O'Connor daydreams of sneaking up behind Costigan with his hurley stick and smashing his head to a pulp. But even just thinking about it makes him wary such is the brute's reputation.

What if he turns around?

What if Costigan loses his temper and does to him what is said to have been inflicted on one of the now departed and infamous Barlow brothers? Francis O'Connor crosses himself and recalls what has been forever immortalised, although only ever whispered amongst the northern underworld as the Ballad of Paddy Costigan.

Suddenly a voice shakes O'Connor from his slumber. 'Good afternoon Francis.'

He looks up and stood at the club door staring at him, flanked by two huge suited bodyguards is Liverpool gang boss, forty-year old Bobby Di Marco. A tall handsome man with black hair and dark eyes, Di Marco rules his empire quietly, but with a bloody hand when required.

His public persona is of a hugely successful and wealthy businessman, whose Italian born parents and grandparent immigrated to this country from Naples to ply a hardworking and highly skilful trade in making cemetery headstones. This he continues with also a massive vested interest in Liverpool's ice cream trade.

More illegal ventures include the city docks where fortunes can be had in contraband. Hardly anything comes off the cargo ships of which Bobby Di Marco does not get a piece of. The man nicknamed the *'Grave digger'* is to be much feared and respected.

'What is a man like you doing washing dirty glasses Francis'? asks a smiling Di Marco.

'A little down on my luck Mr Di Marco,' replies O'Connor. The cards did not fall well and I lost the club.'

'So I heard, I'm sorry for your troubles Francis. Di Marco shakes his head in mock dismay whilst walking towards the bar.

His bodyguards stay at the door.

'Can I fix you a drink Mr Di Marco'?

'So long as he pays for it.' The booming voice of Paddy Costigan cuts across O'Connor and causes all present to stare in his direction. Costigan stands in a plain white shirt with sleeves rolled up and gripping a pipe wrench with cruel intent.

Di Marco holds up his hand. 'Calm down we are not here to cause trouble friend. We come only in peace. I take it you must be Paddy Costigan'?

'I am and who may you be'?

'Paddy for God's sake,' exclaims Francis O'Connor. 'Do you live in a cave man? Surely you know who this gentleman is. This is Bobby Di Marco'?

Costigan has heard of him. Flannery has always spoken well of Di Marco and on the grapevine he has heard this fellow is highly respected by Paddy Mullen also. He lowers the pipe wrench and approaches Di Marco, whose two bodyguards move towards him but are stopped by their boss.

'No lads, relax, we are all good friends here.'

They settle down and a smiling Di Marco and grim faced Costigan shake hands.

Di Marco eyes Costigan with a mixture of trepidation and admiration.

'Paddy Costigan, the legend himself. A man to be respected and feared. It's an honour to make your acquaintance.'

'What can I do for you Mr Di Marco'? answers Costigan, never one for small talk.

'How's John keeping? We never got chance to chat at Tommy Keenan's wedding. I was hoping for a catch up. Is he in good health'?

'He's well.'

'I'm told of your little trouble with the Krays. My congratulations on sending that pair of cockney wide-boys packing. I heard they couldn't get back on the train fast enough'?

Costigan has been informed by John Flannery never to speak about this.

'I'm not sure what you are on about Mr Di Marco'?

'Oh of course you don't Paddy. Of course you don't. Once upon a time in Manchester.'

He laughs. 'It all never happened.

He sits down on a barstool. 'Well the reason for my visit. I'd like you to set up a meeting for me with John and Paddy Mullen. There are others also whom they need to see. We have to get everybody around a table and nail this situation with the Cavern club. It's not healthy.

Too many noses are being put out of joint around here. Me, personally I have no problem, I believe in an open market. So long as our friends from London are not included. No, keep those bastards out of the picture.

But this?

You see Patrick, here in this city it can be complicated. Liverpool is similar in so many ways to my parent's home of Naples. Outsiders stand out like a sore thumb and though you are only twenty-six miles away, it remains a chasm. A tribal thing and if matters are not calmed, they will simply explode out of hand.'

'We explode too Mr Di Marco,' answers Costigan. Mr Flannery purchased this club fair and square.' And what you say about Liverpudlians'? I'm not saying anything did go on, but just ask the Krays how Mancunians deal with unwelcome visitors.'

'That's exactly my point Paddy,' smiles Di Marco. 'Flannery and Mullen will understand how they feel. Sadly not all the locals think as I do. They are a little more protective of what they believe is their property. Their heritage you might say. Your continuing presence here can only serve to antagonise them.

The north is a huge pie Paddy and there's enough tasty pieces for everyone without events spiralling out of control. Do you understand? We have to come together on this.'

Costigan nods. 'I'll ring Mr Flannery.'

'Good man,' smiles Di Marco.

'As a gesture of goodwill I suggest we hold it here in Liverpool at the Cavern. Let my friends see that John and Paddy are not ogres. That they are good, fair and reasonable men.'

'Do your friends include the Clancy brothers Mr Di Marco'? inquires Costigan.

'They do,' he replies rather warily. 'But we all have our crosses to bear. I'm sure you understand that Patrick'?

A comment meant to spear Costigan's soul, but Di Marco totally unaware that this man has not got one.

'Not really Mr Di Marco, but I'll phone Mr Flannery and we'll be in touch.'

Bobby Di Marco's Rolls Royce is parked up outside the Flamenco picture house that he owns. His bodyguards are stood alongside the car chatting and smoking, whilst their boss is inside watching a one man screening of his favourite movie. The1932 Howard Hawks' classic, Scarface, starring Paul Muni. Di Marco sits alone in the darkness, with eyes transfixed on the screen and on Muni in particular, who is based on his hero, Al Capone. He mouths every word spoken by the characters as the white glowing haze of the projection light illuminates Di Marco's hypnotised features.

Like Capone, Bobby Di Marco dreams big, he looks not just to the heavens but beyond them to the stars. He sees no obstacles, just solutions in his quest for power. Already the path to stand alongside the Liverpool hierarchy of John Paul Harris and Frankie Maguire is drenched in blood and littered with the corpses of those who dared to oppose him.

With both of Neapolitan origin Di Marco imagines himself as Capone reborn. He intends to build an empire the likes not witnessed since Capone's stronghold over the Chicago underworld. Through Bobby Di Marco, Alphonse Capone will rise again. And Liverpool will be his Chicago.

And then he will move on Manchester

AN OLD FRIEND

Tommy Keenan steps off the train at Euston Station to be greeted by two men dressed in smart dark suits. Both are mid-thirties with sleeked black hair and give off an air not to be messed with. 'Hello Tommy,' one of them grins wide as the other takes his suitcase off him. 'Welcome to London old son. I have a couple of people who wish to have a little word in your poxy northern ear.'

He recognises them immediately as henchmen who work for the Kray twins. The one who spoke is Charlie Taylor. The other, Eric Lloyd. Both with more blood on their hands then a high street butcher. Tommy smiles. 'How's your luck fellas. Good to see you again. I take it we are off to the East End'?

Neither replies. Lloyd motions Tommy to come with them and they head off through the hurley burley of a Monday morning crowded station. Alarms are going off in Tommy's head. How did they know he was coming to London and more importantly, what do they want? Lloyd is watching Tommy and senses his unease.

'Don't worry Tommy, if the twins held a grudge you'd be dead already. They just want a chat about a little business matter.'
He breathes a sigh of relief, for it appears he is going to keep his fingernails.

Tommy is sat in the back of the car taking him to the Kray's home, whilst Taylor is driving, and Lloyd alongside him. 'You fucking northerners really impressed the twins Tommy,' says Taylor, who is staring at him through his rear view mirror. 'Ronnie said it took balls to do what you and your boys pulled off.'

Lloyd starts to laugh. He turns facing Tommy. 'Reggie said similar. He compared Manchester to the Wild West. 'It's Dodge fucking city lads,' he told us all.'

Tommy smiles and lights up a cigarette. 'We just had to take care of business. The twins left in one piece and still breathing. Job done.'

'Ronnie did mention for a moment he considered slotting you Tommy. Just a passing thought though, he did add,' says Lloyd. 'Much obliged to him Eric,' replies Tommy. 'I'm glad he changed his mind.'

Both Lloyd and Taylor laugh out loud, whilst Tommy takes another drag on his cigarette.

The memories of that nerve wracking day back in Manchester still fresh in his mind.

Finally they arrive at 178 Vallance Road, Bethnal Green. Home to the Kray twins. Lloyd opens the door for Tommy and he steps out. Intrigued and a little wary of why the twins have come calling into his life once more?

The front door is opened ajar. Meeting them in the hallway is the Krays' Mother Violet. A pleasant well-dressed lady with kind eyes in her early sixties.

'Hello Eric, Charlie.' She looks at Tommy and smiles. 'I'm sorry my dear I don't think we have met'?

Tommy Keenan.' He holds out a hand and Violet shakes it.

'Very nice to meet you Tommy.'

'The pleasure is all mine Mrs Kray,' he smiles. Trying hard to believe that this sweet little lady stood before him gave birth to a pair of murderous psychopaths.

'How's your Mother Eric? I haven't seen her around for a while. '

'Touch of the old arthritis, I'm afraid Mrs Kray. Laid up at home, but I'll say you was asking after her. That'll cheer Mum up.'

'Good boy,' replies Violet, gently tapping Lloyd on the arm. She points to the stairway.

'Well go on up, Reg and Ronnie are in their room, I'll bring some tea and biscuits in five minutes.'

'Thank you Mrs Kray,' says Taylor and Lloyd almost in unison. Much to Tommy's amusement. But he daren't laugh.

Eric Lloyd knocks on the door and the three men enter the Kray's inner sanctum. Inside are the twins sat facing each other in comfy armchairs. Both are in shirts and braces. They have obviously been in deep discussion and look up on seeing their visitors.

'Ronnie, Reg,' a smiling Lloyd motions to Tommy.

'We have a special guest.'

Ronnie stands and walks across to shake Tommy's hand. He playfully then slaps his cheek. 'Tommy Keenan, the man who saved Manchester.' He smiles. 'You keeping out of trouble my old son'?

I just got married Ron,' grins Tommy. 'I've no choice now, I'm a reformed character.'

Reg shakes his hand also. 'Congratulations Tommy, we are both very happy for you.'

'Thanks lads.'

'So much that we have a belated wedding gift,' adds Ron.

Here we go, thinks Tommy. Payback time.

'What we are about to tell you may well save your boss's life Tommy,' says Reg.

'So listen up. A few nights ago in a local boozer.......'

NOWHERE MAN

Originally born of German Bavarian parent's, forty-three year old Jewish lawyer Benny 'Cohen' Green came to England in 1936 from Munich to escape the Nazi purges. Benny had distant relatives in Manchester and this Northern outpost soon became a second home.

When war broke out Benny found employment in Blackpool as a young accountant working for a man himself making his way in this world. A tough no nonsense businessman/pt army instructor /part time boxer from Collyhurst Manchester, who was not to be crossed by the name of Paddy Mullen.

Though his formidable reputation went before him Mullen was a fair and personable, bright character who recognised in Benny a talent rare. A head for figures and the law and an enduring ability to talk a blind man into giving up his cane made Benny invaluable in Mullen's line of work.

One that verged ominously at times in the shade between legal and otherwise. He also possessed when required a surprisingly impressive ability to lay out opponents whom dared to tangle with either him or his boss Paddy Mullen. A talent hardly needed but one when witnessed was said to be a sight to behold.

As the world burned around them, soldiers on leave, lonely housewives and every desperate conniving soul known to man descended on Blackpool, as a live for today, we could be dead tomorrow existence occurred. The Nazis were on the doorstep and it was felt only a matter of time before The Prime Minister Winston Churchill's' chilling words. *'We will drown in our blood fighting them'* became a reality in the streets and fields of this green and pleasant land.

And so as the bombs fell and the Battle of Britain raged above, Blackpool, fuelled by an air of imminent catastrophe partied on.

Men like Paddy Mullen provided the necessary essentials to do so. Mullen's name became synomonous with the best of drinking holes and casinos, for when drunk or gambling a fortune on red or black it became easier to forget what lay in wait only a short distance across the channel ready to end your world.

Tommy Keenan is late, so Benny Green decides to go in alone. Dressed dapper in his finest hand-made suit from Weiss gents tailors on Tibb street, and wearing his most outstanding favoured dicky bow and dazzling shiny shoes, the diminutive oily haired figure of Benny, with briefcase in hand enters the impressive entrance of the Dorchester hotel in Mayfair.

He takes off his trilby once inside and gasps around at the stunning interior. Benny is approached by a young, fresh faced, dark-suited hotel employee. Obviously some kind of high class bouncer with a private school education and starting his career here in the Dorchester foyer, almost literally from the ground up.

'Can I help you sir'? he asks, with more than a hint of disdain in the voice. Eyeing Benny like he is some kind of tramp who has wondered in off the street.

'I hope so young man,' replies Benny picking up the disrespect in this fellow's voice. He has heard and seen that look many times.

My name is Benny Green. I'm here to meet Mr Brian Epstein. He's expecting me. Do you think you are capable of letting him know I have arrived, or have you a trained monkey I could speak to'?

Knowing he has made a dreadful error of thinking Benny was nothing more than a mere travelling tinker salesmen looking to sell his cheap trinkets, the hotel assistant attempts to make amends.

'Please excuse me sir, I do apologise. Follow me.' He motions for Benny to come with him.

'Mr Epstein is waiting for you in a private suite on the third floor. I'll take you up in the elevator.'

The two men enter.

Benny eyes this mere slip of a boy who is certain feels people like him should not be allowed through the Dorchester doors. 'Tell me son,' he asks? 'This is just between me and you. What did you think when you saw me enter your hotel'?

The young man appears uncertain. 'I don't know what you are referring to Mr Green'?

Benny smiles. 'Come on now, I can see it in your eyes. Be honest with me. We are both men here. Tell me, it will go no further.'

The young man eyes him with suspicion.

'Go on,' urges Benny. 'You'll feel better for it. I give you my word.'

Feeling he has nothing to lose and happy to bring this old man down a peg or two….

'Okay,' the young man grins. 'But you promise me this goes no further? I don't want to lose my job.'

Benny smiles again. 'I promise, now tell me.'

The young man grins wide. 'Well, when I saw you walk through the door, I thought….. Well I thought, fuck me, how did Hitler miss this one'?

Before he can finish the sentence Benny Green has delivered a left hook that has knocked him out cold. The elevator opens at the third floor and Benny steps over the young man lying in a crumpled heap. He hears him groaning, slowly coming around and stares down.

'My name is Benny 'Cohen' Green.

My parents were Jacob and Martha Cohen and they were murdered by the Nazis in Auschwitz. That was a lesson in manners young man. You'll do well to remember it.'

That said he straightens his dicky bow and runs a hands through his hair. It's time to go to work.

Benny knocks on the private suite door and waits for permission to enter.

He hears a voice. 'Come in the door isn't locked.'

Sat waiting in a lounge chair is the nervous Beatles manager, twenty-nine year old Brian Epstein. He has been dreading this moment since the arrival of the letter yesterday morning. A wary Epstein stands to greet Benny. 'I take it you are the representative I have been informed it would be in my best interest to meet'?

He is clearly apprehensive and ill at ease but trying hard to hide it. Epstein picks up the letter off a table.

'I received this yesterday. It says as follows. Although I'm sure you are already aware of its contents

'Dear Mr Epstein,

'It has come to our knowledge that there are certain irregularities regarding your management contract with the Beatles. It appears not to have been officially signed by your goodself. Thus giving others the option to still speak to the band members. However if you can find the time to meet our representative Mr Benjamin Green

tomorrow at three o clock, then I'm sure we can come to some sort of arrangement, that will suit all parties well.'

Epstein finishes and looks up towards Benny. 'As veiled threats go sir, I have enough here to go to the police with. What have you to say for yourself and who exactly are you working for'?

Benny smiles. 'Come on now that is no threat and informing the police of this matter will only make you appear ridiculous. You have made an error on a legal document from which we wish to speak to you about. Mr Epstein, I can assure you my clients are honourable businessmen. They have just seen an opportunity arise here that they think could be worth investing in. Now I know you are an extremely bright man...'

'Do not dare to patronise me Mr Green,' snaps Epstein. 'I'm not some naïve fool.'

He stares intently at Benny. 'What's your real name'?

'I beg your pardon'? replies Benny, slightly taken aback. He did not expect such a ferocious response coming from this softly spoken and obvious in his mannerisms, public schoolboy.

'Tell me your real name or are you ashamed of it'? demands Epstein.

'Of course not,' Benny replies. 'Why should I be'?

'Then why the lies and the charade'? What are you, a nowhere man? Do you exist Mr Green'?

'Oh I can assure you I exist Mr Epstein. My true name is Benjamin Cohen and I came to this wonderful country back in 1936 from Germany....'

Epstein interrupts. 'And you came because you were being persecuted yes? Because you were a Jew? You were being bullied. The Nazis abused your family and friends. And much worse. Am I correct'?

'Yes you are,' answers Benny. 'Much worse.'

'And yet,' says Epstein. 'You still feel you can turn up here trying to harass and threaten one of your own kind. Am I not right Mr Cohen, is this not what you are doing'?

'Not at all,' replies Benny, trying to recover his composure. 'I'm simply here on behalf of friends to offer you a business proposition.'

'Which involves me doing as you say or I lose my boys right? My God, you may as well have a Swastika on your arm and me a yellow star.

You disgust me Mr Cohen.'

'Let me speak for a moment,' smiles a troubled Benny. Inside he is
reeling at such a comment. 'You lose nothing with this deal but gain
two new business partners who can bring considerable talents to the
table.'

'I have no need for common gangsters. Don't try to sugar coat this. I
fully well understand what's going on here. It's what you people
regard as a shakedown is it not'?

'Not at all Mr Epstein, a shakedown would involve my clients
speaking directly to the band and you being thrown out in the cold.'

'And what makes you think my boys would go along with this? I
think you deeply underestimate our relationship. They trust me. I
have put them where they are today. On the verge of conquering
America Mr Cohen. I'm afraid my answer is no. Absolutely no deal.'

'I take it this is your last word on the matter'? asks Benny.

'Final,' replies Epstein. 'I refuse to be bullied.'

Benny smiles. 'Well I'll bid you a good day then Mr Epstein.'

He offers his hand, but Epstein refuses to take it. He simply stares
at him with disdain.

'Goodbye Mr Cohen, you can see yourself out.'

Benny is reluctant to leave. He is extremely uncomfortable with all
that has been said and unusually stuck for words. It appears Epstein
has struck a particular chord with him. He likes this young man who
outwardly appears a shy and timid individual, but inside possesses a
real hard streak. Benny fears to leave now and say nothing will haunt
him for a long time to come. He has to make things right.

'My dear Mr Epstein, only moments before meeting you this
afternoon I put a young man on his back because he dared to insult
me with a jibe about myself being Jewish. So please rid any thoughts
from your head of me hiding my true self. I'm known to everybody
as Benny 'Cohen' Green. I am proud of who I am and what I am.
You are very wrong to insinuate otherwise. Now we have got off on
the wrong foot today and despite your misgivings, I can assure you
my clients are good men and are prepared to broker a deal which
will see you remain in charge.

Nothing changes. I implore you to listen. I have in this briefcase
here a contract for you to sign and this ends now. You and your boys
carry on as normal, we will simply be silent partners in this exciting
new venture.'

Epstein now views Benny with a more sensitive nature. He realises some of his previous comments were hurtful and he regrets them. Despite this stranger's obvious bad intentions.

'My apologies regarding what I said earlier Mr Cohen.'

This time he offers Benny his hand and he accepts it.

'But my answer remains no. Let me tell you something about this supposed mistake I made on the contract? I purposely didn't sign it. I have a deal with the boys that if they were ever not happy with all that I was doing, then the option was there to fire me and hire somebody else. Now you may consider that not very smart Mr Cohen, but it was a chance I felt worth taking to prove to them I was the right choice, and so far it has worked perfectly.'

And then Epstein breaks into the smile of a man resigned to the fact the game is already up.

'Until now that is.'

Suddenly the fire goes from Benny eyes. The desire that has always burned inside to get the job done has waned. Instead he feels an overwhelming desire to tell this deeply troubled young man not to worry. That all will be well. Benny will simply disappear and life will continue as normal. Whereas the truth is unless Epstein signs with them he loses everything in an eye blink.

Benny takes out the contract. He holds it up.

'Please sign this Mr Epstein? We can work together I assure you. You will be looked after.

I give you my solemn word?'

Epstein shakes his head. 'It is just never going to happen Mr Cohen, and please shut the door behind you.'

He goes to leave only for Epstein to call out his name once more. 'And Mr Cohen.'

He turns around. 'Shalom,' says Epstein with tears in his eyes.

'Shalom my young friend,' replies Benny.

'What the hell happened to you Tommy? I was worried,' exclaims Benny, as the two men meet in the Dorchester foyer. 'Sorry Benny I got waylaid. Two old friends wanted to say hello.'

'The Krays'? asks Benny, suddenly alarmed for his friend's health. He looks him up and down. 'Do you still have your fingernails'? Tommy laughs. 'They killed me with kindness Benny, and told me something really interesting that I needed to relate back to Paddy straight away. Believe me this Beatles scenario is going to blow up in our faces if we are not careful.'

Benny notices the hotel assistant who he had punched previously, now sporting a busted lip and nursing it with a handkerchief. Tommy spots him also.

He points across. 'Is that your handiwork'?

He smiles. 'I had to teach the boy a valuable lesson in manners. One I don't think he'll forget in a hurry. Benny puts an arm around Tommy's shoulders.

'Come on, let's get out of here. I'll buy you a beer.'

In a Mayfair backstreet, away from the madding crowds, Benny and Tommy are sat at the bar in the Iron Duke's pub. Named after the man himself, Lord Wellington, it is a homely little place frequented by characters a world away from what you will find inhabiting the Dorchester.

Its walls adorned with military paintings of past conflicts but all dwarfed by one in particular. A huge sized frame of Wellington directing his troops on horseback at the battle which immortalised him for all time as the Iron Duke. Waterloo.

Both men appear mesmerised by it. 'He looks a hard faced bastard and not one to cross,' says Tommy. They continue to stare.

'Wise people learn when they can, fools when they must,' says Benny. 'That was one of Wellington's famous sayings. Shrewd words in our line of work don't you think'?

Tommy inhales on cigarette and looks towards Benny.

'What's going on? I know you too well. Tell me'?

'It's just something the Epstein kid said to me. I can't get it out of my mind.'

Benny appears troubled. Tommy is not used to this, for ever since he has known the kindly man, Benny Green has always been the first to buy him a drink, tell a joke or to light up his smoke. A constant light in his life. When Tommy's mum died and was buried in Moston cemetery, Benny was one of only three people present at the graveside. Paddy Mullen being the other. The old adage. 'A friend in need is a friend indeed' could well have been invented for Benny 'Cohen' Green.

'Speak to me Benny.'

He tries hard to smile but fails miserably. 'Epstein told me I should be wearing a Swastika on my arm. He cut deep Tommy. And rightly so because what that boy said made sense. I was acting like a goddamn Nazi. I was bullying him. He's a good man, a genuinely nice man and I was trying to hurt him.'

'Steady on Benny,' smiles Tommy. 'let's keep everything in prospective here. Epstein has the option to work for us. He made a mistake not signing that contract, a business mistake. It's not as if we put the contract on a table in front of him and said either your brains or your signature would be on it. You've done nothing wrong.

Everything here, all we are doing, it's just a day's work. You are thinking too deeply. Epstein's comment was deliberate and planned to make you feel lower than a snake's belly.'

Benny goes quiet. He takes a drink and smiles at Tommy. He puts a hand on his shoulder. 'It was July 1946 when I finally had confirmed the fate of my mother and father. Oh I had become resigned to the fact they had been murdered by the Germans, but to have this told me by someone who witnessed their end?

It was a letter post-dated from New York off an old neighbour in Munich. Anna Dahlstein. Anna too had seen all her family decimated. Seven in all. Gassed at Auschwitz.

My parents met the same fate. She told me somebody who knew them watched as they were beaten and prodded but still walked hand in hand towards the place where the black smoke always rose. The fucking gas chambers.'

Benny fights hard to hold back the tears.

'I try so hard to keep these memories locked away in a place marked no entry, but every now and again they escape. Today my friend it has become a flood. A tidal wave that I cannot hold back. I apologise if I've embarrassed you. It was never my intention.'

Tommy shakes his head. 'I'm your friend Benny, if you cannot speak to me who can you talk to'?

'I cannot do the deal Tommy. How do I face my parents again when the time comes? What do I say. How can I justify my actions? I'll tell Paddy the same thing. I have neither the heart nor inclination to go through with this. Epstein put his neck on the line by not signing the contract. Those boys trust and believe in him and I won't be the one to stick the knife in and ruin that.'

Tommy stares at his friend. 'Well if that's how you feel, then so be it.'

He calls across to the bartender. 'Two more beers here please.'

Tommy turns back to Benny. 'You go with your heart, now cheers and here's to your mum and dad.'

Tommy raises his beer.

TICKET TO RIDE

Word reaches John Flannery off Paddy Costigan of Di Marco's invitation. After speaking to Mullen the decision is taken to go. 'Bobby is a good lad John,' said Mullen.

'It will be a good opportunity to iron out teething problems and maybe cross a few palms with silver.'

The meeting will take place at the Cavern club on Thursday. Flannery has been informed the best of Merseyside royalty will be there on show. Bobby Di Marco, The Clancy Brothers, Frankie Maguire and John Paul Harris. Between these men they have Liverpool carved up......Everywhere that is except the Cavern club.

Tuesday: A white Rolls Royce carrying Bobby Di Marco and his bodyguards pulls up alongside the Liverpool docks. Across the Mersey, huge cargo ships are in port being unloaded. Two men stand leaning on the wall rail reaching down towards the water.

They are the much feared and notorious Clancy Brothers, Denis and Billy. Gypsy by blood, they ply a vicious trade in illegal gambling and nightclubs. Theirs' is a small empire, but one they protect through brutality and intimidation.

They also have easy access to guns and contacts nationwide for 'special occasions' that they hire out. Fellow travellers.

Family.

A Clancy speciality is to slice enemies and bad payers with a frightening fervour that horrifies both fellow gangsters and Police alike. Like wild dogs, men such as Di Marco tend to keep the Clancy brothers at a distance on a leash. But today he needs them, for a special occasion of his own is dawning.

A double hit on John Flannery and Paddy Mullen to take over the Cavern club and Beatles contract, and the countless millions of pounds to go with it. Di Marco has also decided to rid himself of the other Liverpool bosses, Frankie Maguire and John Paul Harris. Using the Clancys and their men as foot soldiers, alongside imported muscle from Naples, reliable shooters related by blood, a 'Saint Valentine's day massacre' Liverpool style is dawning.

With the last one standing, Di Marco, ready to step in once the deed is done to take over the dead men's shoes. And then he will deal with the last thorn in his side, the Clancys also.

An unquenchable thirst for power has tipped Di Marco over the edge. Secretly he dreams of a Merseyside empire with himself as the kingpin and nothing or no one will be allowed to stand in his way.

In just one day's work Bobby Di Marco plans to inherit the crown.

A smiling Di Marco steps out the Rolls as a bodyguard opens the door. He strolls across to the waiting Clancy brothers and shakes both their hands.

'Denis and Billy, we stand on the edge of greatness and riches my friends. Are your boys in town'?

They arrived this morning,' answers Denis, the older of the two. Twenty-eight years old with long scraggly hair tall and dark cavernous eyes. He is sporting two ear rings and wearing a black leather jacket.

'We hit Paddy Costigan tomorrow night, all is in place.'

Costigan is a dead man walking,' adds a smiling Billy, the younger brother. Twenty-five years old and in appearance similar to his older sibling, with eyes also murderous and sinister. 'Let's see how this fucking legend deals with five shotguns surrounding him from all angles.'

'Be careful now Billy,' warns Di Marco. 'Costigan possesses a sixth sense. Just get him in the van and out of the city. What happens to him after that I couldn't care less. But I want him off the scene and I say again be on your toes at all times. Boys, watch the mad bastard. Have you decided where you are going to lift him'?

'He has a routine,' says Denis. 'Get this Bobby, first he goes to a brothel on Argyle street. Mary Lannigan's flea pit and then has a couple of pints in the Slaughter house pub. How fucking ironic? Just opposite there is a piece of wasteland and that is where we will be waiting. Don't you worry your pretty little self about the Clancy brothers.

We'll take good care of business and deal with Costigan. You just ensure everything goes to plan your end.'

Di Marco produces a packet of cigarettes and offers them out to the brothers who accept.

He lights both up. 'When this is over boys they will write a song about our deeds in the coming days.

This is our passage to the top. Our ticket to fucking ride'

It is Tuesday evening and Paddy Mullen is sat in his office at the Cromford club when without notice in walks Michael Brady. A surprised Mullen looks up and rises from his seat to go and greet him. They shake hands.

'Michael it's good to see you. What brings you across the water? He points to a chair for Brady to sit down. Can I get you a drink'?

'Cheers Pat, I would have knocked only I forgot. You know how it is'?

Mullen smiles and pours them both from a bottle on a nearby cabinet and hands Brady a glass.

'What shall we drink to'?

'How about the Beatles'? replies a straight faced Brady.

The penny drops. 'Ah right,' says Mullen, sporting a wry grin. 'You have heard then.'

'The Irwell is a river not an ocean Patrick. I think it's only fair after recent events that Salford should benefit from any good fortune likely to come yours and John Flannery's way, don't you think'?

Mullen shakes his head. 'I'm not so sure. Events have turned a little nasty Michael. I think after what I'm about to say, you may not be so keen.'

Brady takes a sip of whisky and smiles. 'Try me'?

'Well the locals have not exactly welcomed us with open arms.'

'Has it sparked'?

'Not yet,' replies Mullen. 'Flannery has placed Paddy Costigan at the club to ward off any potential trouble makers.'

Brady shakes his head. 'That mad bastard should be put down, but I suppose he has his uses.'

Mullen sighs heavily. 'Never more so than now, for the balloon is going to go up Michael.

This can go no further than these four walls.'

'You have my word Pat.'

'I sent Tommy down to London yesterday to help with Benny Green in tying up the Beatles deal. Only he was picked up at Euston Station by two of the Kray's henchmen.'

'Poor Tommy, there goes his finger nails I suppose'?

Mullen smiles. 'Not exactly. The twins believe they owe us and Tommy in particular. It appears one of their business associates overheard a conversation in an East End pub between a gang of gypsies. The name of the Clancy brothers came up. They spoke about a big job that is paying well up north in Liverpool working for a man nicknamed the *'Grave digger.'*

'Bobby Di Marco'? exclaims Brady.

'The very same. He's obviously using out of town killers, heavyweights to do his dirty work. These men are hired shooters for Di Marco. He's planning to take out not just myself and Flannery, but the rest of the Merseyside hierarchy of Frankie Maguire and John Paul Harris. '

Brady appears astonished.

'He wouldn't have the fucking nerve. He wouldn't fucking dare'?

'Mullen shakes his head. 'No mistake, it seems our Bobby has delusions of grandeur. They went on to talk about a mad Irishman called Paddy Costigan. Firstly he was to be got rid of and then the rest of us. In one go he intends to wipe out everybody. Take over Liverpool and with myself, Flannery and Costigan out of the picture, move in on the Cavern club. Not to mention the Beatles contract. And then, Manchester.'

Brady smiles. 'Pat, he would never make it past the Liverbird. We'd have his carcass hanging over the ship canal in a whispered fucking breath. But I have to admit there's a little bit of me that admires the balls of this guy. This is a big call. Are you sure your information is spot on'?

There's more,' replies Mullen. 'I've had this confirmed by Salvatore Rea. He has a regular convoy of trucks working out of Liverpool docks bringing back various goodies from Italy to Manchester. One of his drivers, who luckily happened to be Salvatore's nephew got chatting to a freight loader.

He told him an interesting tale about three men arriving on a boat from Naples last week, whom he recognised as members of the *Camorra*. The Neapolitan Mafia. They were shooters. One of them is of particular interest. A certain Luigi Di Marco.'

'And what are you doing about all this'? inquires Brady. Absolutely flabbergasted at what he has been told. 'You need anything count me and my brother in. You just say the word and the Mersey will run red with Di Marco's blood.'

Mullen smiles. 'We are going to rain on his parade Michael. And Bobby Di Marco isn't going to see us coming.'

'I have someone who maybe can help you out,' says Brady. 'A young man by the name of Damian Quinn. He was one of the boys ready to hit the Krays. A good Salford boy, one of ours and a born killer. Put him on a ferry cross the fucking Mersey with Di Marco and I promise he'll not reach the other side.'

Mullen says nothing. He appears deep in thought…..

But Quinn's name is one he will keep in mind for good reason.

John Flannery rings the Cavern club to inform Paddy Costigan what is occurring. He tells him to be on his guard as big trouble is coming their way. Costigan fumes, but is told to stay calm and to be alert. After initially being informed by Paddy Mullen of Bobby Di Marco's plans to kill them, Flannery's original urge was to let Costigan lose to wreak hell. Only to be persuaded to hold fire by Mullen.

'Let the locals deal with this John,' he said. 'I've a role for Paddy in mind, but for once it doesn't involved causing carnage.'

On the phone going down Costigan is in a fury. For a moment he contemplates taking matters into his own hands and hunting down the Clancy brothers himself. But the thought of incurring the wrath of John Flannery and maybe even more Paddy Mullen, is enough to make Costigan stop and think. These are the only two men in the world he respects.

They act as a calming mechanism on the murderous rage that stirs forever inside him. And so he will wait. For now.

Paddy Mullen has sent word to Liverpool to set up an urgent meeting with Frankie Maguire and John Paul Harris. He will arrange a secret liaison in Blackpool at the Norbreck hotel.

Just after three o clock on Tuesday afternoon, the three men meet in the suite overlooking the vast Blackpool promenade. It is a rainy windswept, god-forsaken day and the beach lies empty, except for the few brave foolhardy souls, whose grim attempts to enjoy their trip to the seaside appears more likely to see them blown off their feet and into the raging North sea.

Mullen, Maguire and Harris are men of a similar age and manner. Old School.

They stand quiet with drinks in hand, staring out through the hotel's huge glass, rain-lashed panelled windows. Mullen has already told them of Di Marco's intentions and now it is time to deal with him.

Frankie Maguire speaks first. 'We owe you for this Paddy. This bastard is going to get his comeuppance.'

'Me too,' adds John Paul Harris. 'I'll not forget this old friend.'

'We need calm in our lives lads,' answers Mullen. 'None of us need this Al Capone clown in the north. What have you in mind'?

'Di Marco surrounds himself with a ring of metal,' says Maguire. 'Two armed bodyguards and now a trio of fucking Neapolitan toting shotgun merchants intent on starting a war. It'll be difficult, but not impossible.'

'We have to get him alone,' answers Harris. 'Then make him disappear. No need for a funeral pyre. Di Marco alone will suffice.'

'No the Clancy brothers have to go too John Paul,' replies Maguire. 'For far too long now they have dirtied the streets of our city with the way they do business. I should have taken care of those two maniacs a long time ago.'

Mullen interrupts. 'Can I suggest an alternative strategy'?

Both Maguire and Harris go quiet.

'I have it on good authority from a couple of good friends in London just where the Clancys are holding out. I also understand that Di Marco was planning to hit them once he had finished with us. Now I think it might be a good idea to visit our gypsy friends this evening, and inform the brothers of this little nugget. Let them know it's their problem to sort out Di Marco. Otherwise'?

Mullen smiles as he offers both men a cigarette. 'What we need for this task is somebody of a certain persuasive manner. Someone likely to make the Clancys believe they have no option, but to go along. Somebody like Paddy Costigan I propose'?

'Your friends in London'? asks Harris. 'I assume you mean the Krays'?

Mullen nods.

Harris continues. 'How can you be so sure about all this Paddy. It's a huge call'?

'I can't for certain,' smiles Mullen.

'But every bone in my body is telling me this is what he plans to do. Di Marco is out of control. He has delusions of grandeur that would put Mussolini to shame. He cannot help himself and when informed of this particular bombshell by Costigan, one can only imagine the Clancys' reaction. I really don't think we'll need a crystal ball to forecast it.

Do you gentlemen'?

Maguire and Harris are both smiling.

'And as for Di Marco,' he continues. 'We simply have to arrange a time and place for the two parties to come together.'

'Paddy Mullen, I have to admit you are a damn genius,' answers Maguire.

Harris laughs. 'With thinking like that Paddy, you could almost be a Scouser.'

'Now, now gentlemen,' grins Paddy. 'No need for insults'!

The Clancy brothers and their gang are holed up in a terraced house on Russell Road off Penny Lane. It is late afternoon and the five of them are in a small living room. Shotguns, knives and baseball bats lie scattered all around.

As does a fair amount of half-filled and empty beer and whisky bottles being devoured for Dutch courage. Much will be needed as the clock ticks ever further down to the kidnapping and murder of Paddy Costigan.

The older brother Denis stands to address his younger sibling Billy and the three out of town shooters. 'All right boys go easy on the drink now. We leave here at seven…..

Suddenly there is a loud bang on the front door. They hear a voice

'I come in peace lads, we need to talk.' Billy peeps out the window.

'Fucking hell, it's Paddy Costigan! What the fuck are we going to do big Brother'?

Costigan continues to shout. 'You need to hear what I have to say to you.'

He puts both arms up in the air. 'I'm unharmed and on my own so open this fucking door will you. Come on now.'

Denis makes a decision. 'We let him in and if he starts trouble we do it here. God is a fucking Romany lads,' he laughs, attempting to hide his fear.

'He has brought the devil to our doorstep to save us the trouble of finding him. We'll listen to what he has to say, but one wrong move and we blast this bastard through the gates of hell.'

Denis heads for the front door and stands behind it.

'I'm going to let you in Costigan, but you dare try anything and you are fucking dead, do you understand'?

Costigan fights hard to keep his temper. Every piece of him wanting to kick down the front door and rip limb by limb these fucking gypsies whom have had the temerity to plan to kidnap and kill him. But he is under orders.

'I give you my word. You have shown you have balls, now fucking open up.'

He hears the sound of the door being unbolted and stood there is Denis aiming a shotgun towards him. 'One wrong move Costigan and I'll blow your fucking head off.'

Costigan steps inside with his hands raised. He walks into the living room where the other four stand with guns pointed. He stares towards Denis.

'I take it you are Denis Clancy'?

Denis nods. 'What the fuck do you want Costigan? You have two minutes.'

'I'm here to give you a message on behalf of Paddy Mullen, John Flannery, John Paul Harris, and Frankie Maguire.

Billy looks towards his brother with a glance of desperation. He is sweating heavily and his hands are shaking. Costigan's reputation having the ability to reduce even the most desperate of cutthroats to gibbering wrecks.

'Calm down Billy lad,' says Denis. 'Go on big man say your piece.'

'They are offering you a way out of this situation and unless you go along you are finished in this city and elsewhere. It may also interest you to know that after ridding himself of the others you were next on Di Marco's list.

Look at you,' sneers Costigan.

'Did you really believe he'd spare a few fucking tinkers who could possibly over a drink too many open their mouths and hand him a life stretch for murder? You are dead men walking, unless that is you agree to what I'm about to tell you'?

'Keep talking Costigan, you have my attention,' answers Denis.

'You take care of Di Marco and his henchmen once and for all and we are equal. The slate is wiped clean.'

'How can we be sure Mullen and the others will keep their word'? asks Billy.

Because unlike you they are fucking honourable men. Besides you have no choice.'

Costigan looks at his watch. He counts down, '3-2-1.'

Outside there is the sudden deafening screeching of four vans arriving and coming to a halt. Denis rushes to the window and watches as twenty armed men gather on the road outside the house.

'You see those men out there Clancy,' says a pointing Costigan. 'They are tooled up to the fucking teeth. Liverpool's and Manchester's best with orders to send you to fucking gypsy hell if you don't agree to go along. Now what's to be your decision'?

Denis stares at Billy and the others.

They all nod.

He turns back to Costigan. 'What about you?

'Paddy Costigan what about you? How can I be sure you'll not come looking for revenge? You do have something of a reputation my friend.'

'Believe me,' replies Costigan. 'If I wanted to kill you, you'd be dead already.'

Denis nods his head and smiles before bowing to Costigan like he was a visiting king.

'The legend himself is amongst us.' He spits on his hand and offers it to Costigan.

'You have yourself a deal Paddy son.' On my oath. A gypsy promise. May I be struck down by lightning from the fucking skies if I break it.'

Costigan accepts and the two shake hands.

'Believe me Clancy if you break it I'll cut your fucking head off,' answers Costigan.

The blood suddenly draining from Denis's face.

'When will you do it'? he asks

'Tomorrow morning at the docks,' replies a shaken Denis. 'There's a meeting planned. I'll kill him there. '

Costigan smiles to make Denis even more nervous.

'Make sure you do.'

Paddy Costigan returns to the Cavern around 12-30am. It is closing time and the remnants of the drunken clientele are being escorted out of the door by Francis O'Connor. He bolts it behind them, leaving just himself and Costigan.

Outside you can hear people singing and laughing in the street. Slowly the noise fades away.

O'Connor walks across to the bar and starts to pour himself a whisky. He shouts across to Costigan who is heading upstairs. 'Would you join me for a nightcap Patrick'?

He turns and walks over to his fellow Irishman.

O'Connor hands him a whisky. 'I propose a toast,' he declares, whilst grinning wide. 'May we both be in heaven a full half hour before the devil knows we are dead.'

A slight smile crosses even Costigan's face on hearing this.

The two down the whisky in one go and slam them back down on the bar.

'There's no heaven and hell. Just here and now.'

O'Connor refills the glasses and smiles. 'Lucky for us both then. Tell the tale Patrick, let me hear it from your own lips. The true story. The one that turns grown men to gibbering wrecks.

The ballad of Paddy Costigan.'

'Do you think you can handle it Francis? Have you got the stomach to hear'? replies Costigan. Seemingly happy to finally reveal his story. One that has intrigued and caused horror amongst the northern underworld for ten years.

O'Connor hands him over his drink. 'Try me,' he says.

Costigan begins. 'Back in 1954, I did a bank job with the Barlow brothers, Michael and Seamus in Belfast and came away with over twelve grand. The brothers were fools and much worse, greedy fools. They made the grave mistake of trying to rip me off by doing a runner to England with the cash.

They disappeared from sight but I managed to track down their Father. With a knife to his throat he let it be known they'd taken a boat to these shores. He never spoke again after that because I cut his fucking tongue out.

It took me a while but I finally caught up with them. One night in Manchester I was sat in a pub and overheard talk of two Irish brothers from Belfast who'd been throwing huge amounts of money about in the casino. And had lost the lot.

The name Barlow was mentioned and it didn't take me long to find them after that.

They'd blown all the cash, including my share and I just couldn't let this go.'

A shocked O'Connor listens transfixed. He is still reeling from Costigan's admission of cutting out their Father's tongue.

'I waited and picked my moment. Late one night I ambushed the brothers at gunpoint in town and took them to a deserted warehouse on the edge of the city.

Once there I handed both a knife.'

Costigan smiles at the memory.

'They were terrified. I gave them instructions to fight to the death but with a twist. Whoever lived I was going to crucify and bleed them till they drained.

At first the elder brother Michael refused to fight, but then Seamus cut him and so it began. Both went hell for leather before Michael had Seamus on the floor and sunk his knife deep into his brother's guts.

I was true to my word and gutted Michael like a fish. I heard a caretaker found him hanging from the wall next morning with nails in both hands. Crucified. Bled dry.

After that nobody ever fucked with Paddy Costigan again.'

Costigan pours himself another whisky and downs it in one. He looks across at an ashen faced O'Connor.

'You did fucking ask.'

O'Connor feels sick. He cannot bear to look Costigan in the face.

'I always thought people had exaggerated over the years. You know how these things work. Everyone adds another layer until the myth becomes that little more real and before you know it's absolute fact. But this'?

O'Connor takes another drink whilst all the time Costigan sits staring at him.

He continues. 'This is just fucking sick. How can you do such a thing and still sleep at night. What kind of man are you Patrick Costigan'?

Finally O'Connor plucks up the courage to look Costigan in the eyes. What he see scars his soul.

For Costigan is laughing.

O'Connor pours another drink. He is shaking and declares with fear in his heart.

'May the devil pray for your soul Paddy Costigan,'

On Thursday morning at 6am, Bobby Di Marco's white Rolls Royce makes its way through the empty dock gates and heads to meet the waiting Clancy brothers. Inside Di Marco, his bodyguard who is driving, and sat in the rear, the three Naples hitmen.

The normal ice cool Di Marco is suddenly nervous. His day of destiny has dawned. Nothing must go wrong, so much preparation but he knows one wrong move and all is lost. The fact so much depends on the Clancys fills him with dread.

Di Marco can only hope the prospect of a huge pay day will entice them to ensure they keep their part of the bargain and dispose of Paddy Costigan. The meeting this morning is to be a final rundown where he will look into their eyes and make sure all is well.

That they are ready and then it will all begin.

A new era and with the old guard swept away he will reign supreme. His time. Bobby Di Marco's time. And then when all has settled the Clancy boys will be dealt with also.

Denis and Billy along with the three other shooters are stood waiting for Di Marco's arrival at the quay. All are armed. The order from Denis is let him step out of the car then on his word open fire. 'Remember boys,' says Denis. 'This bastard was going to send us to hell, so let us return the privilege and deliver him and his fucking greaseballs there instead.'

'Such a shame we cannot carve him up Denis,' replies Billy.

'He deserves nothing less.'

Suddenly they hear the sound of a car engine and from around a corner appears the Rolls.

'On my word,' repeats Denis. 'Stay calm.' The vehicle come to a halt ten yards away from the Clancys. They stand rigid. No one moves.

Bobby Di Marco steps out of the car.

He looks towards Denis who is smiling but the others alongside him appear pensive.

Their eyes are all over the place. As if waiting for something to happen.

Something is not right.

Di Marco stops in his tracks. 'Everything okay Denis'?

All instincts telling him there is a real sense of imminent danger in the air.

Denis smiles. 'I'm fine Bobby. And you. How are you feeling on this beautiful Liverpool morning'?

Di Marco plays it cool. He grins wide. 'A great day has dawned my friend.'

'You are going to betray us Bobby.' The words of Denis Clancy cutting a chill through the early morning air. 'What are you talking about'? asks a shocked Di Marco.

'We had a visit last night off Paddy Costigan. Yes, the man himself came to us. He explained everything. Soon as you had got rid of Mullen and the others, we were next on your fucking hitlist.'

Di Marco remains extremely calm on the outside, but his heart is racing. The fact his plans have been discovered can wait, first he has to deal with the Clancys.

'That's not true Denis, come on think, why would I do such a thing? We shook hands, we had a deal. Costigan is just trying to drive a knife through our partnership. Surely you can see that'?

But Denis simply spits on the floor. 'You are a piece of work Bobby. You're nothing but a lying, fucking greaseball.'

Suddenly the sound of screeching brakes and a small convoy of police cars and vans roar into view. Out of them pour a small army of truncheon welding officers.

They charge across.

The Clancys drop the guns to the ground and put their hands in the air, for there is nothing to be gained from killing policemen.

The Neapolitans and Di Marco's bodyguard are screamed at.

'Step out of the fucking car'!

They do so and are swiftly handcuffed.

Di Marco is thrown onto the boot of the Rolls and searched. A pistol is found in his jacket.

'Oh Bobby, Bobby,' exclaims the veteran, fifty-two year old detective, Sergeant Arthur Hollins. 'Oh dear me, what are you doing with this.'

'Shooting pigeons Sergeant.'

'I like pigeons Bobby, bad answer lad.'

Hollins produces a pair of handcuffs and bounds Di Marco tight with them.

He whispers in his ear. 'I don't like guns and I detest what you was planning Di Marco. I witnessed enough fucking carnage in the war. I was on Salerno beach and I saw my friends torn apart by bullets.

And you wanted to bring that shit to Liverpool. To this city'?

Hollins lifts Di Marco up and pushes him into the arms of two waiting Constables.

A defiant Di Marco smiles at Hollins. 'Nice words Sergeant, but you know as well as I do that I'll be back out on the streets again in no time.'

'Maybe so,' replies Hollins. 'But you'll be so with a price on your head. Hell Bobby, I might even take it up myself. You are finished here.'

The smile drains away from Di Marco's face. 'How much'?

'Fifty grand,' answers a grinning Hollins.

'And not alive, just dead. Maybe I shouldn't say this because it goes against my better judgement. But I will anyway. A little advice. If I was you I'd head for warmer climates and fuck off out of Liverpool. Get on an aeroplane and never come back.
And fast.'

Tommy Keenan and Benny Green are sat at the bar in the Iron Duke pub. After hearing of events in Liverpool from Paddy Mullen on the telephone, Tommy now has a more pressing matter in mind. Mullen has instructed him to go above Brian Epstein's head and speak direct to the Beatles. Thus freezing Epstein out.

He has yet to tell Benny and after his comments the previous evening Tommy feels distinctly uneasy. Stuck between following Mullen's instructions and hurting his friend's feelings.

'So what did Paddy have to say'? asks Benny.

'What do you think? He wants me to go speak to the band. You are my friend Benny, just say the word and I'll ring back and tell him to find somebody else.'

No you have to do it Tommy. My problems are mine and mine alone.'

'Have you said anything to Paddy about this'?

Benny appears a broken man. 'I don't think that's a good idea do you? I owe him everything. What am I going to say? Sorry Paddy, this one time my conscience is telling me not to do the deal. Even though it'll probably cost you millions of pounds.'

Tommy is not convinced and is disgusted at Benny's attitude. 'Shame on you Benny 'Cohen' Green. You should know better than to simply dismiss Paddy like this.

You have known him longer than me. He took you in. Have you forgotten Blackpool? That madhouse. He looked after you, gave you work and most of all friendship. The man loves you like a brother and you should show him a little more respect.'

Benny is taken aback. He is not used to being admonished by Tommy. Part of him wishes he could simply go on as if nothing has happened but it is simply impossible. His heart is broken and he has already made a decision.

'This is one I have to walk away from Tommy. In time I'll square things with Paddy but it's over for me here now.' He takes a huge breath, 'I'm moving to Israel. It's something I should have done years ago. I need to do this to honour and preserve my parent's memory.'

Benny smiles. 'I'll never forget all Paddy has done for me. He's my brother, as are you, and I sincerely hope there's no bad feelings.'

A shocked Tommy is struggling to take in what Benny is saying.

'You're not thinking straight. Just like that you are packing up and leaving? You forget something Benny, we are your family now. Who do you know in Israel? You'll be starting all over again, just like you did when you first come over from Germany. You can honour your mother and father's memory right here, with people who care about you.

Please mate, step back a minute. This is all happening too fast.'

Knowing his friends mind is already made up Tommy backs off and hails the barman for another two beers.

Benny puts his arm around his shoulders. 'Tommy will you do me a favour when you meet the Beatles'?

'Please don't tell me you want their autographs'?

Benny smiles. 'Not for me thank you. I'm a jazz man myself. But it's clear from listening to Epstein that he believes they possess a certain loyalty to him. My last advice to you is get John Lennon on board. There's something special about that young man. Paul McCartney speaks a lot without saying anything. The other two, Harrison and Starr will go along with Lennon.'

'Do you have anything derogatory at all on Epstein that I could use'? asks Tommy.

Benny shakes his head. 'No nothing. He's a good and honest guy.'

Tommy is struggling to figure out how to approach the band. 'Can't we make something up? Maybe put fifty grand in a bank account and claim he's ripping them off'?

They'd never believe it,' answers Benny. 'I'd like to wish you luck with this one Tommy but I haven't got the heart. Do you understand'?

'I do, but business is business Benny old son. You know that. This is what we do. I'm going to say or do anything to get those boys to sign for Paddy and Flannery. No hard feelings I hope.'

'Of course not,' replies Benny.

Tommy smiles and nods, but inside he is far from happy.

However, it is time to go to work.

CAN'T BUY YOU LOVE

Astoria Cinema Finsbury Park: The Beatles, John Lennon, Paul McCartney, George Harrison and Ringo Starr are sat relaxing in their dressing room after a concert. Lennon is reading a newspaper, McCartney is strumming a guitar, Harrison is dozing and Starr is watching the BBC news on a small television bracketed to the wall.

Outside the wailing and yelling of screaming young girls can be heard. For them this is a constant soundtrack to their everyday lives. Beatlemania. But to these boys it hardly resonates anymore.

Lennon laughs out loud and looks up from his paper.
'Lads, it says in here that Elvis is looking forward to meeting the Beatles on their forthcoming tour of America. I better pack my blue suede shoes.'

'The King is keeping an eye on the competition,' replies a grinning McCartney.

'Didn't you nearly get thrown out of school once for your Elvis sideburns'?

'I did and I wouldn't be here today if it wasn't for him.'
Suddenly there is a knock at the dressing room door.

'Go away we are not in,' calls out Ringo Starr.
McCartney starts to strum and sing quietly. 'Someone's knocking at the door, somebody's ringing the bell.'
That's fucking rubbish,' says Lennon.

Again there's a knock and Harrison shouts out. 'Just come in, come in, whoever you are. But don't be boring.'

The door opens and Tommy Keenan enters.

He is smiling wide. 'Hello lads, how's your luck'?

'Who the fucking hell are you'? asks Lennon.

'My name is Tommy Keenan. I'm here representing two business clients who'd like to take over the management of the band.'

'We already have a manager,' says McCartney. 'Now can you leave please before we call security and get you beat up.'

'You heard the man,' adds Lennon. 'Leave and shut the door behind you.'

'I'm afraid you don't understand lads,' replies Tommy. We are your security. Your contract with Brian Epstein is legally no longer binding. My clients would like to take it on and in doing so make you all offers you simply can't refuse.'

The four men are momentarily taken aback by Tommy's words and it's Lennon who speaks up. 'Are you a gangster Mr Keenan? Because you look and sound like one.

And if you are can I see your gun'?

'Tommy shakes his head. 'This is a legitimate offer and no I'm not a gangster, and I definitely don't own a gun. Not a real one anyway.'

'Well you are not boring Tommy, I'll give you that,' says Harrison. Tommy takes the contract out of his pocket. He passes it to Lennon. 'If you read through you'll see it's so much better than the one under Epstein. It's a great offer boys and you'd be mad to say no.'

For a moment Lennon stares at the contract then proceeds to fold it up into a paper plane and send it over in McCartney's direction. He in turn flies it over to Ringo, who does similar to Harrison. None bother to even look at it before handing it finally back to Lennon. He floats it back to Tommy who catches it.

'Where are you from Mr Keenan?' asks Lennon.

'Manchester,' replies Tommy. Knowing this is not going well.

'Thought as much,' says McCartney. 'You can tell by you funny accent.'

You don't speak proper like us,' joins in Ringo.

Lennon smiles. 'look, we have a good relationship with Brian. It's based on trust and we have absolutely no intention of dumping him.'

'He's the fifth Beatle Tommy,' grins Ringo. 'He can't sing or play an instrument but he makes a great cup of tea.'

'You are wasting your time,' says McCartney. 'We love Brian. Go home to Manchester and tell whoever you work for to try their luck with Freddie and the fucking Dreamers.'

Tommy tries to get a word in. 'Your contract with Epstein is null and void. Watch my lips, we are going to double what you earn…..'

'You are not hearing us Mr Keenan,' cuts in Lennon. 'Watch my fucking lips, it doesn't matter how much money you throw in our direction, we are not going to dump Brian. Our relationship is not built on money, it's something far more important. He discovered and believed in us when nobody wanted to know.

Three years ago he took a risk after seeing us perform at the Cavern club and we'll be forever grateful. He told everybody who'd listen that the Beatles will be bigger than Elvis and he's right. We will be, you just watch. Besides he's also stopped us killing each other over time. He's our referee and mum and dad all in one.'

Ringo is right for once, he is the fifth Beatle.'

'Steady on John,' replies Ringo, pretending to be hurt. 'No need for that. And Brian is definitely more of a Mum. A Mary Jane even.'

Tommy pretends to play a violin. 'Do you know what this is? The world's smallest violin playing a sad tune. Look I'm touched by your loyalty, but you are throwing away a fortune here….'

'Is everybody in Manchester deaf Tommy'? asks Harrison.

'And stupid,' says Ringo. 'That's not a violin, looks more like a cello to me.'

'Must be all that billowing chimney smoke affecting the brains,' adds McCartney.

'Have you got family Mr Keenan'? asks Lennon

An increasingly irritated Tommy starts to light up a cigarette. 'I got married last Saturday. I should be on my honeymoon, but instead was sent down here to try and talk you lot round. A fat lot of good that has been. And please call me Tommy.'

'Many congratulations Tommy, we are all very happy for you,' smiles Lennon.

McCartney starts to sing and play on his guitar, The Dixie Cups, Chapel of Love.

'Going to the chapel and we are going to get married.'

'Yes congratulations Tommy,' says Ringo. 'Your wife must be very proud.'

Lennon continues. 'Your wife is your family and Brian is part of ours. It's that simple.

I'm sure you would not appreciate our Ringo here turning up at your house and stealing your good lady'? Not that he would do such a thing eh Ringo'?

'Of course not John,' he replies. 'Because it's just not right.'

Lennon smiles. 'So do you see Tommy? And finally, let's be clear on this, if you do attempt to remove Brian, then this thing we have going on here. The Beatles.

It's fucking over. We'll go our separate ways. Do I make myself clear'?

'Crystal John,' he replies. 'All right lads. Look, cards on the table. A very good friend of mine met your manager this week and after talking to Epstein didn't have the heart or will to cause him grief. And after meeting you four today, now I can understand and see why.'

Tommy holds up the contract, 'I suppose there is only one thing to do with this.'

He rips it up.

'I'll tell my clients it's a non-starter. Good luck in America eh. Say hello to Elvis for me.' Tommy goes to leave only for Lennon to call out. 'Hey Tommy.'

He turns around. 'What's your wife's name'?

'Alison,' he replies. 'And she's not very happy with me at the moment because we should be in a gondolier by now and sipping wine by the Grand Canal.'

All their eyes are upon him.

'Let me tell you something,' says Lennon. 'Money cannot buy you love. Remember those words when you hear us on the radio or the television in the next couple of weeks.' McCartney, Harrison and Starr try hard to keep a straight face.

Tommy notices this, but by now has had enough and just wants to go home.

He looks across to the others. 'Be lucky lads, sorry for the aggravation.' With that said he leaves the room.

Outside in the corridor Brian Epstein stands leaning against the wall with arms folded. He watches Tommy coming towards him and appears nervous.

'Well then'? asks Epstein. 'Have I still got a job'?

Tommy nods. 'I'm sorry Mr Epstein. You'll not be hearing from us again.'

Epstein watches Tommy disappear around a corner. He breathes a huge sigh of relief and appears close to tears. From out of the Beatles dressing room John Lennon emerges. He goes across to Epstein who dries his eyes on seeing Lennon approaching.

Lennon hands Epstein a handkerchief and puts an arm around his shoulders. He kisses him on the forehead. 'It's all over mate, we told them to fuck off back to Manchester.'

It is late Friday night, and Tommy Keenan enters the Cromford club, after returning from London. He heads straight upstairs to Paddy Mullen's office where sat waiting for him is Mullen and John Flannery, who stands leaning against his desk.

'Hello lads,' smiles Tommy.

'What happened Tommy'? inquires a red faced Flannery, clearly not happy after he rang to say no deal.

'They were never going to do it John. All four of them are in tight with Epstein. Lennon even claimed they'd quit if we moved him on.'

'And you believed that'? asks Mullen.

'Yes I did Paddy,' snaps Tommy. 'Look, I was there you two wasn't. They have a bond. The band were adamant in their support for Epstein.'

An irate Flannery is raging. 'And did you show them the contract and explain how much more money they'd be making'?

'I did,' sighs Tommy.

'And what did they say'?

'They made paper planes and passed it around the room,' answers a straight faced Tommy.

Mullen tries hard not to laugh, but Flannery appears close to exploding.

'Are you taking the piss Tommy? Because this isn't a laughing matter.'

Tommy loses his temper. 'Listen, I gave up my bloody honeymoon for this fiasco. It's not my fault they are in love with Epstein.'

Tommy points an accusing finger at Flannery. 'And you should have done your homework.'

'Right that's enough from both of you,' declares Mullen, whilst standing from the desk. He goes to pours three whiskies and realises now Tommy never stood a chance.

Mullen addresses Flannery. 'I'm afraid we are going to have to take a hit and swallow this. It's not going to happen.'

Mullen hands Flannery and Tommy their drinks.

He smiles. 'Most we win, a few we lose. It was always going to be a tough call. Liverpool and, Manchester?

It's a northern thing.

'They did say to try our luck with Freddy and the Dreamers,'? grins Tommy. In an attempt to lighten the atmosphere.

For a moment Flannery glares at him with what appears murderous intent. Only then to smile and burst out laughing.

He puts out his hand which Tommy accepts. 'No hard feelings Tommy'?

'No problem John.'?

Flannery continues. 'I'm getting rid of that damn Cavern club as well. It's not worth the hassle. I've had my full of fucking Scousers.'

Tommy downs his whisky in one. 'Now if you gentlemen don't mind, I best get home to my wife. That's if I still have one.'

'She's waiting for you Tommy,' smiles Mullen. I sent the Rolls to pick Alison and her parents up from Blackpool a few hours ago. Also your flight is booked. You both fly out to Italy at three o'clock tomorrow afternoon.'

He hands Tommy an envelope obviously stuffed with cash.

At first Tommy appears reluctant, but Mullen is insistent. 'Take it and buy Alison something nice and expensive.'

Tommy relents. 'Thanks Paddy, much appreciated. I'll see you both in a fortnight. Maybe a lot earlier if she hasn't calmed down.'

'Mind how you go son,' smiles Mullen, before playfully adding. 'Love to the wife.'

Tommy leaves and steps back into the Mancunian night. Once this time of the evening and this city was Tommy's domain. But not anymore.

'Love to the wife,' he repeats Mullen's words to himself and then smiles wide.

'Very funny Paddy. Very funny'

Back in Paddy Mullen's office talks turns to Bobby Di Marco. Both men are sat facing at the desk. My sources tell me Di Marco is out on bail this Monday,' says Mullen.

Flannery finishes his whisky and refills his and Mullen's glass. 'I should let Paddy Costigan loose on the treacherous fuck. Fifty grand Paddy,' exclaims Flannery.

'The bounty on Di Marcos head from John Paul Harris and Frankie Maguire is huge. Word is it's an open market. I could unleash Costigan and deliver the bastard's head on a plate and claim the money.'

Take my advice John,' replies Mullen. 'Let others deal with this. Besides there'll be a queue of assassins ten miles long for Di Marco. Walk away, Call off Costigan and bring him home.'

'Maybe you are right,' sighs Flannery, who raises his whisky glass.

'To a more peaceful life my friend.'

'We can but dream John,' smiles Mullen.

'We can but dream.'

Liverpool: Monday morning: 11.00Am: After being granted bail it's an extremely nervous Bobby Di Marco who boards the Mersey ferry alone with no bodyguards, and now not a friend in the world. Haunted and hunted.

It's a grim morning and there are dark skies above Liverpool.

The ferry is quiet and thick mist covers the Mersey. The far shore is viewable, just.

Only a handful of people, ten at most are aboard.

This is a relief for Di Marco, who sees potential hitmen everywhere he looks. There is a gaggle of four old ladies, an ageing priest, happily two policemen and three young boys in school uniform.

Di Marco's plan is pick up twenty grand in hidden cash and head out of the city. To go south, giving himself some thinking time on how to remain alive, with every professional and amateur hitman in the north breathing down his neck.

Di Marco glances around constantly at the fellow passengers. A nondescript lot thank God. His eyes searching each of them for the merest hint of danger.

But nothing is forthcoming and Di Marco is able to relax slightly. He goes to find a quiet spot and leans on the railing.

There is no one nearby.

In the near distance, somewhere on board, Gerry and the Pacemakers, *Ferry cross the Mersey* is playing on a radio.

The ferry is midway across the Mersey as it begins to rain a little and Di Marco pulls up the collar on his jacket. His mind racing, devastated with recent events. So many enemies with death in their heart. His death.

The *'grave digger'* feels like he is dancing on the edge of his own final resting place.

All the dreams and great plans now shattered, Di Marco can think only of staying alive. Everything is over. Everything is finished. He thinks to himself.

What would Al do?

Suddenly a voice shakes him back to reality,

'Hello Bobby mate, going anywhere special'? It is one of the two policemen.

It's Damian Quinn and before Di Marco can speak to beg for his life, Quinn has fired three rapid times from a silencer pistol.

Di Marco falls slumped to the deck with despairing eyes of utter shock.

The other supposed policemen walks smiling towards him with a camera.

'Smile Bobby lad. Say cheese because this picture is worth fifty grand.'

The man clicks and then swiftly Quinn and his accomplice pick up the body and throw him overboard.

Bobby Di Marco is sent to sleep with the fishes.

Salford and a little piece of Manchester has come to Liverpool.

As the body falls beneath the water the song on the radio fades out………………..

It is early evening in Venice as Tommy and Alison stroll down the Grand Canal. They are off for a meal, but suddenly Tommy spots a small bar with a television that is showing the Beatles playing. He grabs Alison's hand without really giving her the option.

'Come on let's grab a quick drink.'

They go inside and Tommy puts two bar stools together and orders two glasses of wine.

'He points towards the television. 'I know these fellas.'

'Of course you do Tommy,' she smiles. 'And I used to go out with Elvis Presley.'

The Beatles come to finish a song and amidst the usual backdrop of screaming girls,

John Lennon leans into the microphone and announces.

'This next one is for a friend of mine out there from Manchester and his lovely new wife Alison. It's a new song called 'Can't buy you love.'

As the song begins Alison watches on open mouthed at the small screen, whilst Tommy has a huge grin on his face. She turns to look at him. 'What just happened there'?

He hands Alison her glass of wine. 'Stick with me girl. I promise it'll never be boring.'

Suddenly Tommy gets a tap on the shoulder. He turns and stood facing is a tall bespectacled, dark suited man with an attractive lady next to him.

'Tommy Keenan, I don't believe it! Fancy bumping into you here'?

It's a small world,' smiles Tommy.

He puts an arm around Alison. 'I'd like to introduce you to a very good friend of mine and his lovely wife.

Alison meet Bruce and Frances Reynolds..........'

Tel Aviv: Israel: In the burning midday heat of the Middle East, a white shirted Benny 'Cohen' Green steps off the aeroplane with suitcase and jacket in hand and shelters his eyes from the blinding sun. The roar of the plane engine winding down roars loud and the hot dust sweeps into Benny's face. He walks slowly down the steps until finally his feet are on Holy soil. Benny leans down and kisses the tarmac.

He is crying and clutching tight an old tattered photograph of his mother and father.

Benny 'Cohen' Green has come home.

Three months later, high above Manchester, on the vast Moors that stretch endlessly over the Pennines mountains reaching towards Yorkshire, a lone transit van driven by Paddy Costigan makes its way along a quiet, single, winding, country lane. It's night time and the rain is lashing down. Above thunder roars and lightning bolts strike from the black skies. One illuminates Costigan's face. He is smiling. In the back of the van, sat tied up and gagged are the Clancy brothers. Both have terror etched in their eyes but they cannot scream. Not that it would make any difference for Paddy Costigan has come calling.

It is payback time.

ACT THREE
THE TRAIN ROBBER

ONE DAY TOMMY

Manchester: 1965: The legendary fifty-two year old Detective, Chief Superintendent, Tommy Butler of The Flying Squad and Scotland Yard, steps warily off the train at Manchester's Piccadilly railway station and looks around him. Butler is the man given responsible for capturing the Great Train Robbers. Most have already been apprehended, but the mastermind of this outrageous crime which saw them escape with £2.6 million remains at large.

Bruce Reynolds is the most hunted man in Britain and Butler is under huge pressure from the Home Secretary to bring him to justice. He dare not fail. The train robbery of her majesty's postal service train from Glasgow to London is being viewed amongst the hierarchy as a direct attack against the very pillars of the establishment. Heads are wanted on spikes. Extraordinary jail sentences are being handed out.

It will not be justice but revenge which is carried out against those responsible.

For 1965 Britain remains a nation where everyone, most importantly, the *'Working Class'* must know their place. It does not do to step above your station and so Tommy Butler has to deliver.

Butler nickname is *'One day Tommy.'* Such is the audacity and speed in which he operates to hunt down criminals. This allied to a fanatical dedication to the job in hand has seen him achieve legendary status amongst both the police and criminal underworld. Now, after a tip off from an impeccable source that Reynolds could well be hiding out in Manchester, being sheltered by various underworld gangs, whilst waiting to be smuggled abroad,

he has come north.

Waiting to greet him on the platform is Detective Inspector George Collins, who is not over pleased on being assigned this particular task by his superiors. Collin's last experience of the Met was the Kray affair and he remains highly suspicious of all things London based. However for Butler, Collins has made an exception, for he has heard too many good things off people whose opinions he trusts to believe this man stood before him is anything but a good copper.

And for George Collins that is all which matters.

The two men shake hands. 'Welcome to Manchester Chief Superintendent.'

'I take it you are Inspector George Collins'?

He nods, I'm to be your eyes and ears whilst you are in my city.'
'Your city Collins'? asks a quizzical Butler.
'I like to think so,' he answers. 'I know how it thinks and how it breathes. I keep a good eye on it.'
'And do you think you can lead me to Reynolds in your city'?
Collins picks up Butler's suitcase. He smiles. 'If he's in Manchester I'll find him.'
Collins points down the platform. 'If you'd like to come with me, we have a car waiting to take you to the station.' The two men head out of the station and step into the midst of a beautiful Mancunian, sunlit, late morning.

Butler shelters his eyes to protect him from the sun. 'I was under the impression it always rained in this bloody place'?
Collins laughs, 'You probably heard that rubbish off the same idiots who believe we all walk around up her in flat caps, race ferrets, and with all due respect Mr Butler, live in fucking caves. We have hot and running water as well you may be surprised to know.'

Butler smiles. 'Point taken Collins. No need to be so touchy. How far is it to the station'?
'Bootle Street is fifteen minutes by foot at most.'
'What do you say we walk'? asks Butler. 'Let me get a feel for, as you say, 'your city.'
'Very well,' answers Collins. Not enjoying the sarcasm in Butler's voice. He will give him the benefit of the doubt for now. Collins places Butler's suitcase in the boot of the waiting police car, slams it shut and motions towards the officer in the driving seat to go on without them. He points downwards towards Manchester's heartland, Piccadilly Gardens. Around them the early Mancunian traffic speeds past.

'After you,' he says to Butler, as they head off.
Halfway down they pass a café. 'Can I treat you to a cup of tea'? asks Collins.
Butlers nods. 'Very kind of you.' The two men enter and take a table by the window. The Animal's *The House of the Rising Sun* is playing on the radio. A waitress comes across to take their order as Butler stares at the passers by outside. One man appears to recognise him The two make eye contact before the stranger turns away. Quickening his step.

Butler appears deep in thought.

'A tuppence for them chief Inspector'? asks Collins

He turns around and smiles. 'I was just thinking. Why would Reynolds come north, it makes absolutely no sense? He's no family up here, no business acquaintances so far as we know of. I was convinced we were closing in when suddenly the trail went dead. He could not have left the country, for the airports, the ports, and the docks were all being watched and monitored. Believe me Collins, he wouldn't have been able to leave these isles in a damn submarine without me knowing. I had closed every door and shut every single window of opportunity.'

Can you be totally sure he hasn't slipped the net'? asks Collins. Certainty was something he believed too easily prone to fallibility.

A trait that worried him in people.

Butler appears to resent this question. 'Collins, believe me, what Reynolds and his cronies have done is akin to walking up to the Queen and spitting in her face. Off the record you wouldn't believe the resources I've had placed in my lap to bring him in.

No, he's still here. And just last week we received a break when I had a tip he'd travelled up to your neck of the woods.'

'This tipster, did he have a Mancunian accent'? asks Collins

'Not really, more Eton you might say. No offence but I never reveal my sources identities to avoid any misunderstanding. And maybe finding them dead in a ditch.'

'Fair enough, but I need something. Can I have a name at least'? 'Butler eyes Collins with a slight look of wariness. 'Very well then. Keep this under your hat inspector. A certain Thomas Keenan. Have you heard of him'?

'Oh I've heard of him,' smiles Collins. 'Everybody in Manchester knows Tommy.'

'A friend of yours'? adds Butler, rather scathingly and surprised at Collins' reaction.

'Let's just say if it wasn't for Tommy there would have been a bloodbath with the Krays. All provoked by your glory boys in C11, and God knows what other secret brethren you have going on down there.'

'Is there something you are trying to tell me'? asks a quizzical Butler. 'We are on the same side here aren't we Collins'?

Suddenly the waitress returns with their mugs of tea. They both attempt forced smile towards her and nod their thanks. Butler's comment has clearly angered Collins and he is finding it hard not to lose his temper. 'I'm on the side of the people I consider the good guys. And let me tell you something on that occasion I was ashamed of my badge. I'd like to think someone of your character and reputation, if you knew what was occurring would have acted in the same manner.'

Butler appears fascinated. He leans forward across the table.

'What exactly did you do?'

Collins smiles. 'I upheld the law chief superintendent. I did the right thing.'

The two go quiet and for a second there is a clear standoff. Finally Butler speaks to break the silence. 'I'll pretend this conversation never took place Collins. Now tell me all you know about this fellow Keenan'?

'It just doesn't fit. Keenan is freelance, but works mostly for a local club owner Paddy Mullen. Let's just say his business deals tend to rest in the shade between what's legal and not, but he's no big time villain. It just makes no sense for him to be getting mixed up with the likes of Reynolds. Besides Tommy has just got married. It's an open secret, even to the bad boys up here that anybody even being hinted at having anything to do with the train job, if nicked are going to disappear for fucking years on end. They know normal justice does not apply in this case Mr Butler.

I think even me and you can agree on that.'

Butler ignores Collins' damning last words and returns to an earlier comment. 'Just then you mentioned a Patrick Mullen? '

'I did.'

'I thought so. How is the old rascal'?

'I take it yours and Paddy's paths have crossed before?'

'Oh yes,' smiles Butler. 'I'll tell you a story. 'During the war I wasn't allowed to go and fight because they said I was too good at catching villains and so I spent my time nicking home grown riff raff. Men whom thought they could break the law whilst the world burned and kill, rob and maim to their black heart's content. Well they didn't account for Tommy Butler and I went after them with a vengeance. Small time or big it made no difference to me. It became a crusade. As the bombs fell I went hunting Inspector Collins and I nailed countless of the bastards.

Up and down this sceptre Isle of ours I travelled. I made it my mission in life and no villain was safe. I gave those bastards sleepless nights and wouldn't rest until they were rotting in a jail cell. *'One day Tommy'* they nicknamed me. Not quite, but I was close. One case of a missing kid took me to Blackpool. She'd disappeared from the East End and it was rumoured some sick bastards were passing her around the country for fun. The kid was just

twelve- years old and I had vowed to find her.

And that's where I met Patrick John Mullen.

He ran half a dozen clubs and casinos that were constantly packed with servicemen on leave, or in the midst of a last mad blow out before they went overseas. He always handled any trouble that flared with a strict but fair policy of one warning, then you go through a window. Not really a man you could ever argue with.

When I told him my reasons for being in Blackpool, Mullen's face turned grey. I'll never forget it. He then went hell for leather breaking down doors and I have to be honest a few noses to help me track down those vile scum whom had the girl.

I remember thinking that at one time half of Blackpool must have been working for him. He had this rage, a murderous anger in him. Though I knew he was a good man. Maybe no saint and certainly in matters of smuggling cigarettes and spirits well'? Butler smiles.

'But finally Paddy hunted them down and returned the girl safely in one piece.

Now I had a problem.

I received a phone call off him in my hotel room saying he had these three men. Londoners, all army deserters, bound and gagged and waiting for me to pick up on the end of the North pier. Well off we went to collect them, sirens blazing, truncheon welding coppers, blowing whistles and racing down the pier.

And when we reached them....' Butler stops.

'What,' exclaims Collins. 'What'd you find?' Butler takes a sip of his coffee.

'They were all missing an ear George,' he answers.

Collins is momentarily stuck for words.

'Northern justice I presume,' continues Butler. 'When I asked Mullen why one earth he'd done this he replied. 'They were lucky to keep their heads.'

' So what did you do'?

I had a word in their remaining ear and passed the message best not to mention Mullen's name in court. And not really surprisingly when the time arose his never came up.

'But they were different times,' replies Collins. 'Paddy is a different character now and much more relaxed in matters of business. Unless that is ....'

'Go on,' asks Butler. 'Unless what '?

'Unless you hurt one of his own. Then all bets are off. And Tommy Keenan is one of his own.'

Butler eyes Collins with what can easily be recognised as slight suspicion. He is unsure of this place. Manchester. This northern outpost of intrigue and tribal loyalties on both sides of the law. He will have to tread carefully.

Butler smiles. 'drink your tea Collins, it'll go cold.'

THE GYPSY LADY

Saturday night in The Fatted Calf and this small but always busy city centre pub, just off Market Street, in Cromford court, is packed to the rafters. It's the kind of watering hole you walk in forwards and leave backwards. A raucous atmosphere with pipe and cigarette smoke drifting on the air. A fiddler is struggling to be heard playing for drinks in the corner, and across the floor, a drunken piano player of Irish descent is slurring his words and out of key, whilst singing a song about going home.

The carpet is a deep red for the landlord is sick and tired of cleaning blood up off the floor. So now he just lets be, whilst at the bar it's three deep with customers shouting and screaming to be served more. For nobody has ever had their fill in the Fatted Calf. Forever a minute and a spilt drink or a smashed glass away from a riot. More broken noses on view than on a pugilist outing and into this place, just after nine o'clock, Blind Billy and Boom enter through the door......

All eyes fall upon them. The fiddler man stops fiddling and the piano man stops playing. Blind Billy is forty-two years old, Newton Heath born William Cosgrove. Cosgrove is a former paratrooper who was badly injured at Arnhem. A German grenade relieved him not just of his left arm for which a hook now sits in place. But also the sight in his right eye, which is kept permanently covered by a black patch.

A sinister and disturbing aura surrounds Cosgrove who always wears a long black leather coat. A tall man he soars above his best and only friend in this word, the portly figure of the small, dwarf-like even, but still menacing features of the deaf Frank Matthews. A cruel affliction cursed upon him since birth. Matthews is more widely known amongst the Mancunian underworld as Boom, due to his love of explosives.

Both men were orphaned young and have forged a friendship since childhood.

Placed into a Catholic orphanage run by sadistic and perverted white collared priests, whom spent their nights prowling the dormitories searching for victims.
'It was God's will,' the innocents were told when dragged from their beds and thrown to their knees.

The few fighting back such as Cosgrove and Matthews, kicking and screaming against these unholy men. Refusing their unwanted advances only to receive almighty beatings for resisting. Made to swear upon a supposed bible never to reveal what they had witnessed and suffered, otherwise their souls would go to eternal hell. A pact with the fucking devil seemingly residing behind the white pearly gates.

Together Cosgrove and Matthews found from somewhere the strength to survive such evil and years later, they went looking for revenge. And they found it. The same Priest who had savaged them as children made to kneel and beg for mercy from an uninterested God, then having his throat cut by Cosgrove.

He heard the screams whilst Matthews simply smiled as the last breaths fell from the dying priest's mouth into the back gutter of a Mancunian alley way. The body then swiftly wrapped and weighed down before being thrown into the Irwell. Soon to be picked at by the fishes and rotted by the heinous chemicals from nearby factories that poured into the canals, even changing its colour. The priest's many sins dissolved in a manner he could never have imagined, even in his worst nightmares.

To those in the know Blind Billy and Boom are hired assassins. The common joke made amongst the criminal fraternity is that when Blind Billy misses Boom blows them up. But in reality Billy does not miss. Their reputation for getting the job done is legendary. They never fail and work for the highest bidder and tonight they have arranged to meet a client in the Fatted Calf.

Nursing a large whisky she sits alone in the corner. Anyone attempting to enter her space is met with a fierce 'Fuck off'! Maria Clancy is twenty-six years old, stunningly beautiful with dark hair and eyes that can pierce the soul. She is of gypsy blood and sister to her officially missing and presumed dead brothers, Dennis and Billy. Both men simply disappearing from sight one night in Liverpool, two months ago.

At first Maria assumed they had simply gone to ground after their disastrous partnership with the murdered Bobby Di Marco. But last week she received a letter from an unnamed policemen telling her to stop searching for her kin because they had already been killed by a man called Paddy Costigan.

The letter went on to claim this information was known to the authorities, but not to expect them to act on it. For the Clancys were simply not worth their time or trouble. Too much bad blood had passed for detectives to delve too deep into what they regarded as someone actually doing them a favour. The Clancys hurt people when they were alive. From the grave that problem no longer exists. Finally the letter mentioned two men whom if Maria wanted justice she should turn to.

Thus she now sits alone in a corner of the Fatted Calf waiting for Blind Billy and Boom. The momentarily silence that greeted their entrance ends and once more the music men start up. All others in the pub go back to their business, for it does not do to stare too long at the new arrivals.

Boom points towards Maria and the two head over.

Both men stand looking down and Maria cannot believe her eyes. They sit. Words are forming in Maria's mouth but she daren't utter them. Instead she simply stares.

Blind Billy breaks the silence. 'We hear you wished to speak to us'?

'I have a job for you,' answers a clearly startled Maria.

'You appear alarmed by our appearance Miss Clancy. Is there something you wish to get off your chest'?

'It's just....' Maria stutters. 'You aren't what I expected.'

Blind Billy smiles. He puts a cigarette in his mouth and Boom lights it for him.

'We hear that quite often. Well I do, not so much him. I can assure you, if you ask around our reputation for getting the job done is impeccable. Now we are busy men, if you have something please say, if not, don't waste our time Miss Clancy.'

'I want you to kill Paddy Costigan.'

At that moment the barman brings two beers over for Blind Billy and Boom.

The owner knows best to keep characters such as these onside.

'On the house lads, off the boss.' They both look other and acknowledge the smiling but clearly nervous landlord. Every night for him in here is akin to dancing on broken glass. Something which is a common occurrence in the Fatted Calf.

The two men look at each other in astonishment. They cannot believe what Maria Clancy has just asked of them. If they agree Costigan will undoubtedly be their greatest challenge yet.

Nobody speaks until the barman has gone then Blind Billy leans across the table to within inches of Maria's face.

'What you've just asked of us lady is going to cost you an awful lot of money.'

'How much'? asks Maria, determined not to appear scared by Blind Billy's appearance and him being so near she can smell his stale cigarette breath.

'Ten thousand pounds,' he replies.

'Done,' answers Maria. So abrupt and fast it catches Blind Billy off guard.

'What, you have that kind of money'?

'My brothers did, it's mine now. I want that bastard dead. If you two can't handle it I'll find somebody else who can.'

Boom has lip read Maria. He taps Blind Billy on the shoulder and replies in sign language. 'Fuck me, Paddy Costigan'!

'He won't see us coming old friend,' answers Blind Billy. Ten grand is too good to turn down.'

Boom sits back in the chair, his feet dangling. He smiles and nods in agreement with his friend. 'You have yourself a deal Miss Clancy,' says Blind Billy, who puts his hand out for Maria to shake. He continues: 'Consider Paddy Costigan a dead man walking. For ten grand he's already enjoying his last few days on this earth. I promise you soon we'll despatch him to hell.'

THE TRAIN ROBBER

They were close, so very near to pulling off the perfect robbery and beating the establishment. The biggest two fingered gesture to the powers at be since Thomas Cromwell had the head of King Charles 11 cut off. The underworld's *'Sistine Chapel.'* A work of art and beauty. But it was simply too much money and it belonged to a woman whose power when unleashed was a sight to behold. Like a row of dominoes falling the train robbers were swiftly rounded up as the legendary detective Tommy Butler went to work.

Of the fifteen original gang members only two remain at large. One is Buster Edwards, who has fled the country, the other is ringleader, thirty-four year old Bruce Reynolds. And now appearing unrecognisable from the classic mug shot portrayed across the land in every newspaper and magazine, the newly moustachioed Reynolds sits in Paddy Mullen's office, alongside Tommy Keenan at the Cromford club.

Sat at his desk facing them is an angry looking Mullen. He points a finger at Reynolds.

'You've two minutes to explain what this man is doing in my office Thomas Keenan, before I throw you out of the window'?

'No offence son,' he adds, addressing Reynolds.

One look at Mullen's face and Tommy knows he is in trouble.

'Paddy look. Bruce was desperate. Butler was all over the south like a rash. I couldn't ignore it when he rang for help.'

How the hell did your two paths originally cross'? asks Mullen. Almost speechless with shock and rage for this bespectacled man in front of them could see both he and Tommy doing a twenty-year jail stretch just for harbouring him.

'We met briefly when I was working in London for the Krays, shifting those American cigarettes from Southampton docks. Well one night I had a little bother in an East End boozer when a gang of head cases started to play up rough. They were going to slice me up because of my accent. Can you believe it'?

Tommy smiles but it cuts no ice with Mullen, who has a face of stone.

'Keep talking idiot,' he says.

A sheepish Tommy continues. 'Well Bruce was drinking with his pals and they jumped in to even up the odds. The loud mouths soon backed off and since then we've become mates and always kept in touch.'

Reynolds finally breaks his silence. 'Mr Mullen, I'm truly sorry for landing on your doorstep like a bad smell, but believe me it's only for a few days. I just need time to think out my next move. I have cash and can make it worth your while.'

Mullen stands and walks over to the drinks cabinet. He pours three whiskies and hands both Tommy and Reynolds one before sitting back at his desk.

'Bruce, I don't want your money. It's just you have put me in a terrible situation, but now you are here we'll do our best to help you out. Tommy here has a heart of gold but sometimes the brains of a lump of cheese. You are toxic son. Anybody having anything to do with you, if caught are going to disappear for a very long time. So we are going to have to tread ever so careful.'

Mullen glares at Tommy. 'Does anybody else know Bruce is here'?

'Nobody,' he replies. 'Bloody hell Paddy, give me some credit.' Again Mullen stares daggers at Tommy, who puts his hand up in the air.

'I know, I know' he says. Desperately trying to avoid another ear bashing, if not worse.

'I really appreciate this,' says Reynolds. Suddenly taking the fire out of Paddy's mood.

'I promise you I'll be out of your hair in no time.'

'What are your plans son'? asks Mullen.

'Reynolds shrugs his shoulders. 'There's only one Mr Mullen. To find a way across the channel and stay there. My wife Frances and son Nick kid are with friends already in Spain. I'll send for them when I'm settled and it's safe.'

'The continent will not be far away enough for you,' replies Mullen. 'I'd be looking at Canada or Mexico. Mind you knowing Butler you may consider getting a rocket to the moon.'

'You've had dealings with this copper before then'? asks Tommy.

'A long time ago during the war,' he replies. A bloody good detective. He's like a dog with a bone and one we don't need sniffing around Manchester asking questions. Luckily he's not here. so we can count our blessing for that.'

'I have some more bad news,' says Tommy. Knowing this particular piece of information could well see him launched from the previously mentioned window.

'Go on,' inquires Mullen, dreading what is to follow from Tommy's lips.

He's come north Paddy. One of the boys clocked him having a cup of tea with Collins yesterday morning in Piccadilly.'
Mullen leans back in his chair. How on earth has Butler figured out Reynolds has landed on his doorstep?

Events have just taken a drastic turn for the worse but deep down Mullen relishes the notion of helping Reynolds escape. He feels they, Manchester, owe certain people high in power a bloody nose after the Kray affair. But to pull this off he is going to need help. It's time to call a meeting of the clans……..

Detective chief Superintendent Tommy Butler is residing at the Midland hotel whilst staying in Manchester. Little does he know barely half a mile away his nemesis Bruce Reynolds, is being sneaked out the back door of the Cromford club by Tommy Keenan, and taken to a safe house in Cheetham Hill, in north Manchester. Butler is sat in the hotel bar with a pot of tea reading the Sunday papers. One story in particular intrigues and at the same time horrifies him.

The shocking news of four missing children from East Manchester. Sixteen-year old Pauline Reade, twelve-year olds John Kilbride and Keith Bennett. And perhaps for Butler the most unsettling. The recent disappearance of ten-year old Lesley Anne Downey. All appeared to have vanished into thin air. Nothing is known. To Butler it has all the makings of a mass killer on the prowl. He is due to meet Inspector George Collins in the bar and makes a mental note to bring this up with him and check how the investigation is unfolding.

He looks around the room and the various characters inhabiting it intrigue him. There is the young couple sat canoodling in a quiet corner, who are obviously enjoying an illicit secret liaison. The large overweight businessman sat at the bar alone, always alone with the big red cheeks. The face of a broken man with sad depressed eyes. Already on a pint and a double whisky chasers at just twelve in the afternoon.

No fixed abode and wherever he places the battered fucking suitcase becomes his home.

Then there is the working girl sat watching and waiting. Stalking. The high class hooker out on the game and searching for clients. Lonely husbands away on official business. Men whose wives claim they don't understand them.

Butlers eyes them all, only to be snapped back to reality by the sudden appearance into his midst of Inspector Collins.

'Good afternoon Mr Butler,' smiles Collins. He stares around at the plush surroundings of the Midland interior. It's architecture from another age but the grandeur still evident. The reek of money so prevalent you can smell it. 'I see the Met have not exactly got you slumming it whilst you are away from civilisation'?

Butler takes his newspaper and passes it to Collins. He points to the news piece on the missing children. 'How are events moving with this'?

Collins shakes his head. 'Not good, the Hyde and Ashton boys are climbing the walls.'

'Do you at least have any suspects'? asks a nonplussed Butler.

They tend to keep things tight to their chest up there, but so far as I know, nothing. It's like the kids were here one minute and gone the next. Vanished into thin air. All unrelated cases so far as we can make out and there's not a single shred of evidence to work on. We've a list of names but in all reality they aren't even suspects. Just local head bangers. The normal trash. Nothing adds up and no one knows anything. In all my years I've never known a trail go cold like this.'

'Yes well, anything I can do to help just let me know. Somebody always knows something George. Somebody always knows. After I have Reynolds in custody and behind bars, I wouldn't mind spending some time researching these cases. If that can be arranged'?

'Yes of course and much obliged Mr Butler.'

'Oh please cut out the damn formalities will you and call me Tommy.'

Collins smiles. The cold headed bastard is human after all.

'So,' continues Butler. 'What have you in mind for me today in your city'?

I thought we'd go and see Paddy Mullen? His club, the Cromford is only a ten minute stroll from here and it'll be good for you two to spark off. Maybe reminisce about old times. Even ask him if those ears ever turned up'?

'I don't think so George. This isn't a time for niceties. If I suspect Mullen is guilty of even having spoken to Reynolds he's going down. I'm afraid that's the way of things today. Past deeds mean nothing I intend to nail Reynolds and all who have anything to do with him.'

The two men stand and walk out of the Midland and down the steps. The concierge tips his hat towards them. 'Everybody is so bloody polite up here,' remarks Butler. Must be something in the water.'

'Just decent good manners,' answers Collins. 'You'd do well to mention this hotel to some of your so called colleagues in C11 when you go home. Then stand back and wait for the reaction and the look on their fucking faces.'

Butler stops and turns abruptly towards Collins.

'Let me get something straight here. Whatever happened back then in regards to the Krays in this manor wasn't my doing. I had no knowledge of what was going down. If things went on that you didn't agree with, then you deal with it through the proper channels. I'll be honest with you George. I did hear rumours, bad ones. Vile even of what could have occurred, but because of some local villains, of which, I do not want to hear about, everything went belly up.

Now I'd like to think that if we can't be bosom buddies during this little adventure of ours then you can at least respect the fact that if nothing else, I'm a good copper. I do this job to help people, I don't take money and it breaks my fucking heart when innocent folk, especially kids, get hurt and I can't do anything about it.

If we are going to find Reynolds I need to know if I can rely on you to put away foolish childish things. Such as your all-consuming hatred for the Met and give me a break. Don't tar us all with the same brush. I'm sure you have some hateful bastards with a badge in Manchester.

Now am I clear on this? If not I'll have to request somebody else to assist me in this inquiry. I wouldn't like it, but believe me the way I feel at the moment I'd damn well do it.

Now can I trust you George'?

An admonished Collins feels like dog dirt on a pavement. Only now can he realise the extent of which he has harboured bad feelings towards Butler since his arrival.

'A hundred percent Mr Butler,' replies a repentant Collins.
'Good,' replies a smiling butler. Once again, call me fucking Tommy and now can we get on with what the pain in the arse British publish public pay us to do. And that's nicking criminals'?
Collins smiles. He points in the direction of the Cromford club.
'After you.'
With peace declared between the two they head off in search of Bruce Reynolds.

Approaching Piccadilly, Collins points over towards the gardens. 'See there, in 1940 the Luftwaffe razed this place to the ground. The flames so high they could be seen twenty miles away. People still talk about the red skies. Blood red. It took years for the ashes to stop simmering. Even now if I close my eyes I can still see the fires leaping out of the falling warehouses and smell the burning of the charred wood.'

Butler stares across. Today the remnants of the blitz are still evident all around. Vast mounds of rubble set between buildings that may have survived the initial blitz, but in time succumbed to the sheer shock caused to their foundations by the bombs.

'How the fuck we kept going I'll never know,' says Collins
'We had no choice,' answers Butler. 'It was them or us remember. The German were on our doorstep. That we stopped them is still for me a bloody miracle. Also, bad as it was here in Manchester, what you lot got was only a pinprick in comparison to what the bastards dropped on London.

Like you, thinking back it's hard to believe we recovered but life goes on.

Look around you, people going about their everyday lives. Just going for a walk or a meal. Or going to the pub, or the church, or the Synagogue. It was a hell of a price we paid but we won George.'

Butler turns to Collins. He continues. 'We won and we are going to win again by nailing that thief Reynolds and locking him up. Now let's go and have a word with Mullen.'

It has just gone two in the afternoon at the Cromford club and Paddy Mullen is all set for going home. Suddenly there is a knock on his office door and in walks detectives Collins and Butler.

'Afternoon Paddy,' says Collins. 'Sorry to barge in on you like this, but we need to talk.' Mullen stands from his desk and goes to shake Tommy Butler's hand.

'It's been a long time.'

'Twenty-four years Patrick to be precise.'

'And now what do I owe the honour of having the legendary Detective Tommy Butler in my club'? He motions for both policemen to sit.

'You are an awful long way from home.'

'You know me Patrick,' he smiles. 'No road too long to travel to hunt down the bad guy. Once I catch a whiff of villainy there's no stopping me.'

'I thought you were working exclusively on the train robbery'?

'I am,' replies Butler. 'Thus my reason for coming north and being here in your splendid club today. Where is he Patrick'?

'Where's who'? answers Mullen.

'Tommy Keenan.'

'Why do you need to speak to Tommy'?

'Because I've good reason to believe he knows the whereabouts of a one Bruce Reynolds.

I'm sure you've heard of him'?

'We do have televisions and radios up here Mr Butler,' smiles Mullen.

'And yet I don't see the connection you make between Tommy and Reynolds? I run a tight ship and wouldn't allow any of my boys to have anything to do with him. You know like I do this case is political, and the price paid in terms of a jail sentence would simply not be worth it.'

'I have first class information,' insists Butler. 'Keenan's name came up.'

'Where's Tommy Pat'? adds Collins. 'This doesn't need to be difficult.'

'No idea George,' I'm not his keeper. You are the detectives. You find him.'

'Oh believe me,' smiles Butler. 'I'll find him, and if he's hiding Reynolds then he won't see the light of day for twenty years.'

Collins winces at Butler's remarks as he sees the colour drain from Mullen's face.

'I have listened to you Mr Butler and now you can listen to me. You lot have had your fingers burnt with the train robbery, and I suspect some high up are still sulking about what happened with the Krays here in 63. Now I don't care about your badge or your reputation and I care even less about who you represent.

I have had my fill of that lot for a lifetime.

You are a decent man. You showed me that in Blackpool many years ago. I also believe deep down, although you want to nick Reynolds more than anything in the world, there'll be a part of you thinking something doesn't ring true about the length of jail sentences being handed out. I've already told you once that I'd not allow anyone who worked for me to have anything to do with the train job.

Especially Tommy.

If all you wish to ask of me is the same inane questions about him then you are wasting your time. And now if you two don't mind, I'm already late going home to enjoy Sunday lunch with my family.'

For a moment Butler says nothing but then smiles and stands up. Collins follows.

'Please accept my apologies for keeping you from your family Patrick.'

Butler holds out his hand and Mullen warily accepts it.

'If you do happen to bump into Tommy,' adds Butler. 'Please ask him to get in touch, just so we can clear up any misunderstanding.'

Mullen's features remain of stone. 'Good day Mr Butler, George. You can both see yourself out.'

The two policemen step out the club. Mullen watches them walk off through his upper office window. Butler concerns him. He is convinced trouble is in the air. This man is good. Too damn good and they will have to move Reynolds on, and fast.

'So what do you think'? asks Collins to Butler as the two men enter onto Market Street from Cromford square.

He's lying through his teeth' replies Butler. 'What exactly is the relationship between this Keenan and Mullen?

'Tommy is Paddy's son in everything but blood,' replies Collins. 'He took him in as a kid off the streets at sixteen and they've been together since. I'd advise you to tread carefully from now on. If

Keenan is hiding Reynolds like you seem to think, then this could all turn extremely nasty.'

'Butler stops walking and stares in disbelief towards Collins. 'Who exactly run this damn city George? Is it the authorities or Paddy bloody Mullen'?

'Good question,' replies Collins. He pulls out a pack of cigarette and offers one to Butler, who declines.

'I guess we'll find out before you go home Chief Superintendent.'

In a back street, run down terrace house in Cheetham Hill, far from the madding crowd, Tommy Keenan and the most wanted man in Great Britain, Bruce Reynolds, are sat eating fish and chips out of newspaper and watching the television.

Tommy is laughing. 'One day I'll tell my kids I shared fish and chips with one of the Great Train Robbers Bruce. And the cheap bastard made me pay for it.'

'Whatever happened to that famous Northern hospitality'? smiles Reynolds.

'Seriously Tommy, I cannot tell you how much I appreciate everything you are all doing.'

'Don't worry about it,' he replies. 'Just remember our invitation when you are sat on a faraway foreign beach sipping Bacardi's and cokes. And try not to worry too much because now with Paddy on the case it's just a matter of time.'

'Paddy seems like a good man. How'd you two hook up'?

'Shoes,' says Tommy.

'I'm sorry'? replies a quizzical Reynolds.

For a moment Tommy is lost in the memory of Paddy Mullen a long time ago laying down the law to his Father on their doorstep. Telling him that if he ever laid a finger on twelve-year old Tommy again, he would break every bone in his body.

Tommy snaps back to the present. 'A long story Bruce,' he smiles. 'What we have to ensure now is a false passport and route out of the country. Whoever it was that tipped Butler off has good information. Luckily I'm the only one who knows you are staying here. So keep your head down my great train robber friend. No signing autographs for the locals.'

'Who grassed Tommy? It couldn't have come from my end because nobody knew.'

'Same with me. Unless'?

'Unless what'? inquires Reynolds.

Tommy takes a drink from a beer can then goes into a shirt pocket. He produces a pack of cigarettes and offers one to Reynolds.

Tommy lights Reynolds' first, then his own. He continues. 'Unless my phone was tapped'?

'But who'd do that and why'?

Another long story Bruce,' smiles Tommy. He passes a beer to Reynolds.

'I hope you are sitting comfortably, for this one is special mate.
Once upon a time……'

STAND OFF IN THE FALLEN NUN

Ancoats: It is way past midnight on Sunday night/Monday morning and a police panda car patrols slowly past a row of huge dark gloomy warehouses. The car lights dazzle upon the black roads in front. As it disappears around a corner from sight, suddenly, out of a doorway, his face lit up by a full moon, steps Paddy Costigan. He walks briskly away carrying a plastic bag. Inside is two grand, money owed to John Flannery from the local pubs where he has been collecting. The rules simple. You pay or be burnt to the ground. Irish ingenuity, brutal, straight forward and lucrative.

The Cross Keys, the White Swan, the Edinburgh Castle. Everybody pays Flannery, no exceptions. One look at Costigan and any thoughts landlords may ever have had of refusing to hand over the protection money swiftly disappear.

It's been a good evening's work and Costigan is in a good mood. He fancies a drink, a proper drink and then a woman. There is a place Costigan goes for both. Where men like him can be satisfied. A sanctuary for the mad and the bad and the desperate. Where booze runs on tap and the obliging working girls are willing for money up front to perform the strangest and most perverted requests. When every other drinking hole across the city is calling last orders and throwing drunken punters out on the street, the Fallen Nun unlocks it doors and Manchester's dark knights step through it.

Paddy Costigan is still basking in the warm glow of wreaking revenge against the Clancy brothers. Both made to dig their own graves high up on the vast barren and desolate Moors, above Manchester, before despatching each with a bullet in the back of the head. As ever with Costigan there was twisted logic involved, when with a toss of a coin he made them call heads or tails on whom was to be killed first.

Another depraved act from the circus of evil that existed in Costigan's head.

When word broke from the Liverpool underworld that the Clancys had vanished, Costigan was confronted by John Flannery and he swiftly owned up to their murder. After a raging Flannery had given him a dressing down, a disinterested Costigan answered.

'Is that it'?

His fellow Irishman from Mayo, red faced and wrath vented suddenly realised it was hopeless. Flannery let fly one last riposte. 'Paddy for fucks sake, just try and keep your head down.'

One benefit for Flannery was the fact that Costigan's latest act of monstrous brutality only enhanced his own reputation not to be messed with. It was the same old story. Nobody knew but everybody knew. The legend of Paddy Costigan has grown even more. He is deemed to be invincible. An evil superman who is beyond the law and could not be killed.

But nobody lives forever.

However one man who has finally washed his hands of Costigan is Paddy Mullen He sent word to John Flannery. 'Keep that damned monster shackled and away from the Cromford club.' On being informed by his boss of Mullen's warning, Costigan simply nodded his head. Along with Flannery, Paddy Mullen is the only other man on this earth he respects.

Costigan would adhere to his wishes and stay clear. And so this night as he heads to the forbidden delights of the Fallen Nun, Paddy Costigan is a man content.

Set in a back alley off Oldham Street, reaching towards Piccadilly, is the Fallen Nun. It's entrance up a small set of steps blocked by two burly dark suited bouncers. Their rules are simple. No strangers allowed unless given special dispensation by the manager, sixty-three year old 'Fat' Harry Goldman. Theirs' was already a guest list from a horror movie and Goldman has no desire to add unwanted ingredient to an already explosive concoction.

Suddenly appearing from behind a dark corner comes walking a young couple. They are linking arms. A blond lady and a slim dark-haired man. Both are obviously the worst for drink. They approach the bouncers. One steps forward to block their path.

'Not tonight I'm afraid ladies and gents,' he says. 'Try somewhere else eh. This place is not for you. '

'Do you know who I fucking am'? snarled the man, with a thick Scottish accent.

'Ian leave it,' implores the girl, obviously knowing her boyfriend would be beaten to a pulp by the two bouncers facing them if he carries on.

But he continues. 'You have no idea what I'm capable of. And you dare to deny me entrance into your little fucking hovel.'

The other bouncer enters the fray. 'Big words little man, now fuck off Jock before your girlfriend here sees us bounce you all over the alley.'

The man attempts to swing a punch but is immediately grabbed by the girl who drags him away, whilst screaming into his face.
'Enough Ian, enough! I just want to go home.'

Finally the man calms, he wipes his mouth and stares at the grinning bouncers.
'Look at my fucking face and don't forget it. One day I'm going to be famous.'

He puts an arm around his girlfriend. 'And Myra here too.' She starts to laugh and gives the bouncers a V sign. The two stagger off from where they came, laughing out loud. Passing them comes Paddy Costigan. He glares whilst walking past but they totally ignore him.

Lost in their own little world. A horror beyond words…….

The bouncers step aside for Costigan who does not even bother to grunt and acknowledge their presence. Inside he goes, still clutching the bag full of money from the night's takings.

Sat in a corner of the busy, dark room watching Costigan enter is Blind Billy and Boom. Neither can believe his appearance into their midst, as they have been discussing how to go about killing him for the gypsy girl's money.

Around them Manchester's night owls, some alone, others in small crowds drink themselves into oblivion. Costigan goes to the bar and orders a double whisky. He eyes the stairs leading up towards the brothel on the above floor and smiles. It promises to be a good night. Suddenly he feels a small shove in his back that causes him to turn around. It is Blind Billy. 'Sorry Paddy.' Costigan glares, for a moment the red mist descends but he remembers Mr Flannery's warning and has no intention of disobeying him again. Instead Costigan glowers at Blind Billy. 'Just watch where the fuck you are going,' he growls.

Blind Billy does not move. He stares at Costigan. 'I said I was sorry. You don't scare me Paddy Costigan.' The two men go face to face as a stone cold silence engulfs the Fallen Nun. A showdown between Blind Billy Cosgrove and Paddy Cosgrove.
This will be one to tell the grandchildren about.

Despite wishing to avoid more trouble Costigan's ego does not allow him to back down. Just as he readies to tear Blind Billy apart, a familiar voices makes him look up.
Walking back down the stairs from the brothel, tucking in his shirt is John Flannery. 'Paddy Costigan don't you fucking dare.'

Flannery comes between the two. He turns to Blind Billy and smiles. 'You always took me as a sensible man Billy. Why commit suicide? Let me buy you a drink and let bygones be bygones.
Flannery turns to Costigan. 'Back down Paddy son. There'll be no blood spilt on the floor in here tonight'? Costigan nods and offers his hand to Blind Billy which he accepts. Another time, another place he will rip his fucking heart out, as well as the demented little dwarf Boom, now stood alongside him.

Blind Billy smiles and winks at Costigan.
'No problem big man. I'm glad you saw sense. No harm done.'

Boom laughs and tugs at his long black leather jacket. He motion they should go.

'Have a good night' smiles Blind Billy, and he and Boom are away through the door. Costigan is still raging as Flannery puts an around his shoulders. Another man appears now the trouble has settled down. It's 'Fat' Harry Goldman. His bloated red face sweating, but now smiling wide because his pub has survived being turned into a bloodbath.
'Thank you John,' he mumbles to Flannery. I owe you.'

A smiling Flannery ignores him and turns to Costigan. 'Well done Paddy,' as he takes the money in the bag off him. 'Now let me buy

you a bottle to celebrate the newly reborn Paddy Costigan. A man of calm and forgiving nature. A Mayo saint and long may he live.'
'This is on the house,' interrupts Goldman. 'As is the one after that. And the whores upstairs for Paddy.'
Costigan nod his thanks. He catches the eye of some of the working girls stood watching events on the top of the stairs. Their faces grim and all praying he does not pick them.
Little does Goldman or John Flannery know Paddy Costigan is already picturing in his mind both Blind Billy and Boom hanging from meat hooks.

Outside on Oldham Street, Boom motions in sign language to Blind Billy.
'What was all that about. Why did you antagonise him'?
Blind Billy smiles and replies also in sign language. 'Now Costigan is mad he'll come looking for us. And we'll be waiting…..'
Both men laugh and make their way home up Oldham Road.
Come the morning, a hungover but satisfied Paddy Costigan steps out of the Fallen Nun, with jacket slung over a shoulder. He covers his eyes from a surprisingly blinding sun. It is still early and the city has yet to come to life. In the distance the rattle of trains from nearby Piccadilly railway station hum loud. Costigan has had his fill of whisky and women, now only one issue dominates his mind. He smiles at the thought of the one eyed freak and the dwarf under his knife.
A smiling Paddy Costigan makes ready his plans.

With sirens raging a small fleet of police cars pull up outside 23 Penn Street, in Moston, north Manchester. Out of them swarms dozens of uniformed policemen, whilst from the rear of the terraced house a similar number kick in the back gate and come charging in through the kitchen. They meet in the middle downstairs living room. Others race upstairs but the two bedrooms and bathroom are empty.
When all is secured Detectives Harry Collins and Tommy Butler enter.
Butler stares disdainfully around. He looks across to Collins. 'It appears somebody threw you a false lead old son.' With a hint of annoyance clear in his voice.

Before Collins can reply raised voices are heard coming from outside. Through the window he notices a smartly dressed middle-aged woman shouting loud at one of his officers.

'You best get out there and make sure she doesn't hit him,' smiles Butler ruefully.

'We don't want a riot on our hands.'

Collins glares at Butler then heads out. He approaches the lady who is the next door neighbour. 'Come on now, calm down love.' He gently puts his arm on her, but she is raging. 'Your constable here told me you are looking for the train robber. The policeman in question appears sheepish. Knowing full well he should have kept his mouth shut.

'All this for one man? And what they did was nothing compared to what's going on in Manchester right now. Why don't you go and find out what happened to those poor kids whom have disappeared. Go and kick doors in up there in Ashton and Hyde.'

'You tell them Norah,' shouts a man walking his dog from across the road on the pavement. Then another voice from a facing house. 'Good for you Norah. Well said'! A window cleaner watching from high on his ladder calls across. 'Get your fucking priorities right and three cheers Mrs Quigley'!

Butler stands in the doorway, watching this all unfold.

'They have got a point sir,' says a young uniformed officer stood next to him. With all due respect most people in Manchester would give the train robbers a medal rather than lock them up.' Butler listens but does not admonish him. He realised this is a different world up here. The north is a country in itself.

There is though he thinks, despite his desperation to nick Bruce Reynolds, a truth to what these people are saying. But this is not his manor. Tommy Butler is in town to bring to justice public enemy one Reynolds. However listening to the lady he feels even that line is a contradiction in terms.

For the poor kids whom have vanished.

They are what matters most and nobody wants a happy ending to their disappearance more than Chief Superintendent Tommy Butler of special Branch and Scotland Yard. But now is the time to turn the heat up on Paddy Mullen and attempt to flush the train robber out of the Mancunian sewer he is hiding in and end this.

REUNION OF THE CLANS

It is Wednesday evening and word has gone out across the city and over the river in Salford that Paddy Mullen has called for a meeting of the clans. Mullen knows he needs the co-operation of all the gangs if he is to smuggle Bruce Reynolds out of the country and get Tommy Butler back on the train to London.

Butler has started to turn up the pressure.

A series of Police raid across the city this afternoon at premises owned by Mullen have proved only minor disruptive, but last night's visit to the Cromford club by Butler, who stood outside handing out photographs of Bruce Reynolds with the words
Have you seen this man written beneath has really irked Mullen. Indeed he has taken this as a personal insult.

To the extent Mullen sent a private message to George Collins informing him unless he calls Butler off, their long standing friendship, re-established after the Kray debacle was at stake once more. Collins reply was to return word that his hands were tied. London was calling the shots. Something Mullen had heard off this man before and he was not prepared to tolerate again.

The meeting is taking place in the funeral parlour of Salvatore Rea in Ancoats. All the bosses have been told to come alone, no bodyguards and to ensure they are not followed.

And come they do. The Brady brothers from Salford, Michael and Paul. Harry Taylor from South of town, John Flannery from the north and Jimmy 'the 'Weed' *Da Silva* from Moss Side. On arrival at the funeral parlour each is escorted through a side entrance.

Soon at just gone ten o'clock they are all gathered. Each are clutching a welcoming glass of the finest red Sicilian wine to emerge off this bloodcurdling, if beautiful Italian island.

Nero d'Avola. Rumours exist going back to biblical times, this particular wine was favoured by the mad emperor Nero, who once ruled over three quarters of the known world.

Don Salvatore is determined to help his brother, in all but name, Paddy Mullen. He has been told of what is occurring regarding Bruce Reynolds, and how important tonight's meeting is to ensure matters of business can return to normal.

The train robber has to be moved on.

Mullen enter to a mischievous round of applause from the others. He smiles and raises his hands in mock recognition. 'Gentlemen please, I'm more than worthy.'

They all laugh.

'What's going on Paddy'? asks Taylor.

'Somebody been playing with their train set again'? smiles Flannery. It's all over the city,' adds Da Silva.

The botched police raid in Moston and that loud mouthed constable letting it slip.'

'Where is he Pat'? inquires Michael Brady. 'Where's Reynolds'?

Salvatore Rea stands alongside Paddy Mullen with arms folded and face serious. So much for keeping the train robber under wraps, he thinks.

Mullen smiles wide at Rea and addresses the others.

'Gentlemen thank you for coming. I take it my little secret is out due to the little misunderstanding that occurred in Moston yesterday. No matter, now I have asked you all here tonight for a favour.

Bruce Reynolds is currently holed up with Tommy and I need to find a way fast to get this man out of Manchester, out of my hair and out of the country. Time is seriously of the essence because we have a visitor. The Old Bill have despatched from London their best man Tommy Butler of the Flying Squad up here, and he has our own George Collins alongside him. Now I don't have to tell you this is a double act that would have caught Jack the Ripper.

'One day Tommy'? asks a worried looking Taylor.

'The very same Harry lad,' replies Mullen. 'And let me assure you boys, Butler is on a mission. He intends to nail Reynolds and take him back like the Roman Generals of old, returning to Rome with their beaten opponent caged and paraded in front of the masses.

A warning.

You do not mess with the face on the note.

Now Butler is a good man but he's under orders from the top to do whatever is needed to arrest our friend. And when I say from the top, I think we all know who I'm referring to'?

'The bastards who ordered the Krays hit I presume,' answers Michael Brady.

Oh fuck, not those boys again,' adds Da Silva.

Mullen continues. 'Now I can't talk for you lot, but I feel like there's unfinished business to be had with these people. On top of this Tommy is convinced his home phone was tapped, for nobody else could have known Bruce Reynolds' whereabouts. That one call Reynolds made to Tommy for help was picked up and hence the reason Butler has come north. Now if Tommy's phone has been tapped you can more or less guarantee yours are also.

The Establishment doesn't forget and it doesn't forgive. Therefore I must stress extreme caution from now on when conducting matters of business.'

The bosses appear nervous and angry. 'So what are you suggesting Paddy'? asks John Flannery. 'That we declare war on MI5 and C11, and God knows what else they have got down there'?

'Not a war John,' smiles Mullen. 'Simply a bloody nose in the manner of helping Reynolds get away, and then we let it be known, albeit discreetly to our friends in London of our part in this little escapade. Mullen looks around at the now smiling faces.

What do you say then'? he asks.

'I think it's fucking quality Pat,' replies a grinning Paul Brady. They all nod their heads in agreement. Mullen puts an arm around Salvatore Rea's shoulders. 'Now Salvatore here has a plan. Sicilian cunning that is genius in its simplicity.'

Mullen smiles wide. 'Gentleman, I give you Sicily's finest.'

A white shirted Rea steps forward. He straightens the braces on his shoulders and looks intently into the faces of all present.

He begins. 'Now listen up, we are going to teach those fucking *pezzonovantes* in London a lesson they'll never forget. That this is our city, our world, and our rules.

And this is what we are going to do.....'

It is Thursday afternoon and Jack Butler cuts an annoyed and frustrated figure as he sits reading reports in his office at Bootle Street police station. His is a little boxed off room, whilst outside are a host of detectives working at desks on the case. Neither Reynolds or Tommy Keenan have surfaced and he is tired of receiving phone calls from his superiors asking him what is going on? Such is the rising pressure for results Reynolds has even contemplated bringing in Keenan's wife for questioning.

However on mentioning the idea to his colleague, George Collins, he was immediately shot down. 'That girl is a civilian and I won't tolerate her being dragged into this.' Collins made it known to him any attempt to use Alison as a stick to hit Tommy or Mullen with would not be tolerated. Such was his stance Butler decided against it. He already felt like public enemy number in Manchester. Never mind Reynolds.

He had no desire to antagonise the locals further.

Suddenly the doors swings open and Collins comes rushing in. He is smiling.

'Good news, we have had a tip off that Keenan has been spotted coming out of a house in Cheetham Hill, north of here. This is a reliable source as well, one of mine.'

'Good enough for me George' replies Butler, who stands and puts on his coat.

'Well what are waiting for. Let's go and nick the bastards.'

The two men head out with Collins motioning for a host of other plain clothes detectives to follow.

Collins and Butler step in to the back of a panda car and it speeds off. With sirens wailing, five in all police vehicles race through the city streets, past Victoria Railway Station and down Queens Road to Cheetham Hill.

A voice on the police car alerts Collins and Butler's as it announces loud. 'Another report of Thomas Keenan being seen in Stretford. Also others coming in from across the area. Ardwick, Moss Side, Ancoats and Salford.'

The two detectives stare at each other. Both without talking suspect foul play at work.

'This snitch of yours,' asks Butler. 'Does he work for you or Mullen'?

Collins does not answer, choosing instead to look out the window and quietly seethe.

They arrive at the house only to find it empty as expected. All attempts to question the neighbours proves worthless. Nobody is talking.

A young police constable approaches Collins, whispers into his ear and walks away. Butler notices and comes across. 'What did he say'?

Our boys are answering similar bogus calls all over Manchester,' replies Collins. Somebody is playing games, only they are not fucking funny.'

'Do you know what I think,' says Butler. I think your friend Mullen is sending us a message. You always told me this was your city George, I think today's events prove who this place really belongs to. Don't you'?

Collins says nothing. He knows this is but a mere aperitif and that if they do manage to arrest Reynolds, and Keenan is with him?

They will have a war on their hands.

It is well past midnight on Friday morning and around the city away from prying police eyes, hundreds of posters are being pasted onto lamppost and buildings by shadowy hooded figures. Like a small army of ants they work methodically to ensure the walls on all main roads in and out of Manchester, are covered in pictures of Chief Superintendent Tommy Butler of Special Branch and Scotland Yard.

Beneath the face are the words GO HOME.

Come the following morning, the city awakes to the sight of these splattered in abundance so that they could not be missed. As Butler steps out of the Midland he walks down the hotel steps and is immediately greeted by one stuck on a nearby lamp post. He stares angrily then tears the poster off and rips it up.

As Butler continues on he notices many more covering the walls on Peter Street. Finally arriving at the station, one even covets Bootle Street's outer exterior. Again Butler scrapes it off.

On entering the office a cold silence grips the air with ten pairs of eyes staring towards him. It's clear that what had occurred overnight has been on everyone's lips before Butler's entrance. A smiling Collins attempts to break the ice. 'How about a cup of tea'?

'That would be very nice, thanks you George,' he replies. Whilst not breaking eye contact with those looking at him.'

'What are you lot staring at'? snaps Butler to his embarrassed audience. 'We have a thief to catch. Get on with your jobs.' Swiftly heads turns, whilst others shuffle nervously away and out of his eyesight.

Collins arrives back with two mugs of hot steaming tea and motions to the small office.

'Let's go in there,' he says. Clearly feeling for his London colleague who does not deserve this public humiliation. The two men head in and shut the door.

Butler takes out the crumpled poster from his pocket and spreads it on the desk.

'I'm going to nail this bastard George. If I have to turn this city upside down, I swear to God until Reynolds is in handcuffs and they throw away the damn keys.'

'I'm going off the radar for a couple of hours,' says an equally incensed Collins.

'So far I've played by the rules, but this business with the posters and the false calls? It's not on. Now I told you when you first arrived that this is my city, my fucking Manchester. Well I think it's time I proved it.'

Butlers says nothing. He simply smiles towards Collins and nods. Once outside in the corridor Collins rings Paddy Mullen on his home number.

Mullen answers. 'Hello.'

'Paddy, George Collins.'

'What are you doing ringing me at home George'?

'We need to speak, off the record and not at the Cromford club because that'll be under surveillance. I need a favour Paddy.'

'I'm not in the mood for doing favours. Especially for you.'

'You really do need to lend an ear to what I have to say. This stuff is getting out of control. We have to rein it back in.'

'Very well then,' answers a clearly reluctant Mullen.

'The usual spot in an hour.'

The line goes dead and Collins replaces the receiver.

He sighs, 'Oh no, not that fucking place again.'

Old Trafford: Manchester United football club: A die hard Manchester City supporter, George Collins pulls up onto the forecourt and steps out of his car. He walks towards the staff door where two young men in dark suits nod across to him. Collins recognises them as Mullen employees. He smiles. 'Morning lads.'

'Morning Mr Collins,' one of them replies. 'The boss is waiting for you.'

The other motions Collins through.

As Paddy Mullen stands smoking in the centre circle of the pitch, through the tunnel into view emerges George Collins. He gazes around the empty terraces before heading over to meet Mullen.

'This has to stop Paddy. I won't have Tommy Butler being humiliated. Last night's events were shameful.'

'You tell Butler to go home and the problem goes away,' replies Mullen.

'I think there's something you and whoever pulled that stunt last night with the posters should know. Butler has asked me if he could get involved with those missing kids up in Ashton and Hyde, once the Reynolds case is closed. This is a good man Paddy, you know that. He told me about the young girl in Blackpool during the war. How you helped him and kicked down every fucking door in that town until you found her. And how they were all missing an ear when you left them tied and gagged for the police on the north pier.

Now he let that go. Do you want to know why? Because Butler understands when it comes to kids normal rules don't apply. I want your word there'll be no repeat performance of last night's charade. Otherwise that thin line which exists in our fair city between legal and illegal will disappear for you lot and I'll come down on you all like a fucking hurricane.

'Are you threatening me George? Because that's what it sounds like to me.'

Collins smiles. 'Not a threat old friend, just a kind warning. The bottom line is I'm on the right side of the law. And if that means upsetting certain people in this town, yourself included, well so be it.

We've known each other a long time and it's out of respect I'm here today and to give you a last chance to sort out this mess before the gloves come off.

Cards on the table? You give me Reynolds and this all goes away.'

'No chance George. How am I supposed to square that with Tommy'?

'Oh come on, don't give me that honour amongst thieves bolloxs.'

Mullen smiles. 'I understand what you are saying. I agree Butler is a decent man, of that there's no argument. As for those kids missing in Ashton and Hyde? Maybe you should look a little closer to home, for I'm hearing stories that the boys in blue up there are less than happy with their Mancunian brothers in arms. They say you are not pushing your weight.'

'Internal politics Paddy, it's out of my hands. I've tried to get involved but have been ordered to steer clear.'

Mullen gets angry. 'Don't play the blame game with me, these are bloody kids we are talking about. One man robs a few quid off a family whom have never worked a day in their lives and have no intention of ever doing so and you launch a military scale operation to bring those responsible to justice. And yet some of our own, it could have been my daughter or son, or god forbid yours, vanish into thin air, and you dare to speak to me about internal bloody politics?

This system you claim to represent, this side of the law, it's corrupt. You are a good copper, a good bloke but don't talk this rubbish about right and wrong for it cuts no ice with me. There should be a mobilisation up there in Ashton and Hyde. An occupation force until you either find those poor souls or nick the pond life that's killed them. You should be filling the jails and kicking heads and doors in from Rochdale to Altrincham.'

Both men take a moments respite. Finally Collins pulls out a packet of cigarettes. Mullen produces a box of matches and lights it for him.

'Touché' smiles Collins, as Mullen inhales.

'So where's this place we now find ourselves George'? It feels like no man's land to me.'

Collins shrugs his shoulders. 'Maybe we should just shake hands and say que sera sera?

What will be will be.' He offers Mullen his hand.

'Tell Butler from me this is nothing personal. I'm simply looking after my own.

And bang a few heads together at the station George. Get your people over to Hyde and Ashton. If I, or any of my acquaintances can help just let me know.'

Collins nods in thanks. 'Mind how you go Paddy. He looks around one last time. 'One day I will come to this place and get a result. Bloody reds.'

Don't bet on it George,' smiles Mullen. 'There's only one team in this city and they don't wear blue.'

Collins laughs at this remark, but is unsure where Mullen is referring to the police or Manchester City?

PADDY COSTIGAN'S LAST BREATH
Saturday evening: Six days and nights have passed under Mancunian skies since Paddy Costigan shown the patience of angels

and allowed Blind Billy and Boom to live. The incident in the Fallen Nun, when Costigan was provoked by Blind Billy has haunted his every waking moment since. The promise made to John Flannery simply cannot stand, for the sake of his peace and mind and the thought of losing face, both equally important for Costigan and overruling all else.

And so he makes his way into Manchester to find them and end their world.

Costigan has it on good authority the two men will be drinking in the Fatted Calf and this is to be his first port of call. Outside he will wait and when they show Costigan will decorate the street with their blood.

Little does he know Blind Billy and Boom will be ready. For they knew well Costigan would not have been able to stomach being humiliated and now they also wait and watch by the pub window. Blind Billy has two pistols upon him, whilst Boom is carrying his speciality. Two grenades, primed and ready. The gypsy lady's money will be earned tonight by despatching Paddy Costigan to another world.

Around nine o clock, Blind Billy catches sight of Costigan's huge silhouette in an alleyway. He prods Boom, the time has come. Both men stand and step out of the pub together and head to face the grim reaper. On seeing them Costigan moves to block their path. 'We have unfinished business.'

Blind Billy and Boom don't move a muscle as Costigan pulls out a knife.

'Nobody fucks with Paddy Costigan and gets away it.'

'We'll see about that,' says Blind Billy, as he produces a pistol and fires three times from close range into his stomach.

A look of sheer incredulity crosses Costigan's face as he places a hand low and stares at the blood upon it. Blind Billy fires again and again and he goes down on one knee. Boom takes the grenades, steps forward and places one in each of a dying Costigan's jacket pockets. He removes the pins and both men race clear. A huge explosion thunders as glass shatters from nearby shops. People come flooding out of the Fatted Calf and stare and scream in abject horror at the many body parts of what was once Patrick John Costigan.

Now slain and gone to hell. His sins were just too great and too many.

May you be in heaven a full half hour before
the devil knows you are dead.'

Calmly and without panic, Blind Billy and Boom make their way
down Deansgate, away from the mayhem, whilst alongside them,
police cars with sirens blazing roar to the scene of the crime. They
are heading to meet the gypsy lady and collect their money for this
night's work. Hard earned but executed supremely, Blind Billy
believes it's their best yet. People will no doubt have witnessed their
handiwork but nobody will talk.
Nobody will risk their lives for the sake of a monster like Costigan.
Blind Billy taps his friend on the shoulder. He speaks to him in
sign language.
'We'll have a good drink later on to celebrate tonight.' Boom smiles
in recognition of the words. He replies. 'They'll still be putting him
together when we are old men collecting our pension.'
Both men laugh.

John Flannery is at the Cromford club with his wife Katherine
having a meal when Paddy Mullen comes over to their table. Mullen
makes polite conversation and kisses Katherine, before leaning low
and whispering into Flannery's ear. 'We need to talk. Come up to
my office in five minutes. Flannery nods and Mullen says his
goodbyes and leaves the room.
On his way up Flannery notices more than the usual number of
bouncers and bodyguards lurking in the shadows around the club. It
appears even the normally unflappable Paddy Mullen is spooked. He
knocks on Mullen's door and enters to see the owner staring stern
faced back at him.
'Paddy what's up for fucks sake'?
There's been trouble tonight over at the Fatted Calf John.'
'What kind of trouble'?
'Well it appears one Paddy Costigan has been blown into a thousand
pieces by,
I'm reliably informed Blind Billy and Boom. They are scraping
him off the floor as we speak.'

For a moment Flannery cannot comprehend what he has just been told. The notion that Costigan, who he thought invincible was no more leaves him speechless.

'Costigan had a minor spat with Blind Billy last Sunday night in the Fallen Nun. Luckily I was there and broke it up. It appears he attempted to finish it tonight and got more than expected.'

Mullen hands Flannery a whisky, who smiles. 'The mad bastard will be wreaking carnage in hell as we speak.'

'You do realise,' replies Mullen. 'That once this news gets made public, it'll be the biggest celebration in Manchester since VE day.'

'Do you think this was a planned hit'? asks Flannery.

Mullen shrugs his shoulders. 'Costigan had more enemies than any man I have ever known. If I had to take a guess my money would be that the gypsies hired Blind Billy and sidekick to revenge the Clancy brothers.'

'I suppose it'll be down to me to arrange the funeral,' sighs Flannery.

'Is there any family'? asks Mullen.

'None that give a fuck,' laughs Flannery. 'They hated him more than anybody else did. And here is a frightening thought Pat. Paddy had three brothers and it has always been claimed he was the normal one.'

Alongside the ship canal Maria Clancy is stood alone, clutching a hold all containing the ten thousand ransom money for Blind Billy and Boom. She received the call only an hour ago to say Paddy Costigan was dead. News that made her cry with both joy and relief. Here at this deserted spot near Castlefield locks she now waits.

It's close to midnight and the sky is littered with stars. Maria smiles at the thought her brothers are somewhere up there and now will be at peace with Costigan dead. Then she sees his killers walking towards her. The most unlikely looking double act but one that tonight has made Maria Clancy's heart soar.

She shakes both their hands and gives Blind Billy the money bag. 'Thank you,' she says.

'No problem Miss,' replies Blind Billy. 'It was a pleasure to rid this world of a creature like Paddy Costigan. So rare this job of ours can be enjoyable but tonight was the exception. Now we have one last item of business to take care of.'

Maria appears surprised and a little annoyed. 'I can assure you there's no need to count the cash, it's all there.'

'Oh it's not the money that needs to be dealt with Miss Clancy, smiles Blind Billy.

'I'm afraid it's you.'

With that he shoots twice and Maria drops to the floor. Her eyes full of shock, pain and horror. As she lies sprawled Blind Billy fires one last burst sending Maria Clancy to join her brothers. Swiftly the two men make their escape. Their thinking in double crossing and deciding to kill Maria, being why risk the chance of letting her live and possibly one day incriminate them?

And so ends the last night on this earth of Paddy Costigan and one quite typically drenched in blood and senseless violence.

An epitaph to a monster.

LEAVING ON A JET PLANE

Sunday morning: 'What the hell is going on? We are turning into 1930's fucking Chicago.' Inspector George Collins is livid. Surrounded by reporters he is outside the Fatted Calf, stepping through fragments of broken glass and more than likely Paddy Costigan. Collins turns to the reporters. 'Look lads do me a favour. Soon as we know something I'll let you know, but for the moment just let me do my job eh.

And fuck off.'

Amidst the large crowd of forensic experts and policemen, he spots Tommy Butler and heads across towards him.

'This is something we can do without George. Who the hell was it'?

A local headcase by the name of Paddy Costigan. He won't be missed. Sadly there was another murder last night. A young girl. Shot four times on the canal.'

Butler shakes his head. 'Are these two incidents related'?

'Until we get confirmation of the girl's name I can't say. But I don't like coincidences. Two murders in one night in my city and only hours apart? I'm not having it. Hopefully the forensic chaps can piece together a bullet trace and we can match those with what killed the girl.'

Butler looks around at the chaos. 'A further drain on our resources.'

'Can't be helped I'm afraid,' replies Collins. The two men walk off from the crowds chatting.

'Collins turns to face Butler. 'Tommy, I've spoken to Mullen and I've no doubt they are hiding Reynolds.'

'Well let's go and nick him then' replies Butler. 'What are we waiting for'?

'Nick him for what'? answers Collins. 'Me having a hunch? Besides things have become even more complicated because it's personal now. Mullen and the others are still feeling bad blood over past events. Also I think you should come clean and tell me the name of the snitch who tipped you off that Reynolds had come north'?
'I've already told you, I can't do that George.'

'And I know why,' replies Collins. 'It's because it came from C11. They have been tapping Keenan's phone since the Kray fiasco. And God knows who else's up here. Christ they are probably bugging me. Those people never forget, they are like fucking elephants and have been looking to take revenge since.

Go ahead, tell me I'm lying'?

Butler smiles. He takes off the trilby and wipes his forehead. 'No, you are correct,' he replies. 'They came to me two days after Bruce Reynolds rang Tommy Keenan. But the idiots never acted fast enough. Otherwise we could have simply followed Keenan then grabbed Reynolds soon as he showed up. Hence my later appearance here in your city.'

'You are chasing fucking windmills Tommy. You are never going to get him.'

'I have to keep trying' replies Butler, as he puts his trilby back on.
'I have to keep trying.'

In a safe house in Salford, a backstreet terrace, a stunned Tommy Keenan and Bruce Reynolds are watching the television news as it reports the demise of Paddy Costigan and murder of a young girl, unknown at that time as Maria Clancy.

'What the bloody hell is going on Tommy'? asks Reynolds.
'No idea mate' he replies. 'But I knew Costigan and whoever took him out were either well paid or mad. Or most likely both.'

Suddenly there is a knock on the front door and Tommy rushes to the window. He breathes a sigh of relief and smiles wide. 'The cavalry's here Bruce. Looks like you are on your way.'
Outside stands Damian Quinn and William *'Billy'* Tarr.
Tommy goes to let them in. 'Good to see you both.'
'You too Tommy,' replies Tarr.
'Hey Tommy,' smiles Quinn.
As they enter the living room Reynolds is stood waiting to greet them and Tommy does the introductions.
'Lads, meet the star of our little adventure. Mr Bruce Reynolds.' Tarr and Quinn both shake his hand.
'I've some news for you Bruce,' says a grinning Tarr. He takes a passport from his pocket and hands it over to Reynolds. 'You are leaving on a jet plane old son. From now on you are Mr Keith Clement Miller and off to Mexico this very day.
A back route to the other end of the world.'
'How am I getting there boys'? asks a stunned Reynolds. As he gazes at the passport.
' Well me and Billy here are going to be your personal escort until you set foot on the first plane,' says Quinn. The plan is we take you down to Elstree Airfield. From there you fly to Ostend. A car will then pick you up and drive you to Brussels. You then take a plane with Sabena airlines to Mexico City via Toronto. Now don't worry because we have people in place to help you along.
Courtesy of Manchester you will soon be out of harm's way.'
'And my wife and kid'? enquires Reynolds. 'What happens to them'?
Tarr hands him a piece of paper with a telephone number wrote upon it. 'Soon as you are settled in Mexico, you ring this number and Frances and Nick will swiftly follow.'
Quinn puts an arm around Reynold's shoulders. 'Nothing to worry about Bruce. You are in good hands.'
'I cannot thank you boys enough. All of you.'
'Like I've already told you,' smiles Tommy. 'Soon as the dust settles I want that invite.'
'You can bank on it,' replies Reynolds. Clearly overcome with emotion.
'Right then,' says Tarr, whilst clapping his hands. 'No time to hang around, we have

One day fucking Tommy chasing your arse. Best be off.'

Reynolds and Tommy embrace.

'Don't you be talking to any strangers on this trip Bruce. Especially ones in uniform.

Reynolds laughs. 'Thanks for the advice. I'll keep that in mind.'

'Be lucky mate and stay away from trains right'?

'You too Thomas Keenan. Tell Paddy if he ever needs me I'm there for him.'

The two men embrace and Reynolds leaves the room

The front door slams shut and Tommy falls down on an armchair. He hears the car start up and finally Bruce Reynolds, the great train robber is on his way.

Leaning back he takes a deep sigh and feels like a huge weight has been lifted from his shoulders.

'Right then,' Tommy says to himself. 'Back to the day job.'

That same evening he is walking towards the Cromford club to meet Paddy Mullen, when suddenly two police cars screech up alongside him and out pours several uniformed policemen, as well as Detectives Collins and Butler.

He is immediately grabbed and handcuffed. Collins approaches him.

Tommy smiles. 'Hello George, long time no see. Still upset over the reds wining the league I see.'

Not the time for jokes Tommy,' replies Collins. 'You are in big fucking trouble son. I'd like to introduce you to a good friend of mine from Scotland Yard. Chief Superintendent Tommy Butler.'

Tommy grins wide. 'I recognise you Mr Butler. Your poster was on the public toilets in Piccadilly. Not very fetching. You're a lot more handsome in the flesh.'

Butler smiles. 'I heard you was a bit of a comedian Keenan. Let's see how funny you are in a prison cell. He motions for two officers and they bundle Tommy into the back of the police car.

'What exactly am I being arrested for George'? asks Tommy, through the car window.

'I'll think of something Tommy lad,' smiles Collins. He bangs on the roof and the panda drives off.

'He's too cool,' says Butler. 'This feels and looks to me as though Reynolds has already scarpered George. What are you going to charge him with'?

'Being a pain in the fucking arse, ' replies Collins.

Back at Bootle Street, Tommy is taken straight to the cells and left there until Collins and Butler return. After an hour's wait a policemen appears to unlock the door.

'Come on they are waiting for you in the interview room.'

'If I asked to see my lawyer, what would you say to me'?

''I'd say don't bother Tommy,' replies the officer. 'Everybody knows Reynolds has left town. You'll be out and home before the milkman.'

'Who is this Reynolds fella'?

The policeman laughs. 'Off the record, all this is a waste of time if you ask me. We have the missing kids up in Ashton and Hyde, not to mention last night's events. A lot of the boys think the quicker Butler fucks off back to London and we can get on with catching proper criminals the better.'

They stop outside the room. 'Now in you go,' smiles the officer. 'And not a word about what I just told you, otherwise I'll be working in fucking Rochdale for the next ten years.'

Inside Collins and Butler are sat on one side of a small wooden table with a lone chair at the other.

'Come in Tommy,' smiles Collins. 'We have saved you a place.'

'Much obliged George. But unless you tell me what I'm being charged with, I'm saying nothing until I speak to a lawyer.'

'Oh fucking give me a break son, and don't treat me like an idiot. We know you've been harbouring Bruce Reynolds, and that he's probably well gone now and over the water. Also you are not being charged, we just want a chat.

Okay'?

Tommy sits down and lights up a cigarette. 'First of all there's absolutely no proof or evidence to back up what you've just alleged. I just need to make that clear. Is that understood'?

'Yes lad' replies a resigned Butler. 'Clear as a fucking bright summer's day.'

'Excellent' smiles Tommy. 'Now ask away gents.'

Butler continues. 'Reynolds is no hero. Don't kid yourself. The driver of that train, Jack Mills, was hit over the head with an iron bar. He is fifty-seven years old, a granddad. Older than me for God's sake. A normal working class bloke who was simply doing a job to feed his family, when your mate and his mob laid into him for refusing to help them. They left Jack in a right state. And you,

well you may as well have hit him with the iron bar, because what you did by hiding Reynolds is unforgiveable.'

'I've absolutely no idea what you are on about,' replies Tommy.

'Of course you haven't son. You are an angel. You all are. Everybody up here in this city are whiter than white. The line in the sand between the normal rules of law doesn't apply because for some reason in your world you think you're above it.'

Hearing this Tommy loses his cool. 'You really do make me laugh Mr Butler. You seem to forget I witnessed at first hand this country's rule of law when the Krays came to town. This imaginary line in the sand you speak about? I don't see it and do you know why? It's quite simple really, because it doesn't exist.

Now I'd of thought an intelligent man like yourself would have understood that power corrupts more than poverty ever did. Maybe not in your case, but the people you work for. Or those maybe you don't know you work for? But one thing is certain in my mind, and that is there is no right and wrong in this country.

You just look after your own.'

Those who claim the moral high ground, the establishment, they have less morals and scruples than the worst of the lowlifes, sometimes It has been my misfortune to come across. We have our own laws that are strictly adhered too.

And my world?

What I do for a living? When I go home, well I sleep well at night. Speech over.'

'Where has Reynolds gone Tommy'? asks Collins.

'No idea, like I've already said, I never met the bloke. Now can I go home'?

Collins looks across to Butler, who nods as if to signify let him go.

'Get yourself off Keenan,' says Collins. And we'll be watching you like a fucking hawk.'

Tommy smiles, 'I'd not have it any other way George. I feel safe with you keeping an eye on me.'

'By the way,' adds Collins. 'Paddy Costigan's sad demise. Can you shed any light or is that something else you are not aware of'?

All I know is that his head ended up half a mile from his feet and that the line of suspects could form a line from Old Trafford to Maine Road.'

'Not a popular man then,' smiles Butler.

Tommy stands to leave. 'An acquired taste. Have a safe journey back to London. For what it's worth Paddy Mullen always spoke highly of you Mr Butler. You're just the right copper in the wrong city at a bad time. The cards in your hand have not fallen well.

Bad luck Sir.'

Tommy walks out the door. 'He's a good kid,' murmurs Butler. Almost to himself, but heard by a smiling Collins.

'So is that it then,' he asks of Butler. 'Are you heading back'?

'Looks that way, but before I go, let me have a glance at everything you have on those missing children. Especially the files on the local suspects.'

'Of course,' replies Collins. 'And listen, I know we never got the bastard and have had a few ups and downs, and also that you've had a rough ride up here. But in my eyes you are still the best fucking copper it's been my pleasure to work with.'

Thanks George,' answers Butler.

'Much appreciated. Now get me those files and I'll try to leave you with a going away present.'

A FOUR LEAF CLOVER

Unbeknown to Blind Billy and Boom, just before their moment of triumph occurred, somebody in the Fatted Calf was watching them, watching Paddy Costigan. Even more unfortunate for both hitmen, this person was of gypsy blood and a distant cousin of the Clancy brothers.

Thirty-five year old Fergus Noonan had followed them as they made their way to murder Maria. He watched from afar, but vowed revenge and this night, with the call to arms of his fellow gypsy brothers, vengeance will be had.

It is way past midnight on the Manchester canal path, and Blind Billy and Boom are returning home from Town. Both are very drunk and have been celebrating their recent windfall. They are staggering and each clutching bottles of whisky. Above them a starlit sky, whilst all along the canal bank sit huge warehouses, silhouetted against a full moon that casts huge shadows across the water's surface.

The serenity and peacefulness of the evening is suddenly shaken by the appearance into Blind Billy's and Boom's midst of four armed, masked gunmen with sawn-off shotguns aimed towards them. They are quickly surrounded. Before either can make a move for weapons, the gypsy assassins open fire and Blind Billy and Boom fall in a hellish rakish of gunfire.

Their bodies exploding apart as the bullets from close quarters tear holes in the bare flesh. It's all over in seconds as Blind Billy and Boom lie dead.

The quiet of the night now deafens. Noonan steps towards their shattered corpses and drops a four leaf clover upon the bodies. He smiles. 'Our sweetest regards. That was for Maria Clancy.

May your journey to hell be long and filled with horrors you pair of screwed up fucks.'

His piece said Noonan motions to the others and they disappear back into the darkness from whence they came.

The slate marked clean.

At Bootle Street police station, it has just gone three in the morning and Tommy Butler is still hard at work reading over files given to him by George Collins, about the missing children. One in particular keeps coming to mind, and he places it repeatedly at the top of the pile. Born Ian Stewart on 2nd January 1938, the illegitimate son of a Scottish waitress. His violent personality was shaped by an unstable background.

His mother neglected him and he was raised by foster parents in the Gorbals. Glasgow's toughest slum. After a spree of petty crime as a teenager, the courts sent him to Manchester to live with his mother and her new husband. There he assumed his stepfather's name, continued his criminal activities and developed into a fully-fledged alcoholic.

Time and again Butler stares at the photograph and into the dark soulless eyes.

The young man's previous police record in Scotland has nothing to suggest he is the monster they are looking for, but something deep inside Butler is screaming at him.

The face has it. Manipulative and cruel. He knows, he just knows.
This needs to be followed up. Butler places the man's photograph in his jacket. He intends to give this to Collins before heading back to London tomorrow.

On the short walk back to the Midland hotel he notices two young men in their early twenties, scraping off one of the many posters of himself ensconced across Manchester. He heads over the road to take a closer look.

'What's going on'?

They recognise him immediately.

'Orders from above,' replies one. 'They are all coming down tonight. The war is over Mr Butler sir. Have a safe journey home.'

Butler cannot help but smile. 'Goodnight lads.'

That said he makes his way up the hotel steps for a last night's sleep in a city which despite all has grown immensely on him.

After a brief and eventful if unsuccessful sojourn north, Tommy Butler is now sat in his office at Scotland Yard, catching up with paperwork and events occurring in London. Home turf. However despite Butler's best attempts to concentrate on matters in the capital, his thoughts continually return north and the vanished children. He is convinced they have all been abducted and murdered.

Butler can only hope men like George Collins now take the bull between the horns and start making inroads on the cases. Suddenly there is a knock on his door and a uniformed officer enters holding a brown parcel.

'Excuse me sir, this has just arrived for you.'

He places it on Butler's desk who proceeds to rip open the packaging. Finally its contents are revealed and inside, much to his amusement is a child's train set with a card tied to it that reads:

For Tommy Butler. A decent copper and an even better man.

Regards

Manchester.

Butler smiles. 'Fair play.' He picks up the toy train and holds it high to get a closer look.

Bruce Reynolds may have slipped his grasp for the moment, but Chief Superintendent of Scotland Yard and the flying squad, Tommy Butler, is convinced he will get his man in the end.

The train robber is simply on borrowed time.

Two months on a large parcel arrives at Tommy Keenan's house and he takes delivery at the door. Alison appears from the living room. 'Are you expecting something'? he asks. She shakes her head. Tommy places it on the floor and starts to unwrap it. Inside is a large flat box. 'Well go on then open it,' says an inquisitive Alison. He removes the lid to reveal a huge Mexican sombrero. A grinning Tommy reads a small card attached.

'This is for showing me that famous northern hospitality! All the best Bruce.'

He puts it on, much to a quizzical Alison's amusement. Grinning from ear to ear Tommy declares. 'This is going up pride of place in our living room'!

Three years later on 9th November 1968, Tommy Butler arrested Bruce Reynolds in Torquay Devon. By this time Reynolds had started to run low on his ill-gotten gains and decided to return after planning a similar size heist to the great train robbery. However before plans could be put into action, Butler swooped after hearing rumours sweeping the London underworld that his nemesis was back on these shores. *'One day Tommy'* had taken his time on this one, but in the end justice was served. Bruce Reynolds was sentenced to twenty-five years for his part on what many claimed was the crime of the century.

.

ACT FOUR
THE EIGHTH DAY

NEW ARRIVALS

Tommy Keenan is sitting smoking in a doctor's surgery, waiting for news on his wife Alison, who is currently been seen. He cuts a nervous figure. Around him a host of people in various stages of unwell. Some coughing and spluttering. Others with legs and arms in bandages and plaster. Tommy's eyes turn constantly towards the doctor's door. She has been in there for twenty minutes now. A part of him is raging to just charge in, for the not knowing is excruciating. But he daren't.

Suddenly the door opens and Alison appears. Tommy stands and goes towards her. For a moment she cannot look at him. He fears bad news for Alison's eyes are red and she appears to have been crying.

He holds her hand. 'Well what did the doctor say'?

Finally Alison looks up and stares at her husband. Then breaking into a huge smile she announces loud. 'I'm two months pregnant! Congratulations Thomas Keenan you are going to be a Father'!

He throws his arms around her. Suddenly a tear comes to Tommy's eye and Alison wipes it away. 'Time to grow up my love,' she says.

He hugs her tight. 'I can't believe it,' exclaims Tommy.

'I'm going to be a Dad'!

MY FATHER'S SON

It is Saturday evening in a packed Cromford club. In the downstairs casino raised voices whoop loud as the roulette wheel falls on red and two dark suited men with American accents win again. They are twenty-seven year old Paul Lansky and forty-seven year old, Brooklyn born, Bruno Gianelli. Lansky is the oldest son of legendary Jewish mob boss, Meyer Lansky, whilst Gianelli, a bear of a man, is his bodyguard.

Lansky has been drinking since mid-afternoon and is heavily drunk whilst Gianelli remains sober. For his life would be rendered worthless if ill fate befalls the Godfather's son, so he has to keep his wits about him at all time. For in Paul Lansky's case the apple has fell well out of sight of the tree. Indeed over the hill and far away.

Whereas the father is cool, calm, calculating, and charming even in matters of family business, his heir, when boozing is reckless, uncouth, a drunkard and at times verging on psychotic. Gianelli pleaded with him to go easy but now Lansky is out of control.

All bets are off.

They are in Manchester after meeting with the Kray twins in London to look over potential financial investments in Mayfair. Plans to open a new casino in Berkeley square called the Colony club have been approved remarkably swiftly. This mostly down to the immense power held sway by the twins, whom ensured all obstacles were quickly overcome with a menacing concoction of bribery, corruption, threats and blackmail. Another important factor in the success was that Paul Lansky reneged from the booze. When sober he possesses a modicum of the charm and business flair of his father, but when drinking Lansky becomes a liability. And dangerous.

Also with them from New York is the legendary Hollywood actor George Raft, who after a career playing gangsters on screen, now plies a living as a front man for Lansky's business ventures. However Raft has stayed in London as a VIP guest of the Krays and does not travel north until tomorrow.

On the twins recommendation Lansky and Gianelli have come to meet with Paddy Mullen, in order to discuss a similar proposition in Manchester. A club croupier approaches the Americans and whispers into Lansky's ear. 'Mr Mullen is in his office and can see you now sir. If you will follow me I'll take you up.' Lansky smiles. He motions to Gianelli and they head off.

Upstairs waiting are Paddy Mullen and Tommy Keenan. 'I'm surprised you even agreed to this,' says Tommy, who is leaning on the desk. Mullen is sat behind it.

'These are not the kind of people you turn down Tommy. At least not straight away. I'll listen to what Lansky has to offer and then gently explain it's not for us.'

'I've had one of the lads keeping an eye on them,' replies Tommy. 'They are on a winning streak at the tables. Taking us for a small fortune.'

Mullen smiles. 'A small price to pay. I told Charlie to fix it to ensure when we come face to face, they are in a good mood.'

'You think of everything,' laughs Tommy.

'How are Alison and the baby? She taking it easy'? asks Mullen

'She's well thanks. Although I'm getting earache about getting a job with normal hours. Her Dad owns a couple of shops that specialise in ladies shoes. Wait for this Paddy, you are going to love it. Alison has had a word with him on my behalf about me working there.'

Mullen tries hard to hide a grin but fails badly.

'What, you selling ladies shoes'?

'Tommy nods. 'She reckons I'd be a natural.' Mullen shakes his head. The thought of Tommy working in a shoe shop being harassed by old ladies is an image that makes him smile.

Suddenly there is a knock at the door and Charlie enters. 'Mr Mullen, I have Paul Lansky with me.'

'Ask him in Charlie.' He opens the door wide and a smiling Lansky walks through, with a grim faced Gianelli behind. Mullen stands from his desk and goes to greet them.

He shakes their hands and introduces them to Tommy, before ushering both men to sit down. 'Can I get you a drink'?

'Whisky,' slurs Lansky, whilst Gianelli declines.

'No thank you Mr Mullen.'

Tommy pours three glasses for himself, Mullen and Lansky and hands them over. Gianelli eyes Tommy like an alley cat ready to pounce on an unsuspecting mouse. He notices this and attempts to give a friendly smile in Gianelli's direction are met only with a look of utter disdain.

'So Mr Lansky,' begins Mullen. 'Our two mutual friends in London tell me you have a proposition you'd like to put forward.'

Lansky smiles. 'It's not a proposition of sorts, more I tell you what I want for a reasonable price and you sell it to me. This is how it's going to be. You don't really have a choice in the matter.'
He finishes his whisky in one gulp and slams the glass down on the table.

Mullen smells trouble. He shifts uneasily in his seat. 'I think I'll be the judge of that young man.'
Tommy automatically moves towards Mullen, whilst Gianelli visibly tightens up. Inside he is raging at the disrespect Lansky is showing. This is not how to do business. If it was anybody else's' son, Gianelli would slap him across the face and demand he apologise.

A drunken lopsided grin now appears on Lansky's face. 'I've had a good look around your city today Mullen, and have come to the conclusion you live in a fucking dump. The only place worth shit is this goddamn hole. So name your price'?

He turns to Tommy. 'Hey hired hand, move your ass and get me another fucking drink.'

For a second Tommy contemplates picking Lansky up by the lapels on his suit jacket, but one look at Mullen's face swiftly makes him change tact and instead he bites his tongue, takes the bottle and refills the American's glass.

'The Cromford club is not for sale at any price Mr Lansky,' replies Mullen. Not to you, not to anyone.'

'You do understand who we are Mullen. You goddamn limeys do read the newspapers and can fucking read can't you'?

'I know exactly who you are Mr Lansky, and I know who your father is. The answer is still the same. Absolutely not for sale.'

'The Krays said you were a hard headed bastard, but was someone we could do business with. That's not what I am hearing or seeing here. Now I'll ask you again and I'm getting impatient. Name a fucking price'?

Mullen smiles and has heard enough. He takes a sip of his whisky. 'Not a penny or a million pounds Mr Lansky. You may not know of me, but I think it would have been wise to maybe ask around before coming into my club showing such disrespect, and making veiled threats.'

Here we go, thinks Tommy. The Yank has got Mullen's back up now.

Mullen addresses Gianelli directly. 'It would be a good idea now to get your man out of my club Mr Gianelli, before I really lose my temper.' Gianelli recognises immediately Mullen is not a man to be messed with. His fellow American has chosen the wrong man to try and bully and pick a fight with.

'What the fuck,' rages Lansky. He stands and throws his whisky glass, shattering it on the wall. 'You dare to threaten me Mullen'?

'Go and get some sleep son, you're drunk,' he replies. Gianelli grabs Lansky by the arm. 'It's late Paul, we can continue this another time. Lansky shrugs him off.

'Get your fucking hands off me.' He glares again at Mullen and shouts loud. 'You have no idea of the power I yield. You dare to talk to me like this'? I have a new offer for you. Do you know what it is? Nothing. Tonight you have made the worst mistake of your fucking life.'

Again Gianelli tries to calm him by putting an arm around his shoulders, but is immediately shrugged off. 'Alright Bruno I'm coming.' Lansky turn to face Mullen one last time.
'I am my Father's son.' He grins wide and wipes his mouth on a sleeve.
'You'll be hearing from me again.'
That said Lansky storms out of the room with Gianelli following. His eyes make contact with Tommy, who notices they are almost apologetic. The door slams and suddenly there is silence.
Tommy takes out a pack of cigarettes and offers one to Mullen who sighs heavily and accepts.

He smiles. 'I don't want to worry you Paddy old son, but I think we have just gone to war with the Mafia.'

Once outside Lansky and Gianelli make their way across Piccadilly towards the Portland hotel where they are staying. 'I want you to do something for me before we go home Bruno'? 'Anything,' replies Gianelli.
Lansky looks him in the eyes. 'I want you to kill Patrick Mullen.'

That said he walks off in front leaving Gianelli speechless. So far as he is concerned that is an order too far. Bruno Gianelli will not lower himself to this young scumbag's level. Whatever the cost.

The two men enter the Portland hotel and walk up to reception. Lansky is in a bad way. He is staggering and struggling to make any semblance of sense. Behind the desk is a pretty blond receptionist. Twenty-four year old Sara O'Farrell, and secret girlfriend of married gangster Harry Taylor, who runs South Manchester. Alongside her is fellow hotel worker, forty-five year old Bill Lyons. He takes an instant dislike to the younger yank.

Sara smiles at the Americans. 'Good evening Gentlemen. Have you had a good evening'? Lansky eyes Sara up and down and points his finger at her. 'I want you to bring me a bottle of fucking Jack Daniels whisky up to my room in ten minutes.'
Lyons eyes him with disdain, but she says nothing and remains calm. Dealing with drunken male guests is something of a speciality for Sara. 'All pants and mouth and no balls' is her pet saying for

them. But this one? This one she feels has an aura of danger around him.

Sara knows she will have to tread careful.

'She hands them their keys and addresses Lansky. 'If you'd like to go to your room, I'll be up with your drink shortly sir.'

Gianelli hands his key back. 'He smiles towards Sara. 'I'll help my friend upstairs and then I'm going back out. Please can you keep hold of this until later?

'Of course,' she replies. At least the older one has manners.

Gianelli helps Lansky into the lift. 'I'm going to have that fucking blond,' sneers Lansky. 'Did you see how she looked at me'?

'My advice is get some sleep Paul. We have one day left in this lousy city before flying home. There is still a lot of work to do. George is coming from London tomorrow and we need to make things right with Mullen.'

'Fuck that arsehole,' shouts out Lansky.'I want him dead Bruno. Do you hear me'?

He grabs hold of Gianelli. 'Fucking dead, do you understand'? Gianelli does not answer, he simply nods.

'Thank you,' replies Lansky. 'Oh Bruno, I'm so fucking drunk man.'

They arrive at Lansky's room. Gianelli opens the door and they enter.

'Are you going to be okay'? he asks his young master. Lansky sits down on the bed.

'I want another drink,' he mumbles.

Gianelli shakes his head. If this boy's Father could see him now, this punk would get a beating within an inch of his life.

'I'll see you in the morning.' That said he leaves the room.

Out in the corridor Sara is just coming out of the lift carrying a tray with the whisky bottle and a glass upon it. She approaches a remorseful looking Gianelli.

'I'd like to apologise for my young friend.' He points to the tray. 'I'll take it to him if you like'?

Sara smiles. 'No need sir, but thank you anyway. Gianelli enters the lift and just catches sight of Sara reaching Lansky's room, before the doors shut to take him downstairs. He desperately needs time to breathe and to think away from Lansky. A bad day and one Gianelli did not see coming after the relatively easy dealings with the Krays in London.

Manchester was a place he had never heard of until the twins recommended a visit and meeting with Patrick Mullen. They claimed Mullen was a class act and well worth getting to know. However after Lansky's behaviour early this evening, he doubts now whether it's worth hanging around.

Maybe best to just cut their losses and Gianelli is contemplating ringing the boss, Myer Lansky tomorrow morning and explaining what has occurred. He is sure Myers' advice, once he has stopped ranting will be to get on the first plane back to New York.

Gianelli knew the old man had serious doubts about sending Paul over to England. Worries stressed to him many times by the boss. 'Keep your eye on my boy Bruno. Make sure he shows due respect. Don't let him get lost in the bottle.

Don't let him embarrass me…….'

After tonight's shameful episode with Mullen, Gianelli can only imagine the Godfather's reaction.

As ever with Myer, all is complicated due to him not being Italian, thus unable to become a fully-fledged Mafioso. However there are few in *Cosa Nostra* who demand such respect. A God given ability to make fortunes for his Mafia partners ensures he dines at the top table.

However Lansky is prickly beyond words on the subject. Any under him who bring disrespect upon the family and act as his own flesh and blood have done, could expect a bloody end. For the man lives by one word alone. Respect.

And Paul Lansky has spat on his Father's name tonight.

Gianelli stops at reception where Bill Lyons still stands. 'Hey mac, any idea where I can get a late drink around here'? Before Lyons can answer a voice speaks up behind the American. 'I know a place, but you may need a bodyguard.' Gianelli turns around to see Tommy Keenan stood facing him. Lyons smiles and nods at Tommy.

They know each other.

'I figured after what happened earlier it might make sense for me and you to have a chat.'

For a second Gianelli is wary, but then he remember how quickly this man moved to cover Mullen when it appeared Lansky was set to launch himself on him. Like a son protecting his own father. That alone impressed Gianelli no end.

He smiles. 'I couldn't agree more. I think we may have got off on the wrong foot.' He offers Tommy his hand.

'Let's start again. Bruno Gianelli.' Tommy grins wide and reciprocates.

'Tommy Keenan. Pleased to meet you Bruno. Now let's go and get that beer.'

The two men step out of the Portland hotel and into the Mancunian night.

'Where are we going'? asks Gianelli.

Tommy laughs. 'To the biggest hole of depravity and debauchery this side of Hell my son. I'm taking you to the Fallen Nun.'

Sara O'Farrell knocks on Paul Lansky's door. She waits a moment and then hears the rattle of keys. It opens and a dishevelled looking Lansky stands before her. He pushes it wide and moves aside. 'Come in gal.' At first she is reluctant. Everything inside her screams don't enter, but whether it be professional courtesy, or simply the fact she has been in this position a thousand times before with drunken guests and coped fine, sees her step inside. Lansky immediately shuts the door. And then to Sara's increasing horror she hears him turn the keys to lock it.

'Sir could you unlock the door please'? asks Sara, in what she hopes is her most authorative voice. 'Why the rush lady'? replies Lansky. 'Make yourself comfortable. Sit on the bed and have a drink with me.'

'Sir please will you unlock the door'? By now her voice is cracking and she is clearly scared.

Lansky suddenly snaps. 'I won't tell you again bitch, sit down on the fucking bed! You are going nowhere until I say so.' He starts to unbutton his trousers and realising the situation has become desperate, Sara makes a rush to the door, only for Lansky to grab her. Trying desperate to break free she claws at his face, causing him to scream in pain.

He reacts by lashing out and punching Sara so hard, she is sent reeling against the bathroom door, banging her head. Lying slumped in a heap, Sara is unconscious with blood seeping from the corner of her mouth.

Lansky immediately panics and rings down to reception, his voice stricken with fear.

'We need a fucking ambulance……..'

'Evening Tommy,' say the doormen in unison, as he and Gianelli step inside the infamous drinking house. The Fallen Nun. Tommy acknowledges them. 'How are things lads. Anyone been killed in here tonight'?

'Still early mate,' replies one of them. They enter a packed room and Gianelli looks around, as every face in the darkened room stares back at him. They stand at the bar whilst Tommy orders the drinks. He laughs and says quietly to Bruno: 'Try not to look anybody in the eye and they'll leave you alone.'

'What the hell kind of joint is this'? exclaims Gianelli. Unable to believe he is going to leave the Fallen Nun alive.

'Exclusive,' smiles Tommy. 'Blessed by the devil my American friend. You have to be of certain, shall we say type to get membership in here Bruno.' The two men take their beers and sit down at a small wooden table in a quiet corner of the pub. To ensure he sees any potential trouble coming, Tommy takes the seat facing the crowd, whilst Bruno has his back to Manchester's creatures of the night, all drinking themselves into oblivion.

'Tommy, I'd like to apologise for any disrespect my friend shown to Mr Mullen earlier. Paul cannot handle the booze. He's been under a lot of pressure to seal the deal on the casino in London with the Krays. This is his first major time abroad where he's been trusted by his father in matters of business, and it all just got too much for him tonight. Gianelli takes a drink before continuing.

'The trouble with this kid is that nobody has ever said no to him.'

' Paddy is not even going to consider selling the Cromford club Bruno. Not to Lansky, the queen of England, nobody. Your boy is wasting his time. Now in respect to you and of course his father, what was said in the office is water under the bridge, but take my advice old son. Get Lansky on a plane and home soon as possible. The longer he stays around here, the more likely someone is likely to put a fist in his mouth.'

Gianelli smiles. 'Thanks for the free advice but I'm already on it. We have some friends coming from London tomorrow. Once they arrive I'm ringing New York and hopefully get permission off Meyer to fly back.'

Suddenly one of the doormen is stood at their table. 'There's someone who wants a word outside gents. Says he works at the Portland and that it's important.' Tommy and Gianelli stand and head out the door. Waiting for them is an ashen faced Bill Lyons.

Tommy puts his hand on Lyon's shoulder. 'Bill what's wrong mate'?

An angry Lyons points an accusing finger at Gianelli. 'Your bastard friend has put Sara in hospital. He attacked her in the bedroom and she's unconscious.'

Gianelli turns away in disgust. 'The crazy sonofabitch.'

'Where's Lansky'? asks Tommy.

'The police have taken him to Bootle Street. He even punched a copper in the hotel foyer. Ranting and raving like a nutcase. It took three of them to pin him down and even then he was screaming. 'Do you know who I fucking am'?

Gianelli looks in horror at Tommy. 'I'm going to have to call home and let Meyer know so he can get a lawyer here.'

'What about Sara, you heartless American shit'? shouts Lyons. Gianelli immediately realises. 'Hey I'm sorry, I….'

I'll look after the girl,' says Tommy. You concentrate on calling your people. Has she got any family Bill'?

None that I know of Tommy. But I think there's something you should know about Sara.'

'Go on,' he replies.

'Well she's been seeing Harry Taylor for the last year or two on the quiet.'

Lyons points again at Gianelli. 'When Harry finds out what your sick mate has done to Sara, he'll cut his balls off. And I hope he bloody well does so.'

Gianelli turns to Tommy. 'Who the hell is Harry Taylor'?

'Just so happens to be one of the most powerful men in the Manchester underworld. This is going to be trouble Bruno.'

'The boy maybe a piece of shit Tommy, but he's my responsibility. I cannot allow anything to happen to him. I'd appreciate if you passed the word that Paul Lansky is protected and anybody thinking otherwise will find themselves with me to deal with.'

Tommy looks across to Gianelli and smiles sardonically.

'In all honesty I'm not sure that'll cut much ice in this city, but I'll do as you say.

Welcome to Manchester Bruno lad.'

The next morning Inspector George Collins is settling down in his office at Bootle Street Police station for another long day. With a mug of tea in hand he is being briefed by a young uniformed constable on the overnight incident at the Portland hotel and their esteemed guest, currently rotting in cell twelve. Paul Lansky.
'Any news on the girl' asks Collins'?
'We've been told by the hospital she's in intensive care with a suspected blood clot on the brain. It's not looking good.'
'And the yank has admitted to beating her up'?
The constable nods. 'Lansky was drunk as a fucking skunk sir, but he was actually bragging about it. Kept saying he could do whatever he damn well wanted. And did we know who he was'?
Collins shakes his head in disgust. 'Wake him up and get him into the interview room now. I'm just in the mood to have a word with this arrogant prat.'
'There is something else,' says the Constable. Knowing fully well what he was about to say would shake this man's world to the core. For it is an open secret around the station that this hugely respected and well liked Inspector, has been desperate to help out with the case of the missing children in Ashton and Hyde.
'Go on lad, 'replies Collins. 'Don't tell me it's your fucking birthday and I forgot to buy you a card'?
The Constable smiles. 'We have had a breakthrough up in Hyde. A young couple have been brought in for questioning, after a phone call this morning reporting a murder. They've found a body at Sixteen Wardle Brook Avenue, in Hattersley.
'Any names'?
'The Sergeant on the phone mentioned just one. An Ian Brady. The word is the house is a chamber of horrors. There are rumours wild already up there that they could be responsible for the others.'
Collin's blood goes cold. He goes into his draw and stares once more at the file given him by Tommy Butler. The dead, cold eyes of a man on its front cover.
The file of Ian Brady.
'Who did the arrest'? he asks.
'Detective Joe Mounsey sir.'

Collins grins wide. He is happy for Mounsey is a close friend of his and more importantly one of the good guys. Reminiscent of Butler, he has steadfastly refused to give up on the missing children and has followed through every lead, either big or miniscule that surfaced. Now it appears, hopefully, Mounsey has the break his dogged police work deserves.

Collins stares once more at the photograph of Brady. Butler was adamant this man should be pulled in for further questioning regarding the missing children in Hyde and Ashton. However on informing the ongoing investigation team, he was all but told.
'Keep your fucking nose out.'

Also Collins' repeated requests to his superiors to be transferred over to help with the investigation were constantly blocked or ignored.
'This isn't a Manchester case,' he was informed. 'Let the locals deal with it. We have our own shit to sort.' And so a frustrated Collins has instead concentrated on matters within the city limits, and there is more than enough to keep him occupied.

The horrific spate of murders unprecedented in recent times. The untimely and bloody ends of Paddy Costigan, Maria Clancy, William Cosgrove and Frank Matthews. The latter two more widely known as Blind Billy and Boom. Collins is convinced by some warped link these are all related. And now this business with the yank? He feels his city is sick and it's down to men like him to find a cure.

A BETTER MAN

This same morning arriving at Manchester Piccadilly from London's Euston station are Bruno Gianelli's fellow Americans. Famed sixty-four year old actor George Raft and family lawyer friend of Meyer Lansky. Fifty-nine year old David Schulmann. Gianelli meets them as they step off the train and onto the platform. He shakes both their hands.
'Good to see you guys.'

'Bruno what the fuck is going on? asks Schulmann. 'Meyer is going crazy.'
'It seems Paul tried it on with this girl, she fought back and he whacked her. The local cops have him locked up not ten minutes away. The girl is in a coma. Fifty-fifty, whether she survives.'

'How did this happen. You was supposed to be looking after him'?
Suddenly Gianelli realises he is already being earmarked as a scapegoat if the worst occurs and the girl dies, sending Lansky to jail.

'The kid is out of control David.'
'And it was your job to rein him in Bruno. This is fucking bad.'
If I remember rightly it was your idea to blood Paul on this deal. Maybe Meyer will remember that conversation when we all get back to New York.

Maybe he'll put a gun to your head too'?
A clearly fraught Schulmann wags his finger at Gianelli. 'How dare you talk to.......

'Enough, the pair of you,' snaps Raft. 'This is solving nothing. The only person to blame is Paul himself. Now it's down to the three of us to sort this out and we are not going to do that by fighting amongst ourselves. Now Bruno, take us to the cop station and we'll go and speak to the kid.'

By this time a small crowd of curious onlookers have gathered around Raft after recognising him. One middle aged lady approaches him. 'George I'm a huge fan, may I have your autograph'? She hands him a pen and piece of paper. Raft smiles. Like a turning of a switch the charm comes on. 'Sure can doll, what name is it'?

Word has reached Harry Taylor of what happened to Sara and with his second in command and best friend Billy Tarr alongside him, he has rushed to see her at Crumpsall hospital. Taylor has been seeing Sara ever since that first night when the gang bosses gathered at the Portland hotel to meet George Collins, and discuss the Krays coming to Manchester.
Tarr checks with a nurse for directions and the two make their way along what appears a never-ending corridor. Finally they reach intensive care, but find their path blocked by a burly, stern faced Matron.

'Sara O'Farrell, how is she'? blurts out Taylor. I need to see her.'
'Are you family'? asks the matron
'Not by blood, but I'm the only family this girl has.'
'And your relationship is'?
'None of your business love, now let me go and see her'?

'I'm afraid that's just not possible, I'm terribly sorry sir, Miss O'Farrell is seriously ill at the moment and cannot be disturbed.'

Taylor feels sick. Suddenly a plain clothes detective appears from the ward. He is forty-five year old Henry Manning, who's known to Taylor and has been by Sara's bedside since she came in.

'Who did this Henry'? asks Taylor.

Manning is on the take to Taylor and is the man who broke the news to him of what occurred.

A yank called Paul Lansky. A big shot son of the famous Jewish mob guy. He got drunk, tried it on with Sara, she wasn't having it and he clobbered her. We've got him over at Bootle Street.'

Taylor turns to the matron who is still stood next to him. 'Please can I just go and see Sara for a moment'?

Very well' she replies. A minute only, come with me.' Taylor follows her into the ward. She stops at a side room. Inside is Sara, her face terribly bruised beyond recognition. He enters and walks to the side of the bed. A devastated Taylor takes her hand and squeezes it tight.

'I'm going to get this bastard Sara. I promise he's going to pay for what he has done to you.' Very gently he kisses her on the forehead before turning to leave.

'Thank you,' Taylor says to the matron, stood watching him from the door. He leaves the ward and rejoins Tarr and Manning in the corridor.

'Gentlemen, whatever it takes. I don't care who it upsets. I want that bastard's head on a plate.'

'Harry, the guy is Mafioso,' replies Tarr. 'Maybe not by Italian blood but if you take him out we risk having the entire *Cosa Nostra* lining up against us. Are you prepared to risk a war we could never win over a…'

Tarr goes quiet

'A what Billy? A tart? Is that what you was going to say'?

'Look I'm your best mate. If I can't say this who can? You have a wife and three lovely kids at home. You have women all across Manchester. Now Sara is a nice girl but not family. And in my opinion not worth dying over. All I'm saying is think very carefully and with your head and not your heart.'

'Billy is right Harry,' adds Manning. 'You take this kid out and all hell lets loose.'

Taylor thinks for a moment. Tarr is right, but his mind is made up and damn the consequences. 'Like I said boys.

Head on a fucking plate.'

Detective Inspector George Collins is sat staring across a small table in the interview room at Bootle Street police station, towards an ashen-faced, hungover Paul Lansky.
'Collins offers him a cigarette which he accepts and lights it for him.
'I'm not saying anything until I speak to a lawyer,' says Lansky.
'You have one coming from London. Before then, just tell me. What the fuck was you thinking'?
Lansky simply stares at Collins who smiles back.
'The Mafia,' he scoffs. 'I thought you guys were fucking hard men. Not the sort who beat up on innocent young girls. What, do you get off on it. Does it turn you on?'
Still Lansky says nothing. His expression vacant.
Collins continues. 'I bet you thought you'd come up here from London and do whatever the hell you liked. Out in the provinces, away from the crowds. The boy from New York City, whose daddy is a famous gangster using that immortal rotten line.
Do you know who I fucking am?
Well we do now son and you are going to jail for what you did last night, and I couldn't care less who your damned Father is.'
Suddenly the door opens and David Schulmann enters. 'I'm here representing Mr Lansky,' says Schulmann. 'Can you explain to me what you are doing speaking to my client without me bring present? This is all highly unusual.'
'So is beating a young girl half to death Mr Schulmann. Besides we were just chatting. wasn't we Paul'?
'Yes Detective,' replies a tired sounding Lansky. 'If you say so.'
'Good lad,' answers a smiling Collins. 'We'll speak again later.'
That said he leaves the room.
Schulmann sits down. 'What exactly did you say to him Paul'?
'I said nothing, the fucking cop did all the talking. How's the girl'?
'Not good. The police tell me she is fifty-fifty. Now I need you to remember and tell me exactly what happened'?
'I can hardly remember anything,' replies Lansky. 'I was blind drunk. Just her being in the room. She tried to leave and I wouldn't let her. Next thing I know the bitch is lying flat out on the floor.'

'Do you recall striking her'?

'No.'

'Right then,' says a smiling Schulmann. 'Listen carefully. Our story is she fell and banged her head. You were heavily intoxicated and in shock but still found from somewhere the ability to ring down to reception for an ambulance. Why if you were guilty of anything would you do that? No it's a perfect cover story. Trust me, we'll be back home in days.'

'It's good but that cop will never go for it David. He's got the hots for me.'

'Ah fuck him,' says Schulmann, with a dramatic wave of his hand. 'He's nothing but a mouth with a badge. I have dealt with cops like this all my working life. Trust me your father has had these leeches on his trail for thirty years. It's the limelight. The name attracts them. This limey is no different. Remember you are a Lansky, he's a fucking nobody in a city nobody knows or gives a shit about.

Whereas you my boy are a prince of New York City and a king in waiting. You are a better man.

Now let's get working on this story.'

Schulmann has decided not to tell Lansky that Sara was the girlfriend of local gangster Harry Taylor. He feels it worthless, for if Taylor even hints at taking revenge, Schulmann has instructed Bruno Gianelli to kill him.

Inspector Collins is back in his office when there's a knock at the door, and fellow detective Henry Manning enters after returning from the hospital. 'Hello George, hell of a night.'

'How's the girl'?

Manning sits down opposite. 'Not good. The surgeon says the next forty-eight hours are crucial.'

Collins shakes his head. 'Lansky's lawyer has just arrived from London and appears a real slippery piece of work.'

We have another problem regarding Sara O'Farrell,' replies Manning.

'Which is?'

'Turns out she is the secret girlfriend of Harry Taylor. I met him at the hospital and he's screaming blue murder. Already the word is out that the only way this yank is leaving Manchester is in a coffin. '

'Oh Christ this is just what we need, 'sighs Collins. 'A fucking gang war with the Mafia. You two go back years, can't you talk to him'?

'I'll try but he's really upset over the girl.'

'Well keep an eye on him. I'll have a word with Paddy Mullen. See if he can knock some sense into Taylor.'

Collins stands and starts to put on his jacket. 'Meanwhile I've been invited up to Hyde police station to sit in on an interview with the murder suspect Ian Brady.'

A startled Manning is clearly surprised at this news. 'How the bloody hell has that come about'?

'Guilty conscience I should think Henry. Before Tommy Butler went back to London he pointed out Brady from the files and said then he should be pulled in. Anyway I sent word to the investigative unit but never got a response. That's until about twenty minutes ago when they rang and asked if I'd consider listening to what this Brady has to say for himself.'

In the meantime, whilst I'm up in the hills, I want you to concentrate on keeping Harry Taylor calm.'

'I'm on it guv,' replies Manning. Whilst secretly already contemplating how he can help his hidden employer take his revenge against the yank. Manning makes more money working for Taylor in a month than what he earns in a year as a detective. His loyalty, albeit monetary is to him.

DODGE CITY WITH RAIN

Sixty-three years old Meyer Lansky is the type of man who likes to hear bad news straight away so he can act on it. The telephone call informing of his son Paul's arrest in Manchester England has left him fuming, but also extremely worried. A Father's love exceeds all feelings of disappointment and shame, and all Lansky efforts are now being put into getting his boy home.

Sat in his spacious New York office overlooking the Manhattan bridge, Lansky is surrounded by his closest aides and advisors. He is asking for ideas. An old friend who has been by his side for forty years, Mori Weiss, is first to talk.

'I have spoken to the Kray twins in London, just ten minutes ago Meyer. If we can arrange bail for Paul, they promise to have him out of England on a private plane within twelve hours. One that takes him to Holland where he then boards another direct to Canada. From there we pick him up.'

Lansky has listened intently to Mori. He is not impressed.
'No Mori, tell the boys I appreciated their offer and won't forget it, but I don't want my boy living on the run for the rest of his life. I need whatever these charges are against him to go away. Even if I have to go over there myself to sort this mess out, I'm prepared to do so. What is the name of that god damned place again'?

'Manchester,' answers Luigi Manola. A hotshot twenty-nine year old Italian lawyer who Lansky has high hopes for. 'It's in the provinces of northern England. From what I'm told imagine Dodge City with endless rain and you have it.'

'Do we know anyone in this Manchester'?
The six men present all look at each other, before Lansky's dapper thirty-four year old consigliore, Jakub Goldman speaks up. 'There is somebody Meyer. A long shot but maybe worth a try. He's a second cousin of Charlie Luciano, may he rest in peace.'

Lansky's best friend died three years from a heart attack in Naples. Not a day goes by when he does not think about him.

'Who is he'? asks Lansky.
'Salvatore Rea,' replies Goldman. He fronts a funeral service but Rea is one of the biggest operators in smuggled good over there. He has contacts across Italy and here in New York. Rea is a good man. He flies straight and could well be worth contacting.'

'Ah Sicilians,' exclaims Lansky. 'You all know I loved Charlie like a brother, but why is it with them everything always results in blood and bullets? Keep Rea on hold until further notice Jakub. Let's see how events evolve with Paul before making any decision. But let me be very clear on this gentleman, so there can be no misunderstanding. I swear to you, Paul is not going to be allowed to rot in an English jail.

Whatever it takes or cost I want my boy back.'

DEVIL IN THE DETAIL

Collins' car pulls up outside Hyde police station. Around him there is bedlam with reporters and television camera crews camped out waiting for news. He goes inside. Immediately Collins is spotted by chief Detective Joe Mounsey. The two men warmly shake hands.

'Congratulations Joe, if it had to be anyone who caught this bastard, I'm so glad it was you. What about the girl'?

'Myra Hindley,' replies Mounsey. 'We haven't got enough to hold her at the moment, but she's guilty as sin George. As for Brady, this is one serious and clever, sick bastard. I've never come across anyone like him. He's already trying to blame it on the kid who phoned the murder in. A one David Smith. A seventeen-year old local lad.

He's no angel by a long stretch, and Brady claims he was in on it. But me? I'm not so sure. Smith and his girlfriend, Hindley's sister Maureen, were a pair of nervous wrecks when we picked them up this morning. No, Smith is no killer. It's the other two, I'm convinced of it.

And I want you in there when I interview Brady again.'

'Why Joe'? I mean this is not my patch old mate. That fact has been made pretty clear to me by the boys in charge up here.'

'Because I owe you George. And Tommy Butler too. Fucking in-house politics has got in the way in a manner I never dreamt possible during the last year or so. I'm ashamed and embarrassed. The pressure to get results from above has caused a lot of people involved in the missing children cases to get edgy.

The boss in charge, Chief Inspector Benfield is screaming at people for results. The Brady file you sent became part of that. Stuff got missed because we were jumping all over the fucking place in every wrong direction.

Brady's simply sat on somebody's desk in a never ending pile of other suspects. It was never nothing sinister, just sloppy police work. These are not excuses George, just the truth. I'm sorry.'

'Fair enough Joe,' replies Collins. 'I'll square it with Butler. Now let's go and speak to Brady.'

Mounsey and Collins enter the interview room. A lone, uniformed constable stands guard over a man sat at a small, wooden table, staring into space. A thin, dark haired figure, whose eyes seemingly dead, suddenly flick into life when the two plain clothes detectives come into his sight.'

They both sit opposite Brady who smiles towards them.

'Hello again Mr Mounsey, 'he says with a thick Scottish Glaswegian brogue. 'Who's your new friend'?

'This is Detective Inspector George Collins of Manchester Police. He'd like to ask you a few questions.'

'Good afternoon Mr Collins. Have you come up to see what all the fuss is about'?

Collins ignore this. 'Why'd you kill Edward Evans, Brady'?

'I didn't Mr Collins. It was all an accident that got out of control. Ask Smith. He is who you should be accusing.'

'But you do admit to hitting him with the axe'?

'Only in self-defence. Like I say, things went a little mad. I had no choice.'

Collins meets Brady's gaze. 'I don't believe a word. You are lying through your teeth.'

'What are you a fucking psychic'? laughs Brady.

'No,' replies Collins. 'I'm a copper and a bloody good one. I've been around a little and I have dealt with more murderers than you've had fucking hot dinners. Men who believe they are not just above the law, but God also. Men like you Brady. Messed up fuckers.

I can see the signs. Little give aways. Like now, you are sweating.'

A tiny drop of perspiration falls down Brady's face. He wipes it away and clenches his hands tight together on the table. 'I'll say again. Ask David Smith.'

Collins goes quiet for a full minute. Preferring instead to simply stare at Brady.

Finally he smiles. 'I'm going to throw some names at you. See if you recognise them'?

'Pauline Reade'?

Brady says nothing.

'John Kilbride'?

Silence.

'Keith Bennett'?

Again his features remain rigid.

'Lesley Anne Downing'?

The merest hint of a smile comes to Brady's lips. 'I do read the papers Mr Collins. Very sad. All a terrible shame how they've all just vanished into thin air. Especially the young girl.'

'So you don't know where they are then'? asks Collins.

Brady shakes his head and starts to light up a cigarette from a pack in front of him on the table. He takes a puff and blows smoke rings in Collins' direction.

'Not my fucking doing Mr Collins.'

'Fucking deliver me from evil,' answers Collins. 'I think you know more than what you are letting on. That you killed those kids and are now playing a sick game.'

'We are going to turn that house upside down Brady,' rages Mounsey.

Forensics are all over it like a fucking rash. The devil is in the fucking detail and we'll find something.

And when we do.....'

'Admit it and make things a little easier for yourself,' adds Collins. 'Tell us where they are buried'?

'What are you a fucking double act,?' Grins Brady. 'I've already, said not my doing'?

Collins pushes his chair away and stands up. He has his back to Brady.

'Maybe Myra might be a little more forthcoming.' Collins turns around.

'Was she in on it? The two of you together would have made it so much fucking easier to entice those kids.'

'You have nothing on Myra, she's innocent. I'll repeat again. Ask fucking Smith.'

'You and her are like a pair of parrots,' snaps Mounsey. 'It's all fucking rehearsed. Ask Smith, ask Smith. Well Dave Smith was released an hour ago. You are the one Brady. And Myra. We know you murdered Evans in cold blood and I deeply suspect he is one of many.'

'Scum like you think they are infallible, says Collins. 'Error proof. Well welcome to the real world lad. Four small walls and a lifetime of shit in your food and piss in your drinks awaits.'

Collins winks at him. 'Enjoy lowlife.'

The two Inspectors prepare to leave, only for Brady to call after them.

'Thank you for coming Mr Collins. It's been a pleasure to make your acquaintance.'

Brady's hand shakes badly as he puts his cigarette out in an ash tray.

Collins notices this and smiles. 'The mask drops Brady and the signs show.

The little give aways......Face facts, you are like an open fucking book.'

That said both men leave the room and shut the door behind them.

Once outside Collins punches the wall with his fist. 'Goddammit Butler was right, he's as guilty as sin. You have to nail this bastard over the others Joe. Because he knows.'

Mounsey nods. 'Trust me once forensics have swept the house you'll be the first to know. Why don't you hang around for a day or so? I can fix it with the suits. Believe me we owe you. They'll not fucking say no again.'

Collins smiles but shakes his head. 'Can't do mate, we have big trouble brewing on the home front. But keep me informed on events. Soon as this is all sorted, I'd love to get back involved.'

Mounsey holds out his hand and Collins accepts. 'Take it easy George. Give my love to the city dwellers.'

SPECIAL RELATIONSHIP

'Bail denied'? exclaims Paul Lansky. 'What the fuck do you mean David, bail denied? I have to get out of here, it's driving me crazy.' David Schulmann's attempts to have Lansky released on bail have been refused and in his holding cell at Bootle Street station, the young man slumps down miserably on his bunk with head in hands.

'Be patient Paul, we are working on it. The courts here will not let you out of their sights in case anything happens with the girl. She pulls through you are out of this dump.'

A clearly worried Lansky looks up. 'And if she doesn't'?

'Well then we stick to our story whatever they throw at us.'

'How has my Father taken all this'?

'You are his son. He's working heaven and earth to get you home. All we need is for you to stay calm and keep to the script we worked on. Agreed'?

'Agreed,' sighs Lansky.

'Good boy' smiles Schulmann. 'Now I have to go.'

'Where'?

'Myself, George and Bruno are off to mend bridges with Paddy Mullen. Apparently you two had a bit of a run in last night before all hell broke loose'?

Lansky appears horrified. 'My god I had forgotten all about that.'
Schulmann shakes his head. 'Take my advice. Once this is over stay
off the booze. It's going to be the death of you.'
He ruffles Lansky's hair before leaving the cell.

Outside in the corridor waiting for him are Bruno Gianelli and
George Raft. The latter busy signing more autographs for starstruck
police officers crowding around him.
'Are you famous sir'? asks a young constable of Gianelli. Raft
laughs out loud on hearing this. 'Are you serious'? he says to the
constable. 'This man here is the legend who once stared down Al
Capone. Old Scarface himself would not mess with Bruno Gianelli.'
Suddenly it's an embarrassed Gianelli's autograph they all want!
Into the fray walks David Schulmann.'If you two have quite
finished we have work to do.' A sheepish Gianelli and Raft make
their excuses to the admirers and stroll off behind Schulmann.

At Paddy Mullen's office in the Cromford club, Tommy Keenan
has just finished explaining the previous night's events in full to
Mullen. He listens on open mouthed, unable to believe what he is
hearing.
'Our first problem is to throw a cold towel over Harry Collins and
damp him down. The last thing we need is Harry going all sawn-off
crazy and blowing a dozen holes in our troublesome friend from
across the ocean.'
'I've sent Eric to the hospital to keep an eye on the girl,' replies
Tommy. 'He'll ring soon as there is any updates. Oh and there is
something else I forgot to tell you'?
Mullen eyes Tommy rather worryingly. 'Don't tell me, the
Russians have landed in Salford and are heading our way as we
speak'?
Tommy laughs. 'No chance. They'd never get past the Brady
brothers. It's in regards to the yanks. They are coming over later for
peace talks. You've already met Bruno, the other two are a mystery.
But he speaks highly of them, so hopefully no more hot heads.'
There is a knock at the door and club head barman Frank Lloyd
enters.
'Excuse me Mr Mullen, I have three American gentlemen downstairs
in reception. They say you are expecting them.'

Do they have machine guns'? Tommy tries to stifle his laughter.

'Excuse me'? exclaims Lloyd.

'Oh it doesn't matter Frank,' smiles Mullen. 'Could you show them up please.'

'Yes sir,' replies a confused Lloyd. 'Not really sure what has just gone on.

'Paddy do me a favour, go easy on them eh'? They are a long way from home and going off Gianelli's reaction in the Fallen Nun last night, Manchester is the Wizard of Oz. Another world.'

'Why on earth did you take him in there'? asks a shocked Mullen. 'It's a freak circus.'

'I wanted to shock him' replies a smiling Tommy. 'Showing off a little I suppose.'

'Keenan you have serious problems. Hopefully this baby has not just got the looks of its' mother but her brains also.'

Suddenly another knock on the door and Frank Lloyd re-enters. 'Your guests Mr Mullen.' He motions the three Americans inside.

Mullen stands to greet them and Gianelli does the introductions.

'Mr Raft, I'm a huge fan,' says Mullen

'He is as well George' grins Tommy. 'Paddy models himself on you.' Mullen momentarily glares at Tommy, but then smiles. He ushers the men to sit down.

'Gentlemen, tonight I'd like to offer you dinner on the house here at the Cromford Club.'

'That's very kind of you Mr Mullen' replies David Schulmann.

'Thank you Paddy' adds Raft. May I call you Paddy'?

'It would be an honour George.'

Gianelli speaks up. 'About last night. I'd like to apologise for my young friend.'

He was drunk and did ......'

Mullen puts up a hand to stop Gianelli in mid flow. 'Bruno please, there is absolutely no need. It's already forgotten. But I still must stress that the Cromford is not up for discussion.'

'We would not insult you by mentioning it again Paddy,' adds Schulmann.

'Now can we get down to the matter in hand. Paul Lansky.'

'Of course, go ahead.'

I've spoken to Paul and he's adamant that he didn't attack the girl. She simply fell when there was a misunderstanding and banged her head on the bathroom door. Most unfortunate,

but so far as my client is concerned he is a hundred per cent innocent of committing any crime.'

'Have you mentioned this particular fairy tale to the cops'? replies Tommy.

'I'd pay good money to see George Collins' face when he hears this.'

I take it Collins is the hard ass detective I briefly encountered this morning at the station'? answers Schulmann.

'Hard ass sums George up,' smiles Mullen. 'I'd say that's him.'

'Well then,' exclaim Schulmann. 'It appears we have identified the main thorn in our side.'

'Oh no,' replies Tommy. 'The biggest problem Lansky has is a man called Harry Taylor who is currently planning, the last time I heard, to send him to kingdom come. If I was you I'd concentrate on placating Harry and pray the girl lives.

Otherwise'?

I'm well aware of Taylor and his plans Mr Keenan, I can assure you we have plans in place to deal with him, or any other locals who fancy making a name for themselves off the back of the Lansky name. Schulmann stares over at Gianelli.

No disrespect Mr Schulmann,' replies Mullen. But this is Manchester not New York. Here you are hopelessly outgunned. And I'll not tolerate by either Taylor or yourself any bloodshed in this city. There has been enough lately. I won't stomach anymore.'

He motions over to Tommy. 'Set up a meeting with Harry. Let's try and nip this in the bud.'

'Will do' replies Tommy. He nods over to Gianelli before leaving the room.

'Mind how you go Bruno. Look after yourself.' Gianelli acknowledges, for he likes this Limey. A class act.

Once Tommy has left the room, Mullen turns to address the Americans. He had no desire for Tommy to hear this. 'Right gentlemen, here's how it's going to be. If Sara O'Farrell recovers, then I promise you, I'll move heaven and earth to ensure Paul Lansky is sneaked out of the country to any destination you require. Believe me we have form on this. However, God forbid the girl dies, then all thoughts turn to making sure your boy's story has some credence. Because I don't believe a word of it. And I'm quite certain none of you do either.'

Gianelli lowers his head and Mullen notices this.

'Whether we believe or not is irrelevant, answers Schulmann. It's the police we have to convince. And specifically your friend Collins.'

Mullen says nothing. He goes to light a cigarette and inhales.

Schulmann is smiling. He continues. 'I'm correct then. He is a friend of yours, yes'?

An acquaintance,' replies Mullen. 'Sometime out mutual interests overlap and we
co-operate.'

'And do you think you could possibly co-operate on our problem. Make use of this special relationship'? asks Schulmann.

'I can mention it,' replies Mullen. 'But no promises.'

'None expected. I'm sure you'll do what's right Mr Mullen. And let me assure you when this is all over Meyer Lansky is a man who appreciates his friends. Especially those who go that extra mile for him.'

Mullen is far from comfortable with all that's going on. He understands some things must be done to ensure the status quo in this city continues unabated. If it means him having to do a deal to get the scumbag Lansky out of his and Manchester's hair then so be it.

Patrick John Mullen will live with it on his conscience.

NO GUNS, NO KNIVES, JUST WORDS

The next day, mid-morning George Collins steps one foot into Bootle Street Police Station and is immediately accosted by a young constable who hands him a piece of paper.

Collins reads it and a huge smile appears on his face. 'Thank you son. Great news.' The note was to tell him that Sara O'Farrell has awoken from her coma and is officially out of danger.

Collins decides to go and see Paul Lansky, only to be shocked when on reaching his cell he finds it empty. 'Where's the fucking yank'? he asks the officer on duty.

'Lansky was allowed to go an hour ago Sir. Soon as it broke that the girl was going to be okay, his lawyer arrived with the necessary paperwork and he was out. Apparently word arrived from the hospital she was not pressing charges and that was it.'

'What just like that. Who did Sara speak to'?

'Detective Manning sir. She's adamant it was an accident.'

Collins shakes his head. He suddenly remembers Manning's words about Harry Taylor and races into the duty room. Inside are two plain clothes officers typing away. They both look up on him entering. 'I need two of you on Paul Lansky permanent until he leaves this city.

Get your arses round to the Portland now.' Detectives Wally Lambert and Stuart McCarthy immediately grab their jackets and head off.

Collins is left alone. Something his wife and so many others said about the Americans during the Second World War when stationed on British soil suddenly strikes a chord with him. 'Over sexed, over paid and fucking over here.'

'Couldn't agree more,' he says quietly to himself.

Through Manning, Harry Taylor has been informed Sara is well and that she won't be pressing charges. He, immediately with Billy Tarr, heads to see her. On arrival at Sara's bedside the over-riding feeling is one of relief. He kisses her gently on a battered and bruised cheek.

'Welcome back girl. You gave me quite a scare for a while.'

Sara tries to smile, but struggles. Her face covered in wires and bandages.

She speaks almost in a whisper. 'I'm sorry Harry. I didn't want to cause you any fuss.'

'Tell me, why are you not pressing charges against that bastard Lansky'?

'I know who he is,' she replies. 'The Mafia. Who his Father is. I don't want any trouble. I just want all this to go away. Please don't do anything stupid for my sakes.'

She starts to cry and Taylor holds her hand.

'Everything is going to be alright. Trust me Sara, I'll look after you. You are not on your own no more.' He kisses her again on the forehead. 'Now try and get some rest, I'll be back in tonight to see you.'

The two men head off out the room.

'So what do you want to do'? asks Tarr.

'A part of me still wants him to pay for what he did to Sara. You know as well as I do that bastard could have easily killed her.'

'But it makes no sense to hit him now Harry.'

Maybe not,' replies Taylor. 'But I'd still like five minutes alone, just to let him know what I think of him.'

Tarr smiles. 'Okay then, so let's do it.' But no guns, no knives, just words'?

Taylors grins wide at his best friend. 'I promise. No guns, no knives, just words.'

Paul Lansky is sat drinking champagne on the top floor of the Portland hotel in their finest suite. Also present are Bruno Gianelli, George Raft and David Schulmann. Lansky is in jubilant mood. I can't believe that bitch never pressed charges.'

He refills everybody's glass. 'Hey have we got another bottle anywhere'? Lansky looks around and sees one and immediately goes to open it.

'Don't you think you should go a little easy on the booze Paul'? asks Gianelli.

'Oh come on Bruno, I'm celebrating. I just got a result here.'

'You need to ring your father,' says Schulmann. 'He'll be waiting for your call.'

What and get my fucking butt handed me on a plate David'? I'll speak to him later. Let me relax first. I've had a rough time.'

He raises his glass. 'To British justice.'

The others rather half-heartedly do similar. Gianelli then puts his down. 'I have to go out for a while.'

With that said, he is gone through the door.

'What the fuck is wrong with him'? exclaims Lansky.

Gianelli makes the short journey through Piccadilly Gardens to the Cromford Club. He needs to speak to Paddy Mullen. A thought in his head has been driving him mad. On arrival Gianelli is ushered inside where Mullen is stood at the bar in the empty main suite. He is filling out a betting slip. Mullen approaches.

'Bruno' says Mullen. 'Good to see you. He shows him the slip. 'Just doing my bit to help out the bookies in their old age.'

Gianelli grins. 'I'm a fan of the horses myself. Sadly they are not so keen on me.'

What can I do for you son'?

'I need to ask you something Paddy. Did you take care of the girl and get her to drop the charges'?

Mullen smiles. 'Let me tell you something. When I bet on the horses I always back favourites. That way my odds of winning are increased no end. Whereas others prefer to take a risk in the hope their foolhardy bravery will reap them greater rewards. Dark horses they call them, because you don't see them coming. Well I like to operate in the light with my angles covered and I don't like surprises. And to answer your question.

Yes I paid the girl off. Fifty grand.

A sure thing. I win you, you win, Manchester wins and the problem goes away. However I'd appreciate it Bruno, if you kept this under your hat. No need for the world to know. Let's just call it a result.'

'A result,' repeats Gianelli. 'That's what young Lansky was saying when I left him. He's already half-drunk again. This piece of dirt I work for is not a patch on his father. And if I'm truly honest Paddy, part of me was wishing he'd get his comeuppance over this.'

'Difficult in your line of work to have a conscience Bruno. Maybe you should consider getting out'?

Gianelli shakes his head 'This is not the boy scouts my friend. This is *Cosa Nostra*. Once in, never out. Hey, believe me I'm no angel. Far from it. In this business we all walk around with the mark of Cain upon us. But when I look at this kid? Hell, Paul poisons everything he touches and it's my damned mission in life to keep him alive.

Gianelli smiles. 'Now how about those apples'?

Mullen leans over behind the bar and produces a bottle of Scotch whisky. 'We all have to live with the hand that fate dealt us my American friend. But that doesn't mean we have to like it. Now what says me and you share a glass or two and drink to sure things'?

'I'd like that very much Paddy,' smiles Gianelli. 'And what you said about dark horses and unsuspecting forces? It reminds me of a sad aspect of my job. That when your time is up the button is always pressed by someone close. For the saddest thing about betrayal is that it never comes from your enemies.'

Through the doors of the Portland hotel steps Harry Taylor and Billy Tarr. One phone call from Manning has told them the room and floor of where Paul Lansky is staying. Manning has moved to pull Lambert and McCarthy away from guarding the Americans under the precipice of a suspected robbery in nearby Oldham Street.

Now for Harry Taylor it's payback time and they head for the lift. 'Remember what we spoke about Harry,' says Tarr.
'Just words.'
Taylor smiles. 'Don't worry Billy. I have been saving this one up.'
The two men reach the suite and Tarr knocks on. Schulmann appears.
'Can I help you gentlemen'?
'Yes,' replies Taylor. 'I'd like a word with Paul Lansky.' With that Tarr kicks open the door and they storm in. George Raft goes to confront them.
'Get the fuck out of here before you make me lose my cool.'
At first the two men cannot believe their eyes. Taylor stares in shock at Tarr, who is fighting hard to keep from grinning. 'Calm down George,' smiles Taylor. 'This is not the movies. I just want a word with Paul over there.' He points towards Lansky, who stands petrified, ten yards away.
Taylor walks over to him. 'Me and you need to have a little talk.'
Lansky backs away until against the wall. He looks scared. All eyes in the room are upon him as Taylor continues. 'The Mafia'? He laughs. 'When I was a kid my old man used to take me to see the flicks on Stretford Road to see all the gangster movies. You was in most of them George. You and James Cagney. No offence old son, but Cagney was my Dad's favourite. And mine as well.

I would sit there listening to the click of the projector and then hear the reel of the film humming such a sweet tune. A hush would descend over the decrepit old theatre and on the screen a picture would flicker into life. For a couple of hours I'd sit mesmerised watching the machine gun fights and the beautiful girls, or dames, as you yanks insisted on calling them. I'd imagine I was a bootlegger in Chicago or a Mob boss in New York.

Because these men had style and class They stood for something. Oh they were bad, they were outlaws, but hey, where is the fun in being good? Nobody ever mentioned the word but we knew it. The Mafia. *Cosa Nostra*. *Lucky* Luciano, Al Capone, *Bugsy* Siegel and

Meyer Lansky…. And then there is you. A fucking stain on my childhood memories and a disgrace to your Father's name.'

Lansky daren't move for fear of upsetting this mad Limey more. 'Now you've hurt somebody who I care a lot about. Never mind the fact she claims it was an accident. I know and everybody in this room knows you were out of order. I'd say a prayer boy because today, believe it or not is the luckiest day of your whole miserable fucking life, because this girl is going to be okay.

If, God forbid she hadn't woken up, then your Father would now be mourning a son, instead of simply continuing having to put up with an idiot, who believes his name alone give him freedom to hurt and bully women. So time to go home Paul Lansky, because here in this city there remains a line we don't cross.

And you have fucking crossed it.'

Taylor looks across to Schulmann and Raft. 'Sorry to have burst in on you like this gents, but these words just had to be said.' He nods towards Billy Tarr. 'Come on Bill, time to go home.' They head for the door when suddenly Taylor stops and walks back towards Raft.

'Excuse me George, could I possibly have an autograph. He scrambles around to find a pen and piece of paper on a nearby table.

'Could you sign it To Harry Taylor'?

'Sure can Harry,' smiles Raft. He writes down:

To Harry Taylor from George Raft. One gangster to another

Raft hands the paper over to Taylor, who reads and passes to Tarr.

'Bloody hell,' grins Taylor. 'Don't give up your day job George.'

The two men step out of the suite and shut the door. From inside the sound of them laughing loud is heard. A shamefaced Lansky stands with head bowed, unable to look anybody in the face. Whilst Schulmann goes to console an embarrassed and crestfallen Raft.

'Don't let the limeys upset you George. We think you're one of us and that's all what counts………'

As Taylor and Tarr walk through the hotel foyer, Bruno Gianelli strolls past them. Suddenly from Taylor's suit pocket the piece of paper autographed by George Raft slips and drops to the floor. Spotted by Gianelli he picks it up.

'Hey mister you dropped something.'

Taylor turns around. He walks back towards Gianelli, who hands it over.

'Thanks friend.'

'No problem,' smiles Gianelli, who then strides off towards the lift, content after his chat with Mullen that all their problems are over. And finally they can go home.

Two days later Paul Lansky, Bruno Gianelli, David Schulmann and George Raft arrive back in New York, and a black stretch limousine is waiting outside *JFK* airport, to take them to their Godfather. All four men appear pensive, but none more than Paul Lansky. On arrival his father's consigliore Jakub Goldman greets them.

'The Don is in his office and he's pissed. You best have some answers.'

They go up.

Goldman enters first, to be followed rather sheepishly by the others. Meyer is sat at his desk. Obviously fuming. He rises and comes to face them. Meyer stands inches from his son. He slaps him hard across the face and Paul cannot meet his eyes.

'If I ever see you drinking anything stronger than orange juice again, I swear on your grandmother's soul, I'll beat you within an inch of your life. Is that understood'?

Yes sir.'

He then kisses him on the forehead. 'Now get out of my sight. Go home and apologise to your Mother. She's been crying for a week.' He points toward Gianelli.

'Bruno you go with him.' Paul swiftly makes a beeline for the door. He leaves it half open for Gianelli to follow and Lansky goes back to his desk.

'Sit gentlemen.' Schulmann and Raft pull up chairs as ordered and prepare for the inquisition. Lansky begins. 'So who do I blame for this mess that nearly saw me lose my boy? Is it our friend who has just left the room'?

The silence is deafening from the two men and in that moment Bruno Gianelli's fate is sealed. Okay then,' says Meyer. 'I don't want to see his face again.'

Three days later Bruno Gianelli was shot to death in his apartment by two unknown gunmen.

ALL THE KING'S MEN

Something is troubling George Collins. He has been talking to detectives Lambert and McCarthy. Both men are unhappy with being pulled off the Portland hotel job looking after the Americans, to be sent on a wild goose chase by fellow detective Manning. It didn't ring true with them. That and the fact it became known soon after Harry Taylor and Billy Tarr had entered the hotel at the time they were sent away. Collins smells a rat and calls Henry Manning into his office.

Manning sits facing Collins at his desk. 'What can I do for you boss'?

'What happened the other day when you pulled Lambert and McCarthy off the yanks for some fucking ridiculous robbery on Oldham Street'?

'I got a call at the last moment off a snitch. You know how it is. Some you win some you lose.'

'What was the name of this snitch'?

Manning twitches uncomfortably in his chair.

'Well is it really important George? I fucked up, I can see that. It won't happen again.'

'I want the name Henry'?

'George come on....'

Collins shouts loud. 'Give me the fucking name'?

'Okay, okay,' replies a shaken Manning. 'It was Harry the mouth.'

'Harry the fucking mouth'? replies a quizzical Collins. 'He died of a heart attack three months ago. What the hell is going on Henry. Who are you working for'?

'What are you talking about? I'm a copper, I work for you.'

'And who else have you thrown your hat in with'?

'Nobody, I swear.'

An exasperated Collins let's rip. 'I'm leaving town for a week to help out with the Hyde and Ashton boys. That should give you time to search your conscience and to phone around to get yourself another job. Because when I come back, I want your resignation letter on my desk, Do it, or so help me God I'll make it my ambition in life to put you behind fucking bars.

You get this one chance to walk away because you have a wife and four kids at home. Otherwise I would take your badge off you now and supplant it up your fucking bent arse. Now tell me who have you been working for'?

…………'Harry Taylor.'

'Good, now fuck off out of my face and out of my office.'

Manning stands to leave, but just as he reaches the door Collins calls out.

'Henry.'

He turns around.

Collins stares directly at him and very softly declares. 'Just for the record you have broken my fucking heart.'

With tears in his eyes Manning steps out of Collin's office.

He leans back in his chair. Genuinely shaken and needing a drink.

The phone starts to ring.

'George Collins.'

'George, Paddy Mullen.'

'What can I do for you Paddy'?

'It's more what I can do for you George. I'm speaking for everybody when I say if there's anything we can do Anything at all to help out with those missing kids, you only have to ask.'

'Thanks Paddy, I appreciate that and will keep it in mind.'

'Some things go beyond what is the law and this is beyond evil. There's a code word agreed by everybody. *All the kings' men.* You ring us at any time of day and night and we are at your command.'

'Thanks Paddy. Let's hope we can nail this bastard Brady and forensics do their job in the house.'

'I hope so, speak soon.'

The phone goes down.

Collins is lost for words. He thinks, this of all days when one of his own has betrayed him, the Manchester underworld offer themselves on a plate for the missing kids.

'Only in fucking Manchester,' he smiles and says quietly to himself.

'Only in my city.'

COMMUNION

Hyde Police Station: 15th October 1965: 'We pulled Myra Hindley in this morning. This is off the scale George, it really is.' Chief Detective Joe Mounsey is bringing Inspector George Collins up to date. 'We've found a large number of photographs in the house. Turns out our Ian Brady fancied himself as an amateur photographer, amongst other things. They show both him and Hindley posing up on the moors.'

Mounsey shows Collins the Polaroids.

One in particular catches his eye. Myra Hindley on one knee staring down at the earth. 'Dancing on the graves of the dead,' says Collins, almost under his breath. Another has Brady doing similar.

'We also found an old exercise book full of Brady's scribbling. Lists and lists of names. But there was one that screamed out at us when going through it. That of John Kilbride's. I spoke to Dave Smith yesterday. He and his wife have been up there with them for picnics. I was on the Moors yesterday with Dave and Maureen trying to see if they could point out the exact locations. They gave us something to go on, but not much.

I have lads up there digging now. Not enough, futile some might say, but we have to try.

I've become all but convinced the killing of Evans was a ritual of passage to see if they could trust Smith into joining them. That the kid panicked and came in is, I suppose a blessing. He also told us they disposed of two suitcases full of evidence. Smith overheard them talking about *'missing luggage.'* He also claimed that Brady had a thing for *'Railway stations,'* so we are combing through the locals, and those from here to Blackpool with a fine toothbrush as well. Find these suitcases and hopefully inside will be the answers to all our prayers.

Or should that be fucking nightmares'?

Collins continues looking at the polaroids. 'Do we know where these were taken'?

'Up near Woodhead pass is our best guess. We also found a manuscript full of abbreviations. It's like an A-Z of how to commit the perfect murder and get away with it. They write about cleaning the getaway car from top to bottom, disposing of the bodies and so on. Now Brady can't drive, but a lollypop if you guess who can'?

'Hindley,' replies Collins.

Mounsey smiles. 'Give that man a cigar. Exactly, she's in this up to her neck, I know it. Hindley is hard as fucking nails. Her favourite line about the Evans murder is.

'My version of events of that evening is exactly the same as Ian's.'
'How would you like a go at her George, see if you can chip away at the mask'?

'It would be my pleasure Joe,' answers Collins. Seemingly spellbound by the polaroid of Myra Hindley staring at what he's convinced is a grave.

'It would be my fucking pleasure.'

The two men are heading down a corridor towards the interview room when an excited voice exclaims loud from behind them. 'Mr Mounsey sir.' They turn around to see a uniformed constable racing towards them. 'What on earth is up Johnson'? asks Mounsey.

'Good news sir. He hands him the report. 'I've just taken a call off the British Transport police. They've found the suitcases at Manchester Central Station and are bringing them over now.'

'Good lad' smiles Mounsey, who ruffles Johnson's hair. He passes it over to Collins.

What say we hold fire on Hindley and wait until we find out what's in the suitcases'?

'Fine by me,' replies Collins.'

All are present in the small office as two tattered suitcases are brought in and placed on a table in the middle of the room. A blue and a brown one. Detectives Joe Mounsey and George Collins are joined by the following. Fifty-six year old, Chief Inspector, Arthur Benfield. Head of the criminal investigation into the missing children. Forty-seven year old chief Inspector, Brian Talbot. Local based. Another who like Mounsey has exhausted every sinew of his body in efforts to solve these cases. Also invited in by Benfield is thirty-six year old, Detective-Police woman, Margaret Campion. Everybody in this room thought they had witnessed all horrors possible in their time on the force.

Little did they know what was set to occur?

For a second nobody moves and then Benfield announces: 'Right let's get started.'

Immediately they crowd around as Mounsey opens one and Collins the other. The first item of notice is a cassette tape. Mounsey passes it over to Talbot. 'Do we have a tape recorder in the station'?

He nods. 'I'll go and get it.' Talbot leaves the room.

'Oh Jesus Christ,' exclaims Collins. He is staring in horror at a handful of Polaroids. They are pornographic photographs taken of a little girl, naked and with a scarf tied across her mouth, lying on a bed with her head to one side. Another of her praying and one showing her back to the camera with arms outstretched in a crucifixion pose. An ashen faced Collins passes them over to Mounsey who visibly wilts.

'Oh fucking hell no.'

He in turn hands them to Benfield. Campion leans in to look and her eyes immediately well up. Benfield very solemnly announces. 'I think we all agree that these pictures are of Lesley Ann Downey.' A devastated Collins, Mounsey and Campion nod their heads.

Suddenly the door opens and Talbot returns with a reel to reel machine. All eyes are upon him. He feels them burning in as Benfield hands him the Polaroids. For a second it does not register with Talbot, but then it is like a light going out in his eyes.

'The Fucking bastards.'

Mounsey take the machine off his shaken colleague and sets it up. He places the cassette into the machine and it crackles into life.........The detectives listen on in sheer unmitigated fear, anger and despair.

Thirteen minutes later it finishes and it feels as if hell has descended upon Hyde.

Margaret Campion has tears streaming down her face. 'Excuse me sir,' she sobs to Benfield, before racing swiftly out the door. Talbot moves to follow. 'I'll go and keep an eye on her.'

'Joe, I think now maybe a good time for me to go and speak to Hindley,' says Collins. Mounsey glances towards Benfield who nods his head in agreement.'

'Go now,' he replies. 'You two take her and leave Brady to me. I'm just in the fucking mood.'

Mounsey and Collins barge into the interview room shocking even the uniformed policeman standing guard over the prisoner. Dressed in a white blouse with a green cardigan around her shoulders, the peroxide blond, twenty-three year old Myra Hindley does not move so much as an eyeblink. She simply carries on smoking and stares in disdain at the new arrivals in the room.

'Do you believe in God Myra'? asks Collins. A heaven and a hell'?

'I did once, but Ian taught me we make our own paradise here on this earth.'

'And I suppose these are part of your fucking paradise,' replies Collins, as he throws down the polaroids of Lesley Ann Downey in front of her. Hindley tries to look away, but Collins leans across and puts them under her nose.

'We've just sat and listened to you and Brady torturing this poor innocent little girl for your own gratification. We heard you on the tape threatening to smack her in the mouth if she didn't obey Brady. She referred to you two as her Mummy and Daddy. Did you make Lesley Ann call you that, or was the poor child desperately searching to find a modicum of compassion in your rotten fucking heart'?

'We know you've murdered her Hindley,' says Mounsey. 'You and Brady. Together. And I also believe you've killed and buried the others up on the Moors somewhere. Pauline Reade, John kilbride, Keith Bennett. Saddleworth Moors are for you and him a private graveyard. A place where you can both go and mock the dead. Laugh at their graves and take pictures of them for posterity. Now tell me where Lesley Ann's body is? Show a little compassion for the families and give them something to hang their grief on.'

Hindley is looking at the polaroids. She picks up the one of Lesley Ann praying.

'Where was her God when she was praying for help'? replies Hindley. She kept calling for her Mum. Well what was she doing out so late on her own. What kind of Mother....'

A furious Collins cuts her short. 'Oh please don't you fucking dare.'

She goes quiet and lights another cigarette. One eye continually on the Polaroids. Her hands shaking. '

Collins continues. 'Now we have you banged to rights. Your voice is on the tape as is Brady's. God forgive me for saying this, but if you tell me where Lesley Ann is buried, I'll make sure it goes in your favour.'

'But then you are assuming I killed her.'
So was it Brady that did for Lesley Ann'? asks Mounsey.
'I never said that.'

'Oh come on Myra,' answers Collins. 'He's talking like a skylark and blaming you for everything. Brady claims you led him on. That it was you urging more all the time because you get off on it.'

For the first time Hindley's voices cracks a little. 'Ian would never say that. He loves me.'

'Love'! exclaims Mounsey. 'You don't know the meaning of the fucking word. What you did to that poor girl is beyond all human understanding.

I found this.'

Mounsey takes a key out of his pocket and places it on the table. 'This is the key to the left luggage lock up where you hid the suitcases, from which we found the tape. Do you remember where you hid it Myra'?

Hindley says nothing, but stares toward Mounsey with utter contempt.

'I found it in the back of your prayer book. You say you don't believe in God. And after what I heard on that tape? Well it makes me doubt my own faith also. How could any supreme being claiming to be all things love, let something so evil happened to somebody so young and innocent?

Catholics say that when you take communion it wipes away your sins. We confess to the priest. ''Lord I am not worthy but only say the word and I shall be healed.''

Well for you Hindley there are simply no words and no Communion. Because your poisoned soul is going to hell.

And I guarantee for you one does exists…...'

The two men are talking over a cup of tea in Mounsey's office. 'We desperately need to find those bodies George. Already there are a hundred and fifty officers searching the moors along with volunteers from the public. But Benfield can't allow or afford to let this go on indefinitely. Unless something turns up there's a real possibility they are going to get away with it.'

Where are you looking'? asks Collins.

'Two places. The A628 road near Woodhead and along the A635. A close neighbour of Hindley's and Brady's. Eleven-year old Pat Hodges was taken up there on several occasions. Obviously the girl was too close to home to murder. She has been able to point out several spots of interest and we are concentrating our resources there. The trouble is there are not enough men to cover the area. It's simply too vast. Bog-like and barren and there's a mist that descends so fast you cannot see in front of your own eyes.

It's like there are evil spirits up there colluding to prevent us finding anything.'

'Maybe I can help'?

'What do you know a good psychic to call the demons off'?

Collins smiles. 'Not a demon exactly. More all the king's men. Leave it with me Joe.'

George Collins arrives home in Sale, Manchester. It has just gone one in the morning and he shuts the front door quietly to ensure he doesn't wake his wife and two children. Collins goes into his living room and pours himself a large whisky and slumps exhaustedly into an armchair. His eyes settle on a photograph above the mantelpiece of a family portrait. Himself, wife Joanne and two daughters. Eleven-year old Angela and fourteen-year old Elizabeth. Only now does Collins notices that his youngest Angela, bears a startling resemblance to Lesley Ann Downey.

And then he breaks down in tears…..

Collins looks over to the telephone. He dries his eyes, finishes the drink and takes a deep breath.

It's time to ring the fallen angels.

THE EIGHTH DAY

Early next morning George Collins arrives upon Saddleworth Moor and already finds the area a mad hive of activity. Across the miserable, lifeless landscape shrouded in thick mist, lines of uniformed police officers, detectives and members of the public are stretched out with pitchforks, rakes and spades searching for any disturbance in the earth that might give ruse to a grave.

He spots Joe Mounsey, who is heading towards him with two cups of coffee.

Mounsey hands one over.

'Thanks Joe. A good turnout I see.' Collins points across at the mass of people combing the moors. 'Sadly not enough George. We have great will and heart but not enough bodies. A needle in a haystack doesn't do us justice.'

Suddenly a voice shouts down loud towards them from a police lookout upon a nearby hill. He is pointing at a long road leading from the direction of Manchester.

'Sir Look'! In the distance a convoy of seven coaches is fast approaching.

Mounsey looks on astonished.

'Who the bloody hell is this.'?

Collins smiles. 'All the King's men Joe.'

The coaches draw in and come to a halt. The doors open and out pours quite literally hundreds of men kitted out with long warm overcoats, wellingtons and digging tools.

'All right lads,' roars a voice. 'You know why we are here. Now let's go to work.'

The man in question walks over towards Mounsey and Collins.

'Good morning gentlemen. Mr Mullen sends his regards. Me and the boys are here for as long as you need us.'

Mounsey listens on astonished. 'Much obliged.' He is almost rendered speechless.

Collins points over to a uniformed Sergeant. 'Have a word with him son. The Sergeant will tell you where we need you most.'

The man grins wide and tips his peaked cap. 'Thank you Mr Collins.'

The two detectives watch on in silence as the Mancunian hordes crowd around the shell-shocked Sergeant.

'The poor sod is probably recognising familiar faces,' laughs Collins. 'I bet he's nicked half of them. I know I have.'

'So George,' says Mounsey. 'You are telling me that what we have here is the entire flock of the Mancunian underworld'?

'More or less,' smiles Collins. 'I was told whatever was needed in trying to find the kids just ring. What is it with this fucking city Joe? Everytime I think I know where I stand with that lot, they go and pull a stunt like this.'

This isn't normal villainy George. It's pure evil we are up against with Brady and Hindley. Business will resume in time and for seven days a week we can play cops and robbers again, but for the moment normal rules no longer apply.

For this is the eighth day mate.'

Mounsey puts an arm around Collins's shoulders. 'Come on, let's go and join the great unwashed and grab ourselves a pair of pitchforks.'

That night the body of Lesley Ann Downey was discovered and five days later the remains of John Kilbride was also found and identified by his clothing. On the 6th May 1965, after having deliberated for a little over two hours, a jury found Ian Brady guilty of all three murders and Hindley of Lesley Ann's and Evans. Brady was sentenced to three concurrent life sentences and Hindley was given two. Pauline Reade's body was found in 1985 upon the Moors whilst Keith Bennett's remains undiscovered.......

ACT FIVE
A VERY GOOD YEAR

LITTLE ANGEL

The young and pretty, blond haired nurse smiles wide at the two nervous looking men sat waiting in the hospital corridor. They quickly stand as she approaches.

'Congratulations Mr Keenan. You have a daughter. Both Mother and baby are doing fine. You can go in and see them now.'

For the first time in his life Tommy Keenan is genuinely stuck for words.

Paddy Mullen shakes his hand and embraces him. 'I'm really pleased for you son. Now get in there and say hello to the other new lady in your life.' He gently pushes him in the direction of the maternity ward. As Tommy walks off he suddenly turns around to face Mullen.

'You do know this makes you a grandad'?

Mullen smiles. 'Thanks lad, give Alison my love and regards.'

A nurse leads him towards the room where she lies exhausted on the bed with the baby in her arms. Tommy goes over and sits down next to them. He hugs Alison tight.

'You okay'?

'I'm fine'? she replies, and passes him their baby daughter.

Tommy cradles her tight in his arms. With eyes welling he speaks softly.

'Hello my little angel, how's your luck. Welcome to the world. Now I can't promise that when you are older and want to talk about dresses and make up and perfume, I'm going to listen. You best speak to your mum about that kind of stuff.

But if you ever need a hug or a fiver, maybe even a tip for the horses, then I'm definitely your man.' He kisses the baby ever so gently on the forehead and hands her back to Alison.

'So have you settled on a name'?

Alison smiles. 'Maureen.'

'Well Maureen it is then,' he replies. Tommy holds Maureen's tiny hand.

'Welcome to the family Maureen Alison Keenan. I promise you it's never going to be boring.'

ONE CHANCE LENNY

1966: Forty-six year old Lenny Foyle is one of Manchester's leading and most respected, not to say feared bookies. It takes a brave or foolish man to cross him. Those who do swiftly realise that behind the handsome features, charming smile and hundred pound Saville Row suits, is a ruthless businessman who does not take IOUs or prisoners. A gambling empire of thirty shops around Manchester have made Foyle a rich man amongst once equals.

Born into hardship and poverty in 1920's Collyhurst, he began as a teenager running errands for local bookies. A tuppence here, a penny there, a farthing earned and stashed away in an old whisky bottle for a brighter day. For Foyle swore from an early age the life of his parents was not for him. An Irish immigrant father, dead far too young through drink and a dead end job that killed his chest in the local chemical factory.

A mother so old before her time. Ravaged by the loss of two siblings in childhood and forced to queue for donations from the local church. Begging for scraps of food off strangers in the street to place on the kitchen table for her four remaining children.
Amidst the smoke of billowing chimneys, rat infested dwellings and factory horns sounding like sirens signalling work until you die,

Leonard Foyle vowed this was never going to be the way of things for him.
At eighteen, Foyle had saved and scrimped enough money together to buy shares in a betting shop, owned by a man eight years older called Patrick Mullen. The much more streetwise Mullen was a born operator and he took an instant liking to this young boy from his part of town, who like him was attempting to rise above the choking Mancunian smog to escape a life less than ordinary.

More a death sentence in despair from the day you were born.

They became inseparable. Foyle watched and learned from Mullen until he felt comfortable enough to go alone. When the time came the two parted amicably and an enduring friendship that has lasted thirty years continued unabated.

It took the insane ramblings and murderous actions of the mad Bavarian Corporal in 1939, to derail Lenny Foyle's rise from obscurity into a highly successful entrepreneur.
Twenty-year old Foyle was conscripted and thrown into world-wide carnage where his business acumen mattered little. As the bullets

flew and bombs dropped, Foyle saw action in the retreat from Dunkirk, North Africa and Italy.

He saw men, friends die, maimed and mentally destroyed. A good mate shot in the back for supposed cowardice in France by a young Lieutenant, when in fact he was searching for ammunition. A knife fight to the death at El Alamein, with one of Rommel's Afrika Corps soldiers. When the two men came face to face in a blinding dust storm. Foyle watching the light go out in the young German's eyes as his blade sunk deep. A medal for valour earned at Monte Cassino only coming about because a mad charge ordered by a drunken officer ensued in his entire platoon being all wiped out, except him.

Lenny Foyle learned only two things whilst in the uniform of his country. One was how to kill and that the establishment, whether it be superior officers, politicians or police, viewed him as inferior. He came to the conclusion in this life,

to truly succeed you live by your own rules and the rest of the world can,

for two better words.

Fuck off.

Come the war's end, Foyle threw himself back into the business of building a gambling empire with a fury left over from the blood stained sands of El Alamein, and the ravaged craters, deep slopes and killing grounds of Monte Cassino. He proved himself a ferocious but fair opponent in matters of business. Always prepared to offer a decent price when it came to buying up property for the betting shops.

Foyle earned a reputation as someone you can do business with but, if you valued your legs, or in more serious matters, your life, never dare to cross him. Lenny Foyle lived by one rule. Those who do get one chance to make things right. If not intensive care or the graveyard were viable options.

He became known as *'Once chance Lenny.'*

Soon the hard work came to fruition and Foyle wastes little time buying himself a lavish mansion-like home in Bowdon Cheshire. The raggedy boy from the dwellings was almost there. Fortunes blossomed but fame,

for which he cared nothing, found itself discarded like leaves in the wind.

News reporters in these times of austerity and hardship were desperate for information on this incredulous rag to riches story that was fit for heroes yet to be born.

But nothing was ever forthcoming, for Foyle despised all publicity. The world for him was a closed door. You could knock incessantly, but unless something extraordinary appeared through the keyhole, there was never an entry.

But then came a beautiful, young dark haired lady, whose eyes bore instant access to the heart and soul. The walls of Foyles' kingdom crumbled like a Sandcastle before crashing waves. And the boy from the Collyhurst dwellings committed the cardinal sin one makes when you fall in love. He let his guard down.

Salford born nineteen-year old Pauline Carter was working in one of the bookie shops when one day unannounced as he regular did, Foyle turned up. One glance at Pauline and he felt his heart melting inside him. A brief romance followed before wedding bells rang loud and Pauline entered the inner sanctum of Foyle's world. Foremost amongst the guests at Saint Patrick's church in Collyhurst were two men whom Foyle trusted like brothers. Paddy Mullen and the young Manchester United manager who was swiftly making a name for himself. Matt Busby.

As Foyle busied himself with maintaining and strengthening his empire, Pauline built a home life for the two. She gave birth to a little girl whom they named Susan. Life reached perfection two years later when Susan was joined by a brother. Foyle christened him Patrick Matthew after his two closest friends.

Now his empire had a male heir and this emboldened Foyle even further to expand the gambling business beyond the city limits into neighbouring towns. Only once did trouble flare. One of Foyle's employees was beaten up in a Preston high street and told.

'Fuck off back to Manchester.' A local bookie Trevor Morgan taking exception to this out of towner coming onto his patch.

However the brief fall out ended in mutual agreement that Foyle be allowed to open shops on Morgan's turf. This came around when he was handed the choice of gaining a competitor or losing much more. Foyle holding a pistol to the terrified Morgan's head undoubtedly making his decision easier to arrive at.

Further financial rewards came when in partnership with Mullen, he expanded into the hotel world to buy the Norbreck hotel in

Blackpool. As with anything these two men turned their hand to it proved a huge success. Life for Lenny Foyle and his expanding business empire and family appeared perfect, but in 1958, fate dealt him a helping hand in a way that changed his life forever.

Apart from his family, Foyle found few other forms of relaxation, but one was undoubtedly Manchester United. Whenever possible he'd meet with Paddy Mullen at Old Trafford and they'd sit together with tickets provided by Matt Busby just behind the United bench. Always surrounded by huge swathes of priests and rabbis whom Busby also looked after.

It so happened that in the February of 1958, Manchester United had made it into the European cup quarter finals. The second leg was set to be played in Belgrade and this young exciting United young team that was capturing hearts and trophies in beguiling style in England was expected to go on and conquer Europe in similar fashion.

Two days before the team were set to fly out to Belgrade, a United director passed away, meaning a spare seat became available on the plane. Knowing Mullen dreaded air travel, Busby chanced his hand and offered it instead to Foyle. Hardly expecting him to say yes, due to knowing the workaholic nature of his good pal. To the United manager's delight, Foyle telephoned and said he'd love to go.

Early morning on Monday 3rd February 1958, and Lenny Foyle is in a black taxi cab making his way to Ringway airport, to meet up with the Manchester United party travelling to Belgrade. Suddenly and without warning, two young schoolboys race across the road and his driver is forced to swerve, and in doing so crashes into a lamp post. The impact sees him hurled through the car window and onto the pavement. A shocked and bloodied Foyle staggers out of the cab and goes to help the driver, who is unconscious and bleeding badly from the head.

Any thoughts he had of making it to the airport to catch the flight have now gone. At Ringway, as time comes to board the plane Matt Busby looks at his watch and wonders what has become of Foyle? He shakes his head and joins the rest of the United party to take their seats aboard the Elizabethan charter aircraft *G-ALZU A857*. And a flight into infamy from which many would never return.

The horrors of the Munich air disaster were first made known to Foyle as he was recuperating at home by a telephone call from

Paddy Mullen. Their mutual friend Matt Busby was reported to have survived the crash, but deemed critical in a German hospital. Mullen was at the hub of everything in trying to find news on survivors for relatives. He set up camp at the Busby home as the stark reality of just what had occurred broke like a nightmare storm from a devastated, black Mancunian sky.

For Foyle it was the ultimate what if? It was most likely that he would have been sat next to Matt Busby, and in time Foyle discovered the man in the seat, United Trainer, Bert Whalley, was killed outright. In time a recovered but badly scared Busby, both mentally and physically and the few survivors returned home. Foyle never spoke to him about the crash unless Matt brought it up. However between himself and Mullen it was often the topic of conversation. Foyle many times relating to his pal. 'You get one chance in this life Paddy. Just the once chance.'

Behind the scenes they helped Busby and the club out in ways only men of their standing were capable. United Players misbehaving around town. Whether it be those with drinking, gambling or women problems were noted and kept a wary eye on. Manchester's pubs and clubs became littered with a network of spies whom reported back to Mullen and Foyle, whom in turn told Busby. Always, no matter the difficulties, anything that arose was resolved in-house, quietly and effectively. Nothing was too much for Paddy Mullen and Lenny Foyle to deal with.

But then came George Best and all bests were off.

ROMEO IN FOOTBALL BOOTS

'George, have you been listening to a damn word I've been telling you'? A raging Matt Busby has spent the last five minutes in his Old Trafford office venting his spleen at the twenty-year old Irish genius George Best, who is clearly not taking the slightest bit of notice.

'Er, yes boss.'

'Well then what have I just said'?

Best shrugs his shoulders. He cannot answer. His mind elsewhere on a dark haired, beauty called Susan from Bowdon, who he has been seeing quite a lot of lately. Sara has telephoned too say she has a surprise for him, so they are meeting later for lunch.

'Busby leans back in the chair and throws his pen on the desk. 'What time did you go to bed last night'? Best scratches his head; he dare not tell the boss the truth.

'About half past ten boss.'

'Oh really'? smiles Busby. He reaches for a notepad, puts on a pair of glasses and looks up towards Best 'These are all after you supposedly were tucked up in bed George.'

Busby starts to read off the paper. 'You were spotted with Mr Michael Summerbee in the following. Ten-forty-five in the Grapes. Eleven-fifteen in the Twisted Wheel. Twelve-ten in the Jigsaw club. Ah, it appears young Summerbee has now had the sense to go home. But not you George. It goes on. One o'clock in Mr Smiths and finally at the ripe old time of one-forty-five you were witnessed staggering out of the Jigsaw club, with two blond ladies very kindly holding you up.'

The old man is slipping thinks Best, because one of the girls was a brunette.

'So what have you to say for yourself,'? asks Busby.

I'm sorry boss, it won't happen again,' replies Best, in his most apologetic voice.

'Get out George and straight home. You need to rest up because we have Benfica coming up in the European cup soon, and I don't need to tell you what this competition means to me and this club'? We'll need you at your very best against the Portuguese. Never forget this competition nearly broke Manchester United. We owe it to the lads who lost their lives at Munich to win it.'

'I'll be ready for the Stadium of Light. I promise you.'

'Good lad,' smiles Busby. Again finding it hard to stay mad for any length of time at this young boy from Belfast, who constantly drives him to despair, only then to make his heart soar time and again on a football pitch. And for a man such as Busby still haunted by the loss of lads he considered sons in the air crash,

such moments are treasured and needed.

A nervous eighteen-year old Susan Foyle is in love and a week late for her period. She sits waiting for George Best at a corner table, in a small and quiet side street café in Hale village in Cheshire. George is her boyfriend, or at least she likes to thinks so, for they have only been out together twice.

The first time Susan told him she was not that kind of girl. Whilst on the second date, feeling he was getting bored with her, Susan gave in. She has convinced herself that once George discovers her little secret, he will declare undying love and ask for Susan's hand in marriage. At least she hopes so, for if he dares say no and her father finds out, Lenny Foyle will personally break both his legs.

Susan hears the unique purring engine of George's E Type Jaguar pulling up outside.

He looks up, spots her through the window and waves. Sara takes a deep breath as a grinning George enters the café. Luckily she is the only customer. He kisses Susan on the cheek and sits down facing.

'You look tired George.'

He smiles.' The boss has been overdoing us in training. He's a bloody slave driver.'

'So it's nothing to do with all the stories in the newspaper then. The late nights and all those other girls'?

'You know you're the only girl for me Susan,' he replies, with that twinkle in his eye she simply cannot resist. Her Romeo in football boots. She thinks best to hit George early with the news.

She grabs his hand on the table. 'I have something to tell you.'

George hopes the news is Susan fancies a repeat of the last time they met up. So let her say she loves him and they can get on with it.

'Well come on then, tell me. I love surprises.' He squeezes Susan's hand tight.

'George I think I'm pregnant.'

He swiftly lets go. The words hitting him like a left hook off Cassius Clay.

'How long'?

'Does it matter'? snaps Susan. Her heart breaking at his question and the look of horror currently etched on George's face.

'Of course it does. We can sort this Susan. I know people.'

'What kind of people'? She knows what he is hinting at but wants George to come out and say it.

'Oh come on Susan,' he replies angrily. 'Do you want me to spell it out for you'?

At this she fails to stem the tears. 'Fuck you George'! she screams. That said a sobbing Susan stands and races out of the café. George contemplates going after her, but only for a moment.

The door opens and Susan reappears to point an accusing finger towards a startled looking George. 'Just you wait till my Dad hears about this George Best.

Just you wait'!

Her piece said she steps back out, banging the door behind her. Suddenly the penny drops with George. 'Lenny Foyle?

Fucking hell'!.......

It is early evening and Paddy Mullen is in his office at the Cromford club, when he hears a commotion going on downstairs. Suddenly the door flies open and Lenny Foyle appears. 'That little bastard has gone too far Paddy. I'm going to find him and when I do.'

'Len what's going on'? asks a shocked Mullen.

Foyle rages. 'George Best. George fucking Best'!

'What about him'?

'My daughter Paddy. My little girl.'

Mullen's mind clears and he stands to calm his friend. 'Come on sit down, I'll get you a drink. Foyle does so whilst Mullen pours them both a whisky. He returns to his chair.

'So what has the little sod done'?

'He's broken Susan's heart. Treated her like dirt that's what. She maybe expecting Pat. We'll know for certain tomorrow. When Susan mentioned it to Best he wasn't interested.'

'Doesn't sound like the George I know,' replies Mullen.'

'My Susan doesn't tell lies mate. Look, even if she isn't pregnant I cannot let this go. He needs to be taught that you can't treat people like this. He's getting a good hiding.'

'Oh come on Len, that's a little over the top.'

'No I'm serious, he's getting it. I've got my boys looking for him as we speak.'

'Have you spoken to Matt'?

'No not yet, but I'm telling him what I'm saying to you. My friendship with yourself and Matt means the world to me, but this is family Paddy. The Belfast boy has taken a diabolical liberty. I cannot let this stand.'

Mullen decides to stay quiet and wait until his old friend has calmed down a little. Soon as Foyle leaves the building he will start phoning around because he needs to locate Best and put him in a safehouse. Otherwise Mullen fears Lenny Foyle is one man marker even the sleight of foot 'Georgie boy' will not escape from.

And if so he will be running down the wing no more.

MY KIND OF TOWN

The angels are smiling down on Ancoats, for Salvatore Rea feels as if he has been blessed by God. To be chosen for such an honour is for him beyond words. Frank Sinatra is coming to Manchester to perform a one off show and Rea has been asked by a mutual friend, Johnny Roselli of Chicago, to arrange overnight accommodation and ensure that the great singer's every whim is catered for. But most importantly, as a known man of respect, Rea will be entrusted to provide protection.

Four armed bodyguards from the moment Sinatra arrives until he leaves. The Mafia have placed the life of Francis Albert Sinatra into Salvatore Rea's arms. Everything must go off to perfection, and to ensure this Rea is set to ask his brother, in all but blood for help. For if there is one man in the city who can make this all go smooth it is Patrick John Mullen.

As for choosing the men to guard Sinatra? Rea will pick from his own sons and nephews. The nearly catastrophic visit of Paul Lansky's brief but eventful sojourn in Manchester has not been forgotten by the Commission. A disaster resulting in the clipping of Bruno Gianelli, by unknown hitmen on his returning to New York.

He understands a repeat of the Lansky debacle could have equally serious recriminations. Ancoats, 'Little Italy' are afraid of no one or nothing, but even they have no wish to take on the entire *Cosa Nostra*.

Salvatore Rea dares not even contemplate failure…...

When this is all over and he is back in America, Frank Sinatra has to declare when asked by Sam Giancana and the boys that Manchester is 'My kind of town.'

ANYONE SEEN GEORGE?

The Foyle manhunt for George Best takes in every pub, club and café in Manchester, but he is nowhere to be found. George's good friend, hairdresser, Malcom *'Waggy'* Wagner's salon, The Village Barber on Bridge Street, is first on the list to be searched. A second home for Best. 'If you see George,' Waggy is told in no uncertain terms by a bear of a man, an ex-wrestler called Pug nose Nelson. 'Tell him Lenny Foyle would like a word in his ear.'

'Will do Mr Nelson,' replies Waggy. Knowing to call this well-known lunatic by his first name, Pug Nose, could see him hurled head first through the Village Barber's window. Satisfied Best is not hiding under the hair-drying machines they finally leave. When out of sight Waggy opens up a stock cupboard, and in there, crouched down with head between his knees is George Best.

'George, what the bloody hell have you done. Please not Lenny Foyle's wife'?

He smiles. 'Worse than that Waggy. His daughter.'

A shocked Waggy cannot believe it.' Of all the girls, in all the bars, in this fucking city you pick the one whose father is one of Manchester's biggest gangsters. And one who favours, if the rumours are true, hanging those who displease him on meat hooks. You have surpassed yourself this time. Congratulations.'

'What am I going to do Waggy'? asks Best, clearly at his wit's end.

'For the moment get back in the stock cupboard George. Even you can't get into trouble in there.'

The Salon phone starts to ring and Waggy picks it up.

'Village Barbers.'

'Malcom, its Paddy Mullen.'

A horrified Waggy puts his hand momentarily over the phone and mouths Paddy's name to Best. He goes back on the line.

'Hello Paddy, to what do I owe this pleasure'?

'Don't play games with me Malcom Wagner, I've known you too long. Now you know my feelings regarding our mutual friend from across the Irish Sea. And that I'd never allow harm to come his way. But unless you do exactly as I tell you Malcom, I cannot protect him. Is that understood'?

Yes Paddy,' Replies Waggy. Realising the serious in Mullen's voice and sure of his good intentions.

'Now where's George'?

'He's in our stock cupboard.'

Best cannot believe what he has just heard. 'Waggy what the fuck'! 'Good lad,' answers Mullen. 'Tell him to stay there. I'm sending a car right away to take George somewhere safe until I can sort this mess out.'

The phone line goes dead and Waggy puts his receiver down. He stares at a disbelieving Best. 'Do you realises what you have just done? Paddy Mullen is Susan's Godfather. He and Foyle are like brothers. Thanks Waggy, thanks for nothing.'

Best goes to leave.

'George wait.'

He turns around to face Waggy.

'Where are you going to go? Come on think about it. Paddy Mullen is not the type to screw you over. He's going to look after you. I can't do that. I wish I could George, but it would only be a matter of time before Foyle's mob come back and find you.'

A car pulls up outside the Salon. Immediately the driver beeps his horn.

It is Tommy Keenan. Best recognises him and smiles. 'I was at Tommy's wedding. The bridesmaids were something else.'

'Fucking hell George, do you ever stop'? Waggy embraces him. 'You take care of yourself. I'm sure Paddy will smooth things over.'

Best does not look so sure. He steps out the shop and swiftly runs around the car and jumps in alongside Tommy. They drive off.

'Where are we going Tommy'? asks Best.

'You're coming home with me for a day or two George.' Tommy smiles. 'You ever changed a nappy'?

Matt Busby is walking across the Old Trafford forecourt towards his car when he hears a familiar voice. 'Hello Matt we really need to talk.' It is Paddy Mullen.

Busby smiles wide. 'Paddy you old rascal. How are you'? They shake hands.

'We've got a problem,' sighs Mullen.

'Does this problem speak with an Irish accent'? asks Busby.

'Afraid so.'

'He wasn't at training this morning. What has George done now'?

'There's no easy way of putting this. He's done the deed with Lenny Foyles' daughter and is now, shall we say, running away from his responsibilities.'

'Dear God, 'exclaims Busby. How has Len took it'?

'Like a rampaging elephant that has just been stung by a swarm of bees. He's taking Manchester apart looking for him. But don't worry George is safe. I got to him first.'

'Much obliged Paddy. And Susan is'?

Mullen shakes his head 'Not definite, they find out this morning.'

'Well I suppose in this case it's better for both if the lass is not pregnant.'

'Might just save George having his legs broken Matt,' answers Mullen.

'Why does he do it Paddy? I can't tell you how many times I've has the boy in my office and tore a strip off him. George has been handed a god given talent that even the lads who were killed in the crash didn't possess. Denis and Bobby are special but Best is blessed. He really is. And yet such a gift appears to come weighed down with a curse.

So what happens now'?

'We wait on news of Susan,' replies Mullen. 'I'll ring Lenny later today and we take it from there, but I'm going to need your help.'

'Of course. Hopefully this is the wake up call George needed.'

'I don't think you understand the seriousness of this old pal,' replies Mullen.

'This is not a wake up call. If Lenny Foyle in current mood gets his hands on Best, he'll put George's lights out and the Belfast boy will be lucky if he ever kicks a ball again.'

A nervous Lenny Foyle is sat in a Hale surgery waiting room when wife Pauline and daughter Susan enter back in from seeing a doctor. A tearful Susan runs straight into his arms sobbing loud. He catches Pauline's eye who shakes her head and mouths. 'No baby.'

A slight smiles comes onto Foyles' face, though any relief he feels at this news is tempered by the cries of his heartbroken daughter. He strokes Susan's hair.

'I have got some important business to take care of my love. But I'll see you both at home later.' Foyle kisses both Susan and Pauline and heads off to continue the search for George Best.

At Tommy Keenan's house the greatest young footballer in the world is being taught by Alison how to change Maureen's nappies. She smiles as Best screws up his face.

'Oh come on George, it's not that bad. He is proving hopeless so finally she takes over. Alison playfully chides him. 'Men'!

'Come over here on the sofa with me George,' smiles Tommy. 'Ignore the wicked woman.' A grinning Best sits down next to him. He stares at the Mexican sombrero above the living room fireplace. The same one given to Tommy as a gift off Bruce Reynolds for helping the Great Train Robber escape abroad. 'Where'd you come across that Tommy'?

'It's off a good friend.'

'Is there a story behind it'? asks Best.

'Oh yes George'! smiles Tommy. 'A hell of a tale.'

'I don't suppose you can tell me'?

'Not really lad. You are in enough trouble.'

'What exactly is it you do for a living'?

Alison immediately looks up on hearing this. 'Very good question George. What exactly do you do Mr Keenan'?

Tommy laughs. 'I suppose you could describe me as a little like Robin Hood without the bow and arrow.' Alison raises her eyes. 'My god he thinks he's Errol Flynn now.'

'Never mind what I do replies,' Tommy. 'You've got to sort yourself out lad.'

'You should do right by that young girl George,' adds Alison.

'I tried to Alison, honestly I did, but Susan ran off before I got the chance to explain.'

'What exactly did you say to her'? asks Tommy

'It all came out wrong. You have to remember I was in shock. I mentioned I knew people who could help out and she took this to assume. Well...'?

Tommy and Alison look at each other. Neither can believe what they are hearing

'George you silly fool,' says Alison.

He continues. 'I can't believe she'd think I'd even suggest that. My ma and da would disown me.'

'Well why didn't you explain to her and we wouldn't be sitting here now hiding you like a bloody fugitive'?

'I panicked because I suddenly realised who Susan's dad was. It had never dawned on me before. Instead of thinking rationally I got straight in the jag. Parked it up in a garage off Deansgate and headed for Waggy's.'

'And you were planning on spending the rest of your life in the stock cupboard'?

George smiles. 'Seemed like a good idea at the time.'

Tommy shakes his head and tries to hide a grin. He starts to put his jacket on.

'I have to go and speak to Paddy and get this all ironed out.'

Tommy kisses Alison and then Maureen's too. He strokes the baby's head and smiles. 'What are we going to do with your Uncle George eh girl'?

THE PROMISE

'He said what'? exclaims Paddy Mullen, as Tommy explains Best's comments.

Mullen smiles. 'This should sort matters out. Susan is not pregnant by the way but Lenny stills wants a 'word' with George. I'll speak to him and organise a sit down. Peace talks. Matt will come along and hopefully his will be the calming influence. Tommy, I want you to go back home and take him to Old Trafford. Then, when the time comes and I know everything is safe you bring George in to apologise.

No, to grovel to Len.'

'Will do' says Tommy. 'The poor kid is petrified.'

'Good,' replies Mullen. 'Maybe, just maybe it will teach the randy little sod a lesson.'

Tommy laughs. 'Oh for a quiet life eh'?

'We wouldn't know what to do with ourselves lad.'

'Paddy, when we settle this thing with George, myself and Alison have something to ask you'?

'If this is about calling me grandad, then Alison, and Maureen when she can talk, I have absolutely no problems with. But you, don't even think about it.'

Tommy laughs. 'No, it can wait.'

'Good,' replies Mullen. 'And give that little daughter of yours a big hug off me.'

The meeting is called for Matt Busby's office at Old Trafford. Paddy Mullen telephones Lenny Foyle who agrees after hearing what George Best has had to say, to come along. He gives Mullen his word that Best would not be harmed. 'If the kid is genuine then he's off the hook Paddy.' Mullen then contacts Busby and everything is arranged. At just gone three O'clock in the afternoon, Lenny Foyle's Rolls Royce turns off Chester Road and pulls into the Old Trafford forecourt. At the wheel with Foyle alongside him is Pug nose Nelson. A Manchester city supporter and devastated after being told by his boss that it appears the manhunt for George Best is set to be called off.

Mullen is already sat with Busby in his office enjoying a cup of tea when there is a knock at the door and Foyle enters. Both men stand to greet him.

'Thanks so much for coming Len,' says Busby. 'This is all highly embarrassing and I'm sure hurtful for yourself and Pauline and Susan.'

'Matt, you are a gentleman,' he replies. 'I should be apologising and thanking you for helping to finally sort this out.'

'No problem old pal,' smiles the United manager. 'Believe me, the boy Best won't know what's hit him when he returns to the training field at the Cliff.'

'I second what Len says,' adds Mullen. 'You have enough on your plate running this football club. We owe you.'

'You owe me nothing lads,' replies Busby. 'Now let's get down to business. The three men sit.

Mullen smiles wide. 'George bloody Best! Now first Len, I have to admit I've been keeping George out of your way for the last day or so.'

'You don't say,' answers Foyle. He smiles.

Mullen continues. 'Now I've spoken to Tommy Keenan, who George related his story too and I'm convinced the boy has been badly misunderstood on the matter. I think he deserves a break Len, and I don't mean his legs.'

'Best give him a call then,' replies Foyle. 'Let's hear it from George's mouth.'

'I don't have to ring him,' smiles Mullen. 'He and Tommy are in the next room.'

For a second Foyle glares at Mullen in utter incredulity, but then bursts out laughing.

'You're never boring Pat, I'll give you that.'

Mullen stands to go and fetch George Best and Tommy. 'Excuse me for a moment gentlemen, I shall go and grab the motley pair.' He leaves the room and Busby smiles over at Foyle.

'Even I didn't know they were in there.'

'As ever our Paddy has keeps his cards close to his chest,' replies Foyle.

Mullen enters the room where Tommy and George Best sit waiting. He points towards a nervous looking Best. 'Come with me son.'

The three men step out.

With the most pensive of steps George Best enters into sight of Lenny Foyle and his manager Matt Busby. Foyle glares at him. 'Take a seat please George,' says Busby. Himself, Foyle and Mullen sit opposite. A Mancunian inquisition. Tommy stays standing near the door, feeling a little sorry for Best. Though also at the same time thinking he has got away with a good result. For it could have been so much worse.

'Hello George' says Foyle, in dramatic sarcastic fashion. 'Fancy meeting you here.'

'How are you doing Mr Foyle. I'd like to apologise for any offence I may have caused to you and your family. Susan in particular. Any chance I could say this to her in person.'

Suddenly Foyles' until now calm persona snaps. 'You ever even attempt to come anywhere near my daughter again Best and I'll…..'

Mullen interrupts. 'Now, now Len. Don't let your temper get the better of you. We all know George is only trying to say and do the right thing.'

Busby listens on like a wise old sage. 'Best you stay well clear George lad. Let Susan move on eh. You just concentrate on your football.'

Foyle straightens his tie and begins. 'Okay then here comes the speech. Are you listening Belfast boy'?

'Yes sir,' replies a sheepish Best. Silently praying for this to be soon over.

'You are such a lucky lad to have two great men like Paddy Mullen and Matt Busby fighting your corner. If not then circumstances could be well be very different now because when it comes to my family, I act rash and without thinking problems through. People can get hurt. But these two got to me just in time.

Anyone else, I would have ignored, but I have too much respect for Paddy and Matt to not take into account their feeling and opinions. And so we are here today and you still have your legs.

And now you owe me nothing. We are straight. Paddy? You own an apology. But to that man over there.' Foyle points toward Busby.

'You owe him the world and everything in it boy. You have no idea how he's suffered for this football club. Lads of your age and younger ripped from his grasp by a horrible plane crash. You with your talent have helped him to come back and to keep going and now, don't you dare spit on his hopes and dreams.

Don't you dare young Best.

The great Eusebio and Benfica are coming up in the European cup on their own patch. The Stadium of Light. The Portuguese have never been beaten on home soil but you are going to end that George. For Matt, you are going to electrify the crowd with your God given talent and that will be your apology to my friend.

I want to see genius, I want to see pride, passion and guts in a red shirt, and I want you to ignite the world with your performance.

One so goddamn brilliant, even the Busby Babes, God bless them, will look down from the gates of heaven and say he's not bad this kid. He's a red. He's one of us. Now is there anything you don't understand George'?

'No Mr Foyle,' smiles Best. 'I promise you I won't let the boss, you, Paddy or the lads killed down. I swear to you I will turn night into day in the Stadium of Light.'

' Good lad, you are off the hook, now get the hell out of my sight.' He stands to leave.

'Yes sir.' Tommy opens the door and follows Best through.

It slams shut.

'Great words Len old pal. Thank you,' says Busby.

'No, thank you Matt. Thank you.'

'Right then gentlemen, smiles Mullen. 'Now that's finally settled, my treat. Dinner at the Cromford with a bottle of Ireland's finest and many to follow. God knows we deserve it after the last couple of days.'

Tommy's drives off the forecourt with Best looking extremely pleased with himself.

'You are grinning like a Cheshire cat George. You haven't won anything son, you only survived by the skin of your teeth and have to calm it down a bit.'

Best is grinning wide. 'I'll try Tommy, but there's a lot of temptation out there. One thing is certain though, I'll be checking girl's surnames from now on. Where are we going anyway'?

'Back to the house so you can pick up your things, then you're free again George. Free to hunt and pillage and no doubt in time, if you haven't been listening to Len, get your legs blown off by another irate father or husband.'

Best laughs. 'No I'll be careful. Thanks for the advice Tommy, but you are only young once.'

'No problem, but promise me you'll look after yourself.'

'Maybe' says Best. 'All depends what she looks like.'

Suddenly an angry Tommy pulls the car to a screeching halt. He stares Best straight in the eyes. 'Promise me George. I mean it or by God, you think you had a problem with Foyle, well so help me.....'

Never having seen this side of Tommy, Best is taken aback and a little afraid.

'I promise Tommy. Jesus, I promise'!

'Good lad,' smiles Tommy, reverting like magic back to his normal happy, go-lucky self again. 'You are a Good lad George, but your brains are in your trousers. Don't ever think or even dream again about taking the piss out of men like Mullen, Busby or Foyle.'

They drive off. An unnerved Best finally realising that behind the cool happy exterior of his driver, Tommy Keenan is a gangster.

And one not to be messed with.

Once back home Tommy leads Best into the living room, where Alison sits with Maureen in her arms. Tommy smiles. 'Our house guest is leaving us I'm afraid. This short but sweet time together is over.' A laughing Alison stands up.

'Thanks for putting up with me Alison.'

'It's been a pleasure George.'

'I have something for you George,' says Tommy. He takes the sombrero off the wall and hands it to Best. 'Take this for luck and you score a goal over there for our Maureen'!

A clearly emotional Best is choked. 'I promise Tommy, believe me, I'll look after this.'

He holds the sombrero up.

'Well put it on,' smiles Alison.

'Oh no not yet,' he replies. 'When you finally do see me wearing this, remember it's for your little Mo.'

The three share an embrace before Tommy leads Best to the front door.

'What did you mean'? asks Tommy. 'The next time you see me wearing this? What are you planning you Irish rogue'?

'Like I told Len Foyle,' replies a grinning Best. 'I'm going to light up the world and this,' he holds up the sombrero. 'This will keep me in the shade. Take care Tommy, look after those two beautiful girls.'

'You too Bestie.' The two men shake hands. The gangster and the footballer.

You too lad.'

STRANGERS IN THE NIGHT

Chicago: The supremely powerful Mafia mob boss, fifty-six year old Sam Giancana, is sat in his office peeling an orange, waiting for the world famous superstar, fifty-one year old Frank Sinatra, to come pay homage. Giancana enjoys rattling Sinatra's chains when the mood takes him. Ever since ensuring Frank was handed an Oscar winning starring role in the Hollywood blockbuster *From here to Eternity*, he has taken great pleasure making him dance like a puppet on a string.

Sinatra: the name alone pure gold amongst the showbiz elite. A world Giancana likes to dip in and out of now and again. Notably emerging with a starlet to use and abuse. None more than Marilyn Monroe. His notorious affair with Monroe coinciding with her seeing the President of the United States, John F Kennedy.

Giancana out to prove anything he desired was not beyond him.

But now Sam Giancana's luck has finally run out. A refusal to testify before a grand jury in their investigation into organized crime has resulted in a one year jail sentence. And despite being rumoured worth over a hundred million dollars, Giancana knows such is the government eagerness to nail him, he requires financial security. A back up plan for the worse possible scenario in case they bleed him clean whilst inside.

And with this in mind Giancana has an idea for which '*Old blue eyes.*' is perfect.

For the answer to this problem lies far away in England. A city in the north of that country called Manchester. Here Frank will sing his songs at a one off concert under the guise of a charity concert. Whilst at the same time be the catalyst to an ingenious plot to smuggle diamonds worth $5 million dollars from a London bank account back across the ocean.

For who in their right mind would dare to check the great man's suitcase?

There is a knock on Sam Giancana's door and a smiling Frank Sinatra enters. He comes over to Giancana, who remains seating as they shake hands. Sinatra leans across and kisses his Godfather on each cheek. Giancana hardly moves, instead he simply finishes peeling his orange before taking a bite.

Sinatra stands, unsure whether to sit until asked.

'Do you like oranges Frank'? Giancana catching him unaware. He motions Sinatra to take a seat.

'Thank you Sam, yeah who doesn't'? grins Sinatra.

'I'll tell you who doesn't, Robert fucking Kennedy. That Irish sonofabitch blames me for everything that happened to his degenerate brother. Let me tell you Frank, I never pulled the fucking trigger, but maybe I know who did? Hell every broad he fucked, apart from his wife, I fucked.'

Giancana stares hard at Sinatra. 'Fuck him, people die in my line of business every day. November 6 1963 was nothing to do with me. I've lost so many good men simply for being in the wrong place at the worst time. Maybe that's what happened in Dallas with John boy? Nobody liked him there. In fact they hated his fucking guts, so no surprise somebody filled him with lead.

'Now down to business. you all set for England'?

Sinatra lights up a cigarette. 'We fly out tonight. I've been there once before, this Manchester? A long time ago.'

'This has to work. Those diamonds are my insurance against a very wet and rainy fucking day. Joe Maximillian will travel down from London once you arrive and will make the switch. You perform, then you get back on that fucking plane and you come home. No screwing around Frank. I need you to come through on this one for me.......'

'Don't worry,' replies Sinatra. 'I won't let you down Sam.' With as much sincerity he can muster. Whilst inside his heart is pounding. This sonofabitch has him manacled. Sinatra knows if he is found with diamonds upon him a twenty-year stretch awaits. For the price of an Oscar he sold his soul to the devil in the shape of Sam Giancana.

The excitement of being around these men has long since worn off. But once in never out , the chain is tugged and Francis Alberto Sinatra sings to their tune.

Giancana goes into his desk drawer and produces another orange. He throws it towards Sinatra who catches it.

'I like that new *Strangers in the Night* song Frank. One of your best. You got real talent kid.

'Thanks Sam.'

'Just one thing,' replies Giancana. His hawk-like slits eyes boring into Sinatra's soul.

'Don't you fucking disappoint me.'

Salvatore Rea is walking through Piccadilly gardens alongside Paddy Mullen. It is late Saturday morning and the city is alive with shoppers. Buses and cars roar past as pedestrians lain down with shopping bags risk life and limb to get across the roads. He has asked to speak to Mullen on a matter of the most urgency. So much that Rea insisted on meeting out in the open where there is no chance of them being overheard or bugged.

'Well my old friend,' says Mullen. 'What's so important that you turn down the opportunity of lunch in the Midland on me for a walk around the gardens with the great unwashed'?

A smiling Rea points around at the crowds. 'These are my customers Patrick. They don't know it yet but will be one day.'

Mullen laughs. 'Never off duty Salvatore. A man after my own heart.'

'Patrick, I would like to ask a favour'?

'For you anything.' replies Mullen.

Rea puts an arm around Mullen's shoulders. 'Very well my friend. Frank Sinatra has agreed to perform at the Opera house for the British Italian society. Now as I'm sure you are aware Patrick, Sinatra is controlled by people similar to whom we came across last year.'

'How can I ever forget'? sighs Mullen.

'Exactly,' smiles Rea. 'A man called Johnny Roselli has presented me with the honour of organising Sinatra's protection whilst he's in town. *'Old Blue eyes'* is my responsibility until he steps foot back on the plane to Chicago. I have my four best boys ready. They are special Patrick, my own flesh and blood. Sinatra is safe so long as they are around him.

But my need for you is to surround the Midland with an invisible iron curtain. Men on every corner, in every doorway. I cannot afford the slightest thing to go wrong, otherwise the price I pay is not one I worry for myself, but my family. Ancoats has a big heart and we fear no enemy. But taking on the entire *Cosa Nostra* is not a war I desire or could ever win.

The two men stop walking and Mullen offers his hand to Rea.

'Consider it done. I promise you a small army will be on the streets that night. Neither friend or foe will enter the hotel without our knowing.'

The two men shake hands. Blood brothers: Sicilian and Mancunian. Apart formidable,

Together?

A match for any.

Only half a mile away down Deansgate, Ancoats born, Saint Freddie *'the fingers'* Finnegan is busy doing the rounds. Fifty-three years old and a man who simply cannot resist the opportunity to help himself, if the opportunity arises. Equally adept in all the Manchester large stores such as Lewis's, or amongst the unsuspecting shoppers. A purse here, wallet there, Freddie the Fingers is a legend amongst the Mancunian underworld.

Surprisingly though, not for his remarkable sleight of hand, more for the fact almost every penny he steals, goes to the church or local orphanages. Freddie keeping only a small pittance to live on, and for the odd half a bitter in the Fatted Calf. Seemingly resigned to remain small time he is set to unknowingly embark on the biggest adventure of his life.

Maybe he is not blessed by God but they say the lord loves a sinner and

Freddie *'the fingers'* Finnegan is truly a saint amongst thieves.

Thirty–two year old New York, Brooklyn born, Joe Maximillian, is sat staring at the diamonds on his bed in a lavish suite, in the Savoy hotel on the strand London. Maximillian looks around at his stunning surroundings. Originally built in 1889 by impresario Richard Doyle Carter, with profits from his Gilbert and Sullivan operas, it remains easily the finest of its type in the capital. Famous guest have included Edward V11, George Gershwin, Enrico Caruso, Charlie Chaplin, Humphrey Bogart, Harry Truman, Joan Crawford and Maximillian's own, Frank Sinatra.

It is the night before Frank is set to land in Manchester and ring for him to travel up with the diamonds. $5 million dollars 'worth for their boss Sam Giancana's retirement fund. For a fleeting second Maximillian thought of absconding. Such wealth would enable him to disappear with a new identity onto another continent and live like a king. Then reality hit with the realisation if he did so, Giancana would wipe out not just immediate family, but uncles, aunts, nephews, even friends in revenge.

With a mother, father and two sisters still ensconced in Brooklyn, Maximillian swiftly rid his mind of such treachery. He snaps back to reality. A lawyer by trade he has but one client. An investment specialist Maximillian is based around Europe buying up high class property for the Giancana empire.

The diamonds come courtesy of a Parisian bank heist when the mob joined partners with some junior revolutionaries, before despatching them when the job was complete. Che Guevara fanatics thinking it clever to do a deal with the devil, only for the horned ones to end their world with a bullet in the back of the head when no longer required.

Now as the evening draws on Maximillian must be content with the finest scotch the Savoy has to offer and a pair of high class, Strand prostitutes set soon to call. A friendly porter handing him their phone number. It is a long way from Brooklyn Bridge, thinks Maximillian as there is a knock at his door and the sound of girls giggling can be heard.

A smile comes across his face that turns into a huge beaming grin as he opens it wide and lets in two stunning ladies of the night.

All courtesy of Big Sam. Not that he will ever know of course.

At just a little after seven am on a miserable rain-sodden northern morning, the private jet carrying Frank Sinatra and his entourage touches down on Mancunian concrete, and for the first time since 1953, he has returned. Memories of that early period still so fresh in Sinatra's mind. When he slept on the sofa of a kind hearted Manchester Policeman, Constable Harry Cooper's home after a late night drinking session which he has never forgot.

A boozing night with the beat bobby after they met at the Palace theatre.

A thirty-eight year old Sinatra, who had yet to hit the heights of world-wide superstardom at his lowest ebb, having performed in front of an unimpressed half-empty theatre. The slow claps and heckling like a dagger to his heart and threatening to derail a British tour.

Feeling down and needing a drink he spotted the uniformed officer having a go to bed jug of beer at the stage door and asked if he could join him.

'I sure could do with one of those friend.'

The policeman smiled, shook his hand and a member of staff got him a second pint and one for Sinatra. The bobby briefly returned to Bootle Street police station to clock off, then came back and the drinking continued in the theatre bar until 2am. A by now sozzled Sinatra couldn't remember where he was staying, so Cooper took pity and invited him to his home in Newton Heath, where the singer crashed out on the sofa.

Cooper staggered into bed, accidentally woke his wife Beryl and told her who was downstairs. Thinking he was just talking drunk and it was a bad joke she went back to sleep. The next morning a hungover Cooper woke early for his shift and roused a snoring Sinatra. The pair then headed into Manchester in a taxi, where Frank finally found his hotel keys.

The two said a last goodbye and went their separate ways.

Sinatra always regretted not asking the policeman for his surname. He just remembers him as Harry and that he lived in a place called Newton Heath. And that fate intervenes during his short time in Manchester for them to meet again.

Waiting for the singer and his entourage in the airport is Salvatore Rea and four sons and nephews. All dressed immaculately in dark suits. Looking mean, serious and ready if ordered to fight the world.

Rea looks on proud, for no man could have finer more handsome and loyal blood. Surrounded by his entourage, Sinatra approaches and Rea steps forward to greet them. He puts out his and the two shake. 'Mr Sinatra it is truly a great honour. Welcome to my home of Manchester sir. My name is Salvatore Rea and my family here will guarantee your time amongst us is without trouble'.

Sinatra smiles. Clearly impressed with this small phalanx of bodyguards and Rea himself. 'Thank You Salvatore and please call me Frank. Your boys are a helluva sight.' Inside Rea bursts with pride at this comment.

'We have a side-entrance prepared so you can avoid the press and television people waiting. And a car to take you to the Midland hotel. There the entire top floor has been put aside. My oldest son Anthony is assistant manager and he'll meet you on arrival.'

'And you and your others boys'? asks Sinatra.

'We shall be following in a car behind. My family will be your shadow Frank.'

Sinatra puts an arm around Rea's shoulders and the two men walk off slowly out of earshot of the others. 'Salvatore I need a favour'?

'Anything.'

'Thirteen years ago I played the same joint I'm at tomorrow. That night there was this guy. He was kind to me when I needed it and I'd like to repay the favour.'

'Who was he'? asks Rea.

'A cop,' answers Sinatra. 'He was on the beat outside the theatre. Around his mid-forties, I got his first name. Harry, but that's all. He came from a place called Newton Heath? I know it isn't much to go on at, but I would appreciate if you could at least ask around'?

Let me make some inquiries Frank and I'll get back to you.'

'Thank you Salvatore,' smiles Sinatra. 'You are a good man.'

As a heaving mob of newspapers and television crews lie in wait for the great crooner, little do they realise he has already been swiped away and out of their grasp.

'Old blue eyes' has returned to Manchester.

Joe Maximillian has had the call to say Sinatra has landed and feeling a little bleary eyed and hungover after his previous evening shenanigans with the whisky and call girls, he prepares to travel to Manchester by train. With the diamonds in his suitcase, a nervous

Maximillian rings down for a cab to take him to Euston station. All he wants now is to hand these fucking things over to Sinatra and get away on a plane to Europe and relax a little.

The pressure on him from Giancana has been immense. He thinks the sooner the old fuck goes to jail and his mouthpiece thug, Johnny Roselli is running things the better. Giancana is under the impression he is going to live forever, well in their line of business you live not even for the length of the day, but the moment.

Manchester? The thought of travelling to this grimy northern outpost causes him to scowl with distaste. Maximillian takes a last look around the hotel room. He smiles and thinks, thanks for the memories, and is gone out the door.

Frank Sinatra arrives at the Midland hotel. He and his entourage are swiftly ushered up the main steps and through the foyer into the lift. On the top floor which has been totally given over him, Anthony Rea waits to greet his idol. He straightens his tie and rolls his hands through his oily sleek black hair. This kid could have been born in Palermo, never mind Ancoats.

Suddenly the lift door opens and there stand Sinatra with alongside him Giancana's eyes and ears, Jonny Rizzo, his personal bodyguard Jerry 'the crusher' Arvenite and long-time business manager, Mickey Rudin. A smiling Sinatra steps out first.

'You have to be Salvatore's boy Tony'? You guys are like peas in a pod.' He offers a shocked Rea his hand. The two shake.

'Welcome to the Midland Mr Sinatra. It's a real honour.'

'The honour is all mine kid, now where's my room? I could murder a bourbon on the rocks.'

Rea motions for Sinatra and his entourage to follow. 'This way please.'

Along the corridor there are several suited men. Again all handpicked. Sinatra nods to one and he returns the gesture with a wink. 'Are this lot family also Tony'? asks Sinatra.

'No sir,' replies Rea. 'Just good friends and all big fans. All the boys you see here and others around the hotel are simply looking out for you.'

They arrive at Sinatra's suite and Rea opens the door. He smiles at the American guests.

'After you gentlemen.' They enter. Already inside is Salvatore Rea and the bodyguards.

A shocked Sinatra looks on in disbelief. 'Salvatore how the hell did you get in here before me'?

'Like I said at the airport Frank,' smiles Rea. 'Whilst you are our guest my boys are your shadow.'

GHOST IN THE CROWD

Joe Maximillian steps off the train at Manchester, clutching tight onto the briefcase carrying the diamonds and his suitcase. He looks around at the hurrying and scurrying passengers around him on the platform. Maximillian's eyes shifting from person to person. The man is a nervous wreck. He makes his way through a heaving Piccadilly station. His heart beating so loud, Maximillian is convinced it is set to burst from his chest.

He walks fast, perspiration dropping from his forehead. Not looking where he is going, Maximillian stumbles and trips, falling flat on the floor and banging his head. Inadvertently letting go of the briefcase. Lying in an embarrassed heap an elderly gentleman and a young girl bend down to help him. 'Are you okay lad'? he is asked, whilst the girl gathers up his suitcase and puts it at the side of him.

Maximillian panics, his mind clearing and thinking of the briefcase. He scamper to his feet, his face bleeding. 'The case' he exclaims a voice filled with panic. 'Where's the fucking briefcase'? But it has gone.

The old man puts a hand on his arm. 'Take it easy you have had a bad fall.'

Maximillian brushes it off 'Get your fucking hands off me'!

'Don't you talk to him like that,' screams the young girl. 'He was only trying to help.'

But Maximillian is a man possessed. Many faces are staring, but only out of astonishment at this strange man with the American accent cursing loudly. Hearing the commotion a policeman come across. 'Calm down sir and please watch your language. Now what's going on'?

'What's going on'? rages Maximillian. 'Some lousy sonofabitch has had it away with my briefcase. I have been robbed. That's what's fucking going on.' The officer looks around at the curious bystanders. 'On your way now please ladies and gents,' he calls over.

'Nothing to see here.'

Instantly they melt away, content the show is over. 'So would you like to report it stolen sir'? I'll need a description. He takes out a pen and pad from his breast pocket. 'Your name is'?

Realising the horrific situation he now finds himself, Maximillian resolves to just get away swiftly as possible.' It really doesn't matter officer. They are only work papers. I would rather just get to my hotel and lie down for a while.'

'If you are absolutely sure'? replies the policeman. A little dubious that this yank is as squeaky clean as he is trying to come across. 'Yes I'm certain. Can you hail me a taxi for the Midland Hotel'?

'Of course, follow me.' He picks up the man's suitcase and they make their way out of the station. The world is collapsing around Joe Maximillian's ears.

What the hell is he going to tell Sinatra?

Worse than that, Sam Giancana?

Freddie *'the fingers'* Finnegan has had a result. Whilst hanging around Piccadilly Railway station, looking for easy pickings, he is only yards away when a man from the London train trips to the ground and let's go of his briefcase. Swooping in inimitable style Freddie has it away and is gone. Disappearing like a ghost in a crowd, he calmly steps out the main entrance and is now back in his Ancoats home. He stands in stunned silence and cannot believe his eyes. Diamonds! Freddie quickly shuts the case. Then opens it again to make sure he wasn't imagining things!

No, they are still there and Saint Freddie *'the fingers'* Finnegan believes his boat has finally come in. There is only one place to take these. The one man in Manchester he can trust not to stitch him up and give a fair price. Then to do right in the eyes of God, but first though Freddie will put on his best suit, and take the short ride back in to town on the 112 bus to the Cromford club,

and an audience with Paddy Mullen.

After taking a deep breath and informing a shell shocked Frank Sinatra and Giancana's man, Johnny Rizzo that he has lost the diamonds, Joe Maximillian retires to his room and in a short time has already finished off half a bottle of scotch. Sinatra was simply too stunned to talk, whilst a seething Rizzo called him every name under the sun and more.

'You goddamn sonofabitch. You have one task to complete and you fuck it up. Wait till Sam gets to hear about this. Me and Frank are not taking the blame for this Joe. You are on your fucking own.'

Maximillian cannot believe that somewhere out there in this lousy, Limey city, a two bit thief has signed his death warrant.

There is no doubt Giancana will lash out in fury, and Maximillian can only hope he takes out his wrath on him and not his family. Only this thought alone is keeping him from running. Suddenly there is a knock on his door and Maximillian stands with glass of scotch in hand to answer. He opens and stood before him is a grinning Salvatore Rea holding up the briefcase.

'Joe Maximillian'?

He nods.

'Joe,' smiles Rea. 'This is the luckiest day of your life.' He hands him back over the briefcase.

Only minutes after being informed of Maximillian's misfortune by Salvatore Rea on the telephone, and planning to put the word around Manchester of a huge reward for the diamonds' return, Paddy Mullen found himself face to face in his office with Saint Freddie *'the fingers'* Finnegan, and the already infamous briefcase. Not knowing whether to laugh or cry, Mullen listened on to Freddie telling him. 'My dear Mr Mullen, you are the only man I can trust to give me a fair price for the diamonds.'

It was with no little sympathy that Mullen explained to Freddie that he had just ripped off the Mafia and was now in mortal danger. However if agreeing to just hand them over for a small fee, then Mullen would consider the matter closed. In a moment of spiritual weakness and obvious self-preservation, Freddie went along and with fifty pounds shoved in his pocket from Mullen, he headed to the Fatted Calf. With thirty notes set aside for donations, the rest was for *'Fingers'* to drown sorrows and calm his nerves.

Freddie was now of the mind that sometimes the Lord truly works in very mysterious ways.

EPITAPH

Joe Maximillian takes the briefcase off Salvatore Rea and invites him into the room. Rea explains his good fortune and Maximillian can only sit on the bed and listen in relief.

Finally he speaks. 'Salvatore, I can only offer you my deepest heartfelt gratitude. You have quite simply saved my life.'

'It was not my doing Mr Maximillian. A good man called Patrick Mullen is who you should be thanking. I'm just glad that everything has been resolved.'

Rea offers him his hand and the two shake.

'Just one more thing. Regarding that.' Rea points to the briefcase. 'Now what is your business is not mine. And that serves for the rest of my family who are currently protecting yourself and your friends. It would deeply upset me if any of my boys get in trouble over whatever is in that briefcase. So I ask you with all respect.

Please, up your fucking game. Do I make myself clear'?

Maximillian nods. There is something in this man's eyes that makes him not dare question Salvatore Rea's words. This is no local hick talking. He is undoubtedly a man of honour.

And one not to be messed with.

'I understand,' replies Maximillian. 'Can you arrange for me to meet this Mullen and thank him personally'?

A huge grin appears on Rea's face. 'Of course, Patrick will be at the concert tomorrow night.

It will be my honour to introduce you to my greatest friend.'

Tommy Keenan pulls up in his car outside 27 Scotland Hall Road, in Newton Heath. He is there on behalf of Patrick Mullen. A brief chat with Inspector George Collins regarding Sinatra's vague memories of the Police Constable swiftly resulted in him being traced. For years Harry Cooper has boasted about the night he got drunk with Frank Sinatra, but few ever believed him. Now, as Tommy goes to knock on the door and the recently retired policeman opens it, the myth will shortly become Mancunian legend.

Wearing a cardigan, carpet slippers and holding a mug of tea, a smiling Cooper recognises Tommy. 'Mr Keenan how are you. Keeping out of mischief I hope'?

I'm doing my best Mr Cooper,' grins Tommy. 'It's good to see you.'

'You too son, but what do I owe the privilege'?

Tommy hands him two tickets for the Frank Sinatra concert at the Palace theatre.

These are VIP tickets off an old friend of yours. A thank you for a gift of kindness many years ago.' Cooper's wife Beryl, appears behind him. She too never truly believed Harry's story regarding Sinatra. Even the fact he had slept on their sofa. Harry shows her the tickets.

'They are off my old mate Frank.'

Beryl appears bemused. She looks towards Tommy as if for proof.

'It's true Mrs Cooper, Frank has invited you both to come as his personal guests and would like to say hello at the end. If you could possibly hang around'?

'Oh we'll bloody hang around Tommy,' laughs Harry. 'You can count on that '!

'I have to go,' says Tommy. 'Good seeing you again Harry.' The two shake hands.

He goes to walk back to his car, only for Harry to shout his name and make him turn around.

'Hey Tommy, what you did with the Krays….That took guts.'

Tommy simply smiles and nods a goodbye. Sometimes he feels that long, gone, Monday morning, three years ago. Once upon a time in Manchester will be his everlasting epitaph.

DELIVERED FROM THE ANGELS

That same evening, sixteen hundred miles away in Lisbon. At Benfica's world famous *Estadio Da Luz*. The Stadium of Light. Matt Busby is giving a last minutes team talk before battle resumes again in this European cup quarter-final second leg. United hold a narrow 3-2 lead from the first game at Old Trafford, but history is not on their side. For the Portuguese champions have never been beaten on home soil and they have amongst their ranks one of the greatest footballers in the word. The formidable *'Black Panther.'* A striker of ferocious power, pace and shooting ability who causes fear in the hearts and eyes of the finest defenders.

The magnificent Eusebio.

Kick-off has already been delayed twenty minutes whilst Eusebio receives the European player of the year award on the pitch in front of a raging, passionate 100,000 crowd.

All is designed to make the Mancunians even more edgy before the contest begins. Matters hardly helped in their dressing room when Paddy Crerand accidentally smashes a mirror whilst kicking a ball against the wall. 'Fucking hell Pat,' screams Nobby Stiles.

'As if we haven't got enough problems you've just gone and cursed us seven years bad luck'!

'Aaagh calm down Nob,' smiles Crerand. We'll beat this lot, no problem.'

Suddenly Busby's assistant, Jimmy Murphy, calls them all together. 'Right lads come on,
the boss is going to say a last few words. Let's have your attention now.'

The players sit down and all eyes fall upon their manager in the middle of the room.

'Boys, I'm going to keep it short. Tonight I don't want you to take any chances for the first twenty minutes or so. Keep the ball and take the heat out of the game. Don't give their supporters anything to get excited about. Then, as the game goes on we shall see. Do the simple things we have always taught you and you'll be fine. Pass to a red shirt, for this is not a night for heroes. Especially you George.'

Busby looks over to his boy wonder. 'Don't be greedy son. We cannot afford to lose possession.' A smiling Best stares back at his manager.

'George are you listening'?

'Yes boss.'

'What did I just say'?

'Not a night for heroes boss.'

'Good lad' replies Busby. 'Now all of you get out there and do your jobs.'

What happens next is the birth of a supernova as a stunned Stadium of light watch on in awe, as George Best ignores his manger's pre-match word words and within twenty minutes of the game rewrites the history books to announce his arrival on the word scene. A one man performance on a football pitch, unmatched and unrivalled.

A beguiling display of electric speed and trickery not out of place in a conjuring show, Best takes on the Portuguese and beat them on his own.

Scoring twice as United finish the first half 3-0 and utterly rampant. Come half time the away dressing room is in uproar, even his own teammates are unable to believe Best's performance. Crerand playfully slaps him around the top of his head. 'George you bastard, the boss said we were supposed to be keeping it fucking tight. Do you ever listen'?

Everybody laughs as Crerand continues. 'Hey Nobby, so much for seven years bad luck'?

Stiles grins. Manchester United are nearly there. Busby cannot take his eyes off the young Irish boy sat quietly in the corner. Hardly, it appears out of breath, and the calmest person in the room. He remembers his own words from before kick-off.

'Not a night for heroes.'

Even Busby cannot help but smile. This boy is not just a hero, he is a genius.

Back in Manchester, in Paddy Mullen's office, he and Tommy Keenan have been following the astonishing events from Portugal on the transistor radio. Both are speechless after listening to the commentator describe Best's incredulous first half showing. 'Looks like our George is keeping his promise Paddy.'

Mullen shakes his head. 'Matt always said this boy was delivered from the angels. Sounds like he is singing a right tune over there tonight.'

Twenty two miles away in Bowdon, Lenny Foyle sits in his mansion with a glass of wine in hand, listening to the same commentary. The smile on his face wide in the knowledge that the boy Best has kept true to his word. 'Good lad George. You took notice after all. This was your one chance to show the world, and you have taken it with both hands.'

The second half sees no respite in the magic show. Born in Belfast but reared in Manchester and now his wings were in full flow. United continue to run riot and ultimately win 5-1. Come the full time whistle Portuguese supporters charge onto the field to mob George Best. One chases after him with a knife, but only for a lock of hair and Best produces his faster sprint of the night, before finally the man is tackled to the floor by police officers.

Amidst the hysteria and madness of screaming crowds desperate just to touch him, the myth of the fifth Beatle begins. No guitars, drums or vocals, just the beauty and the sheer quality and the dancing feet of Georgie boy. '*El Beatle.*'

The first of the footballing superstars.

Back in the Cromford club, a beaming Paddy Mullen switches off the radio. He turns to Tommy. 'Well I didn't expect that! Matt will be ecstatic. I'm so pleased for him. He's coming to the Sinatra concert tomorrow night. As are you with Alison I presume'?

'Oh yes, we wouldn't miss it for the world Paddy,' replies a smiling Tommy. Alison's parents are babysitting. I cannot wait to see the look on old Harry's wife's face when Frank notices him.

Besides we both still need to ask you something'?

Mullen eyes him with joking suspicion. 'What are you scheming'?

Tommy is laughing. 'Don't worry, you'll find out soon enough.'

'All the other lads are coming too,' replies Mullen. Lenny Foyle amongst them. Front row. Manchester's finest riff raff. Salford, south and north, Moss side. Even George Bloody Collins has declared a truce and is putting in an appearance.'

'Everybody loves '*Old blue eyes*' Paddy. He's almost as popular as you'!

'Get out of my office now Keenan,' exclaims Mullen. 'And straight home lad.'

'Yes grandad,' grins Tommy, as he ducks swiftly out the door, with a pencil thrown by Mullen just missing his head.

The next morning the aeroplane carrying Manchester United back from their glorious victory in Benfica lands amid great fanfare and pomp at Ringway airport. It appears the entire city has turned out to welcome their heroes home. But in reality all eyes are watching out for just one man. An Irish waif sprinkled with gold dust.

A hundred photographers stand waiting with cameras at the ready as the plane's door are wedged open and the air hostesses come into view. Smiling wide they wave down to the waiting masses.

'Come on ladies,' shouts a newspaperman. 'Get out of the bloody way and let's see George.'

Suddenly the man of the moment appears and he is wearing the huge sombrero given him by Tommy. Grinning wide, Best makes his way down the steps. There is a mad barrage of cameras going off as they flash and click, flash and click, flash and click…………

So begins the phenomenon soon to be heralded as Bestmania.

And a promise kept.

Tommy Keenan is at home with Alison watching events on the television. Both can do nothing but stare incredulously at the screen. 'He promised me he was going to do this,' says Alison. 'George said he would wear it for Maureen. I love that boy.'

'You and every other girl in Manchester,' answers a smiling Tommy.

God bless you George lad.'

QUALITY

Frank Sinatra is sat alone in the Midland suite with a whisky in hand, staring at the diamonds in the briefcase. One thought is in his head. If, by misfortune an over zealous or curious airport worker decides to check his bags for contraband then the party is over. He will be singing the carols at the New Jersey state prison Christmas party, for the next twenty years. Then a knock at the door makes him shut the case.

'Come in,' he says hastily.

Entering is Johnny Rizzo. Mafioso. Thirty-two years old, handsome and debonair with a killer's cold heart. A smiling Rizzo heads across to speak to Sinatra.

'Hey stop worrying, it's written all over your face. No one is going to check your bags. You are a God, a fucking world superstar. Just forget about it and relax.'

'Maybe you want to put it in your bag John'? replies an angry Sinatra.

'Come on calm down,' says Rizzo. Ain't no big fucking deal.'

'Easy for you to say, it's my ass that will be doing a twenty year stretch if I do get caught.'

Suddenly Rizzo's smiling features turn to stone. 'Do you really want me to ring Sam and tell him you are having second thoughts Frank? Because I can guarantee you, he won't be a happy man.'

Sinatra takes a large swig of his whisky, then shakes his head.

'Good man,' grins Rizzo. 'Now I'll leave you alone to get ready for tonight. knock em dead superstar.' His piece said Rizzo leaves the room. A seething Sinatra has grown to hate this man. 'Screw you Rizzo,' he says. Almost under his breath, before refilling the glass.

'Screw you.'

It is early evening and around Manchester's Palace theatre the atmosphere is electric. Newspapermen, television cameras and photographers are gathered *en masse* around the main foyer, waiting for the city's great, good and notorious to arrive. Hundreds of onlookers wait with autograph books in hand to capture the signatures of movie and pop stars, footballers and television celebrities.

The greatest show in the world is in town. The Beatles and Elvis may have captured the teenage market but for those of a certain vintage, Frank Sinatra still reigns supreme. His is the hottest ticket in town and the touts are cleaning up with prices ten times their original value.

On Scotland Hall Road, in Newton Heath, a Rolls Royce pulls up outside Harry and Beryl Cooper's house. First to spot it is Beryl whilst looking out of the window. She hopes the curtains in every house in the road are twitching. Especially Mrs Marks at number 23. This will give the nosey old cow something to gossip about, thinks Beryl.

'Well shall we go Mrs Cooper'? asks Harry. Looking splendid in a smart suit and tie.

Equally elegant in a red dress Beryl holds out an arm for her husband to link.

'Yes Mr Cooper.'

Together they step out their front door. The chauffeur opens up the rear door for Harry and Beryl. Once back in the driver seat the chauffeur looks through his rear view mirror.

He is smiling. 'Would you like me to take you twice around Newton Heath before we head for the theatre house'?

'Oh yes please,' laughs Beryl. She clutches hold of Harry's hand. 'Don't forget to wave as we go past number 23 my love'!

A grinning Harry thinks this comment is hilarious and indulges Beryl as the Rolls moves ever so slowly away.

In the Midland Hotel, Frank Sinatra prepares to make the short journey to the Palace Theatre. Sinatra checks himself in the mirror. He has decided to put the diamonds out of his mind and just concentrate on performing. Give the people of this city something to remember him by, for deep inside Sinatra thinks if he is caught, then here tonight, this hour long show could be his last live audience not consisting of killers, rapists and thieves for a long to come.

And so *'Old blue eyes'* smiles and is ready to roll. He finishes the whisky in his glass and takes a last glance in the mirror. Frank likes what he sees. He straightens his tie and winks at his image. Francis Albert Sinatra is ready to reign supreme and knock them dead in the rainy city.

He steps out of the suite and waiting for him in the corridor is his entourage and Salvatore Rea and the bodyguards. A grinning Sinatra shakes Rea's hands.

'How far to the theatre Salvatore'?

'It is two minutes in the car.'

What say we walk'? he replies, whilst looking at Rea's sons and nephews.

I'm not sure,' answers a worried looking Rea.

'Oh come on Salvatore,' smiles Sinatra. With your boys looking out for me, the devil himself wouldn't dare chance his arm. Come on my friend. Show me a little of your great city.'

'Very well,' sighs Salvatore. His mind racing with the thoughts of everything that could go wrong. 'As you wish, but I insist on walking by your side. And I'll be honest Frank, if a fucking cat runs across our path, I'm going to instruct one of my boys to shoot it.'

Sinatra looks at Rea in mock bemusement. 'Remind me never to get on your bad side Salvatore'!

'Rea smiles. He addresses the bodyguards. 'Bring Mr Sinatra and his entourage down to the foyer and wait for me there.'

Back at the Palace, Paddy Mullen is at the theatre bar holding court with the rest of the Manchester bosses. All stood shoulder to shoulder drinking champagne and chatting away. Michael and Paul Brady, Harry Taylor, Jimmy *'the weed'* Da Silva, and John Flannery. Amongst them, a rather, sheepish, Inspector George Collins.

Keeping a beady eye that no prying newspaperman snaps a photograph of him in the midst of this Mancunian criminal hierarchy. 'Jesus Christ,' smiles Collins. If the Commissioner could see me now'? He looks down the line. 'The nights I have dreamt of getting you lot on an identity parade. Where's my fucking handcuffs when I need them'?

They all laugh. 'Come on, you don't mean that,' replies Flannery. 'We've all got feelings George. I'll have trouble sleeping tonight after hearing that.'

'Yeah comments like that are hurtful George,' smiles Da Silva. 'Anyone would think we were common criminals.

'Heaven forbid,' says Collins. 'But may I make a toast gentlemen.' He raises his glass.

'To Manchester.'

In a sweep the bosses do similar and repeat. 'To Manchester'!

'Good lad Harry,' replies Paddy Mullen, 'I've a toast also. For a man whom we all respect. Whom we consider a pain in the arse, but our pain in the arse. To Bootle street's finest.'

Mullen put his glass in the air. 'To George Collins.'

The rest follow on. 'To George Collins'

'A good copper,' calls out Michael Brady.

'Here here,' adds his brother, Paul. 'A fucking good guy, if a pain in the arse.'

Collins is secretly moved by these remarks but remains composed and strait faced.

'I hope you bastards don't think I'm going soft. So Long as you rascals always remember this is my Manchester and not yours then we'll continue to get on just fine.'

The last good cop in the city George,' say Harry Taylor.

'Oh yes,' answers Collins. And unfortunately for you Mr Taylor we have unfinished business. He is referring to Detective Henry Manning, who before being made to resign was on the take from Taylor for five years.

Collins grins wide. 'But not tonight Harry, our situation can wait. For tomorrow is another day.'

Taylor raises his glass towards the policeman, who reciprocates. The atmosphere suddenly becoming a little cold. Paddy Mullen moves quick to clear the air. 'Well gentlemen I believe it's nearly time to take our seats. Don't forget we are invited to the after concert party at the Midland on the top floor. Just show these beauty's to the security in the foyer and you'll be escorted up.' He hands out tickets to all.

'And please don't shoot anybody up there,' smiles Mullen.

When stood next to Collins he leans close and whispers into his ear. 'Not tonight old pal eh. Peace in our time. What do you say'?

Collins nods. 'Like I said Paddy, it can wait.' Mullen puts an arm around his shoulders. 'Tonight you are sitting next to me. Make sure you don't go nicking any troublesome Mafia types. I'm getting too old to go through all that hassle again'!

Collins cannot help but smile. 'Fair enough. A truce old friend.'

Surrounded by the Rea clan, Frank Sinatra and his entourage are led briskly through the huge kitchen of the Midland. Chefs and waiters watch on in astonishment as they step through a side door. Waiting outside is another large group of suited men. They form a circle around the American party and it's obvious many of them are armed.

Salvatore Rea appears and looks around. Paddy Mullen has been true to his word for a small army of men await his orders. Rea motions for them to move and with an escort worthy of a visiting American President, Frank Sinatra makes his way to the Palace theatre.

Harry and Beryl Cooper are led to some of the best seats in the house by a theatre usher. Four rows back and straight in Sinatra's eyesight. Harry is in a state of bewilderment, whilst Beryl remains in delayed shock! They sit down. I still think I'm dreaming,' she says. Whilst taking in the lavish surroundings and splendour of the theatre house. The audience is filling up fast as time ticks down for the show to begin. Beryl notices someone coming towards them from the middle aisle.

'Oh my goodness,' she mouths, as Matt Busby and his wife Jean take their places next to them. Busby smiles towards her. 'Good evening.' Beryl blushes whilst Harry, a fanatical Manchester United supporter cannot help himself. He leans across his wife.

'Congratulations on last night Mr Busby. I thought Bestie was brilliant. A great win.' He offers Busby his hand and the two shake. Harry Cooper is the name. I'm a good friend of Frank's.' Beryl raises her eyes whilst Busby simply smiles and with typically grace and style whispers back to Harry. 'Your friend has a magnificent talent. I'm so looking forward to hearing him sing.'

Whilst quietly thinking this Harry Chap is a bit of a dreamer!

Through a back entrance Frank Sinatra is smuggled into the Palace just fifteen minutes before he is due to go on stage. Already comfortable with the setlist, Sinatra calls for a meeting with the famed Mancunian band leader, Hugh Gibb, to make just one change. He hands him a slip of paper with the name of a song on it.

'This is for an old friend of mine out in the audience.'

Gibbs smiles. 'No problem Frank. The boys are well aware of this one.'

The lights go out and a hush goes over the Palace Theatre. Suddenly the music starts up and Frank Sinatra enters stage left. For the next thirty minutes he holds the audience in the palm of his hands. They sit transfixed, as if glued to their seats. Truly magical. Sinatra asks for a towel and a pretty young hostess appears on the stage carrying one, plus a glass of whisky.

To the crowd's delight and the girl he thanks her with a kiss on the cheek. Sinatra wipes his face down. He looks out onto the crowd.

'Can I get the spotlight on these beautiful people out there'?

Illuminated, Sinatra stares hard at the faces and suddenly he stops at one.

Harry Cooper, whose heart is beating like a drum.

Sinatra smiles wide. 'Hey Harry, how are you doing'?

Harry stands up. 'I'm fine thanks Frank. Glad you got home alright.'

Listening on the audience are in uproar, 'It's good to see you again my old friend. Is that your lady sat by you'?

'Sure is. She's called Beryl.' Harry tries to make her stand but a red faced Beryl politely declines! Being simply too embarrassed.

Sinatra continues. 'Well Beryl, you won't remember this but many years ago your husband took pity on a miserable and drunken American and let him stay the night on your sofa.

That was me.'

The crowd erupt in applause. Nobody claps harder than Matt Busby, now realising this friendly chap sat next to him is not mad after all!

'I would like to dedicate this next song to both Harry and Beryl. Ladies and gentlemen. This is *Strangers in the night*.'

Take it away Hugh.' The music restarts and the greatest night in Harry and Beryl Cooper's life continues.....

Later that evening at the after concert party in the Midland suite, Sinatra pulls Harry aside. 'In my life old friend, I have encountered so many bullshitters and con artists. Trust is a word that doesn't fucking exist in this business. Sometimes I look in the mirror and the only person I can count on is staring back at me. So what you did that night for me stands out and has stayed in my heart Harry.

And will do forever more. If you and Beryl are ever in the states you have to look me up.'

Harry smiles. 'The same goes for me Frank. You ever find yourself back in Newton Heath, feel free to nip in for a cup of tea. Or maybe something stronger.' The two men laugh and shake hands.

'You are a real class act Harry Cooper. A one of a kind.'
Beryl watches on with tears falling down her cheeks. Never again will she doubt her husband's words! Out of the corner of his eye Sinatra spots her and goes across.

Face to face with her idol, Beryl thinks she is going to feint. Suddenly the words blurt out of her mouth before she can stop them. 'I would have made you a cup of tea and a bacon sandwich if I had known you was downstairs Frank. I do apologise.'

Sinatra smiles. 'Harry is a lucky man Beryl. Lucky he got to you before I did'!
Beryl has just died and gone to heaven!

Tommy and Alison ambush Paddy Mullen the first moment he is alone. He grins wide.
'Right out with it you two. What is it you want to ask me'? Tommy nudges Alison but she gives him back a look, as if to say. You do it. He smiles. 'Well Paddy, as you know it's little Maureen's christening next month and both myself and Alison would be delighted if you agreed to be our daughter's Godfather'?
For one of the few times in his life Mullen is almost moved to tears.

'I would be honoured,' he replies. 'Truly honoured.' Alison immediately hugs him whilst Tommy looks on. When she finally let's go the two men embrace also.
Salvatore Rea sidles up to the three and Mullen senses it is important. He puts an arm around both Tommy's and Alison shoulders. 'We'll speak later.' They both smile and move away, knowing for Paddy Mullen business never ends.
'My good friend. What can I do for you'? asks Mullen.
'Patrick, I have someone who would like to say hello. This is Joe Maximilian. You retrieved some lost luggage for him.'

'It's good to meet you Joe,' The two men shake hands.
'Mr Mullen, I would just like to say thank you for all your help.'
'Glad to have been of service.'
A grateful Maximillian goes into his pocket. 'Here's my card. If there's ever anything I could help you out with, please feel free to get in touch. And I mean absolutely anything.'
'Well there is something,' replies a smiling Mullen.

Paddy Mullen asks Maximillian if he could speak to Frank Sinatra to see if he would agree to a group photograph with all the Manchester gang bosses. When approached by Maximillian, Sinatra instantly replies. 'No problem Joe. I'm not going to turn that lot anything down. They scare the goddamn hell out of me. I only ask they keep it for themselves and not make it public. Hell I could soon be in enough trouble without being linked to this crowd. They make the Mafia look like a gang of fairies.'

The bosses wholeheartedly agree to this and so the great man takes his place in the middle of Paddy Mullen, Harry Taylor, Michael and Paul Brady, Jimmy *'the weed'* Da Silva and John Flannery.

A photographer is called to capture the moment for posterity. Sinatra looks both ways up and down the line. All the bosses dressed dapper and immaculate. Manchester's dark knights and kings of their domain. A law unto themselves and the wrong side but not all necessarily bad guys.

'*Old blue eyes*' smiles wide. 'Hell you guys look like the damn Quality street mob.'

Post Note: Frank Sinatra made it safely home with the diamonds and when asked by Sam Giancana, what he thought of Manchester? He replied. 'My kind of town'!

ENCORE

Brass Handles Pub: Present Day: Paul Brady has sat open mouthed listening to Tommy Keenan's wild but magnificent tales. 'And you all lived happily ever after'? he asks.

Tommy Keenan lights up a cigarette. 'Not really, over the years Manchester went crazy. Too much blood. No class. The old boys moved aside or were taken out. It was carnage. I got out before the decision was taken for me.'

'I've never seen the picture of the lads with Sinatra,' says Brady. Tommy smiles. He takes out a crumpled black and white polaroid and hands it over.

'There you go.'

It is the one of Frank Sinatra surrounded by the bosses. Brady's finger points to his father and uncle. 'They never mentioned this. I swear Tommy, this is the only photograph I've ever seen with dad and uncle Paul together.' He continues to stare for a while before attempting to hand it back. But Tommy puts his hand up.

'Keep it. A nice family memento.'

'Thank you,' replies Brady. Appearing genuinely touched. 'And how's Mrs Keenan. She still keeping well these days'?

Tommy take a long drag on his cigarette. 'I lost her last year. Cancer. That's why I all but live in here with you reprobates. An empty house is not a home.'

'I'm really sorry Tommy, I had no idea. She sounded like a beautiful lady.'

'The best,' he replies. 'The very best.'

'Tommy, I have a favour to ask. There's war in the air and Manchester is going to explode like never before. There's going to be a fucking eruption. The Syrians, Russians, Ukrainians, Albanians. Nigerians, the Chinese? Christ, not even counting our own.

We, Salford are outmanned and outgunned. It's already begun with today's events. You've been there and done it. Worked with and against the best. I could really do with your help as a consigliore. What do you say?

For old time's sakes.'

Tommy shakes his head. 'Afraid I'm much too old lad. Besides I always did my bit to prevent trouble. I'd be no good to you. My one piece of advice. Don't go looking for a war, but do anything you can to prevent one. There's nothing cowardly about trying to keep the peace. Paddy Mullen taught me that.'

Brady smiles, but it is one of sadness. 'Too late old friend. It's kill or be killed for us now. We are in this up to our necks.'

Shaun Barlow comes over to their table. 'Paul it's time to go mate. We have a name and address in Longsight. A Syrian fuck called Azil Aturak.'

'Longsight, my God. Allah's country,' smiles Brady. 'Well not for much longer.'

He puts out his hand and Tommy accepts it. 'Thank you Tommy Keenan, it's been an honour and a privilege to have listened to your stories. Hopefully if I live long enough we'll talk again.'

'Much obliged for the drink,' says Tommy. 'Mind how you go son.'

Brady puts on his jacket as Barlow and two bodyguards stand waiting.

Finally they head for the door, only for Brady to turn around and look back at Tommy one last time.

'Just one thing. You talked about angels in your stories. Maybe once upon a time, but in this city today, no one is clean. Everybody takes Tommy. Even the angels have dirt under their wings.

Be lucky old man.' Brady leaves the pub.

Tommy checks in his pocket for loose change and has enough for a last half. He accidentally pulls out a picture of Alison, taken when she was shining beautiful in her
mid-twenties. So full of life and stood alongside him at the Cromford club back in 1963. Tommy stares for a moment and smiles.

He gently puts it back in his pocket and very quietly, says almost in a whisper.

...........'Fallen angels.'

THE END

Printed in Great Britain
by Amazon